MATHEMATICAL ECONOMIC TEXTS

1

DYNAMIC PROGRAMMING

MATHEMATICAL ECONOMIC TEXTS

Editors

K. Arrow, Professor of Economics, Harvard University, U.S.A.

F. Hahn, Professor of Economics, London School of Economics, U.K.

J. Johnston, Professor of Econometrics, University of Manchester, U.K.

J. Parry Lewis, Professor of Economics of Regions and Towns, University of Manchester, U.K.

R. M. Solow, Professor of Economics, Massachusetts Institute of Technology, U.S.A.

Students of mathematical economics and econometrics have two unnecessary difficulties. One is that much of what they have to read is spread over the journals, often written in different notations. The second is that the theoretical and the empirical writings often make little reference to each other, and the student is left to relate them.

The main object of this series is to overcome these difficulties. Most of the books are concerned with specific topics in economic theory, but they relate the theory to relevant empirical work. Others deal with the necessary mathematical apparatus of economic theory and econometrics. They are designed for third-year undergraduates and postgraduate students.

The editors are drawn from both sides of the Atlantic and are people who are known both for their contribution to economics and for the emphasis they place on clear exposition.

Titles in the series

1. Dynamic Programming: D. J. White
2. Uncertainty and Estimation in Economics—Volume I: D. G. Champernowne
3. Uncertainty and Estimation in Economics—Volume II: D. G. Champernowne

Other titles are in preparation

DYNAMIC PROGRAMMING

D. J. WHITE

Professor of Operational Research
University of Strathclyde
Glasgow, Scotland

OLIVER & BOYD
EDINBURGH AND LONDON
HOLDEN-DAY
SAN FRANCISCO . CALIFORNIA

SBN 05 001624 5
Library of Congress No. 69–13418

First published 1969
© 1969 D. J. White

Copublished by
OLIVER & BOYD LTD
Tweeddale Court   Edinburgh 1
and HOLDEN-DAY INC.
500 Sansome Street
San Francisco, California

Printed in Great Britain by
Aberdeen University Press

CONTENTS

ACKNOWLEDGEMENTS

I would like to record my indebtedness to the following people who have been concerned, in one way or another, with the preparation of this book:

to Professors Johnston and Lewis, Manchester University, for their reading of the manuscript and for their helpful suggestions and encouragement;

to Dick Bellman, whose works have been a constant source of inspiration since I became interested in this subject, and from whom I have learnt that D.P. is a way of life;

to John Norman who was a constant companion during the preparatory stages of the manuscript;

to Rosemary Leach, who prepared the first draft and to Pauline Turner who prepared the final draft, and to whom the mathematical typing was probably a nightmare.

I hope Dick Bellman will forgive me for the following:

to Hazel Margaret

for whom the Principle of Optimality does not hold.

Chapter 1

INTRODUCTION

DYNAMIC PROGRAMMING, as an optimising procedure, has been around for a few years now, and, perhaps, the main reason that it is still with us arises from Bellman's inexhaustible supply of examples, both realistic and imaginary, which may be analysed using this approach. For reasons, which will be discussed later, D.P. (as it will be referred to in the remainder of this book) has not met with the approval that L.P. (Linear Programming) has among people actively engaged in decision analyses at any level of the company or nation. This is due partly to the, sometimes severe, computational problems which arise in its use, and partly to a misunderstanding of the advantages it has to offer over other approaches, these being perpetuated by the inappropriate choice of examples sometimes chosen to illustrate the approach, examples for which standard approaches are quite obviously considerably better.

It is the main purpose of this book, and, in particular, of this chapter, to present briefly, not only the nature of the main contributions in the field of D.P. to date, but also the relative advantages and disadvantages of other approaches. A much more detailed and comprehensive coverage of D.P. can of course be found in Bellman's three books [9, 12, 16] where his examples and exercises cover almost every form of optimisation problem.

Let us first of all remove one cause of confusion among, particularly, newcomers to the Operational Research or related fields, viz. D.P. is not comparable with L.P., although there are optimisation problems which can be tackled both ways. The backbone of all discrete optimisation problems, at least those in which differentiability is valid, is the Differential Calculus, from which the traditional L.P. results can, with appropriate modification, be derived.

The Calculus approach reduces a classical discrete optimisation problem to one of solving a set of 'equilibrium' equations. The Principle of Optimality in this approach is equivalent to the statement that certain derivatives are zero. In the Appendix, pp. 157–158, a statement and Calculus solution to this type of problem is given. The D.P. approach, however, uses an entirely new Principle of Optimality (referred to simply as *The* Principle of Optimality), expressed, not in terms of the solution variables, but in terms of their consequences via a value process. D.P. is, in a sense, a dual form of the Differential Calculus approach.

Roughly speaking the principle can be expressed as 'when certain variables have been determined, the remaining variables are optimum for a derived problem'. This is achieved by embedding the original problem in a sequence of related problems.

The 'solution of equations' expression of optimality equivalence is now replaced by a 'functional equation'. In the Appendix (pp. 158–159) the difference between simultaneous point equations and functional equations is clarified for the interested reader.

The following chapters deal essentially with means of solving certain of these functional equations. Let us state, briefly, two of the problems we encounter later on.

A production manager has the choice of two machines to meet a known uniform demand for some product over n periods of time. Each machine has different cost characteristics, depending on the time worked (age) since last overhauled. When a machine is not in use it is overhauled, within a unit time period, at a certain cost. How should he sequence the use and overhauls of the machines to minimise the cost of satisfying the known product demand over n periods of time, using only one machine at a time?

Consider the following problem. A barge owner has a fixed capacity c, and a set of packages of different types. Package type i weighs w_i and has value v_i. How should he load the barge to maximise the value of the packages loaded?

These problems, as they are formulated in their respective sections (viz. 2.6, 4.1), have a common feature. They are seen as sequential decision processes in which control variables are chosen in a given order, and the common feature is that, once the first so many control variables have been chosen, the remainder are chosen to optimise a residual problem generated by the first so many decisions. Thus the production manager will make all his future decisions from any given time onwards to be optimal from then onwards; the barge owner, once he has allocated so many packets of a given type, will choose the remaining packets to make the best use of the remaining capacity. As simple as this may seem, this Principle of Optimality, is, indeed, very powerful.

As will be seen in Chapter 4, the continuous counterpart of the Differential Calculus is the Calculus of Variations which expresses the optimality of a control function in terms of partial differential equations, which are usually formidable to solve, especially with two or more boundary conditions imposed. These differential equations can usually be derived, formally at least, using D.P. However the stages prior to this derivation provide a computational routine for solving the problem which must be considered as a realistic competitor of the equation solution approach despite computational redundancies, if only because there are absolutely no procedural problems in getting a solution. D.P. provides a routine, if sometimes laborious, general procedure for a very wide class of problems.

Recently another approach to control analysis has been put forward as expressed in Pontryagin's 'Maximum Principle'.[38] This is applicable to problems where, for one reason or another, the Calculus of Variations approach fails. As with this approach, however, we still face severe difficulties in identifying a computational procedure for solving the partial differential equations derived, and thus, again, D.P. does present a competitive alternative.

We have stressed the advantages of replacing the solution of equations approach generated by Calculus methods, by the D.P. approach. It is interesting to note that Bellman [20] suggests that, even outside problems of optimisation, problems of solving sets of equations which are unstable may profitably be turned into an optimisation problem and solved using D.P.

The main criticism against the use of D.P. is that it carries out a large number of redundant computations. In terms of the language used in Chapter 3, it considers too many possible paths (although of course it considers by no means all paths). As we have pointed out previously, there are situations in which D.P. is still a preferable approach to any other, especially when real difficulties arise in applying such procedures in practice, even more so when we want integer solutions, and when solutions lie on the boundaries of the allowable regions or when discontinuities prevent differentiation. However, there are even classes of problems in which the solution to every problem in a class of related problems is required. One such class of problems is discussed in Chapter 2.

It is perhaps worth pointing out that, in problems in which some uncertainty exists in respect to the number of stages in the problem, D.P. offers a ready made sensitivity analysis with respect to the number of stages, whereas other approaches need a complete recomputation each time (see Chapter 4).

Although, in some cases, the criticism of redundancy may be correct for deterministic problems, when we turn to stochastic problems the criticism fails to hold, since we need to know what to do in any possible contingency at any time, i.e. we need an 'optimal policy' as distinct from an 'optimal path'.

Before the advent of D.P. (and to a very great extent even now) the approach to policy determination has been to assume a particular form and either analytically, or by simulation means, find the parameters which give the best policy in this class. In general we do not know the form the optimal policy will take, and hence a most definite form of sub-optimisation is introduced. This approach cannot, in practice, cover all possible policies in any case, for these cannot be put in a one-one correspondence even with an infinite dimensional Euclidean vector space.

Even if we consider a system defined by a 3-dimensional vector, with 10 levels of discrimination in each component, and if 10 alternative actions exist for each state, there are 10^{10^3} possible policies (see Chapter 3 for definition of a policy).

D.P. on the other hand makes no such presuppositions—a policy obtained this way is always an optimal policy globally. Arguments are sometimes offered that, since the model is only an approximation to reality, why go to the trouble of deriving a global optimum, especially in view of the heavy computation involved in some problems. This, of course, is a complex problem answerable only in the context of the decision problem centering on model construction. Why should we hedge on computing the true optimal solution to a problem thought to be only an approximation to reality? If this sort of reasoning is valid why not select any feasible solution? Leaving this one for future study, if we accept the problem as the true problem, then the choice of solution procedure should be treated as a decision problem itself, and any computational cost should be compared with some loss measure through sub-optimising. In choosing a class of policies to analyse, in most cases, without a priori reasons, we simply do not know the possible sub-optimisation losses, and, as a consequence, the decision not to use D.P. is a partially uninformed decision.

As an example of the dangers which lie in restricting policies to a specific class, it can be shown (see White [51]) that if we restrict ourselves to the class of linear decision rules we can have an infinite ratio between true optimal performance and linear sub-optimal performance.

Manne [32] offers another way out of the sub-optimisation problem by using an L.P. approach. This is discussed in Chapter 5 although work is needed to compare them properly (see Norman [33]).

Perhaps the main disadvantage of D.P. is its inability to handle general stochastic constraints. There are some constraints which it can handle however, and a suggestion for handling these is given in Chapter 5. However, a closer examination of constraints in general shows that breaking constraints results in a penalty of some kind and hence in many cases we can still use D.P. providing we can modify our objective criteria to account for penalties arising through breaking constraints. There will be difficulties of course, but value theory, particularly von Neumann's theory,[43] can help here. Even in adaptive type problems (a special form of stochastic problem) we can cater for constraints via value theory, e.g. in traditional batch sampling a special class of sampling policies is usually considered, and the optimum chosen subject to fixed probabilities of accepting and rejecting specified quality batches, and these constraints imply some penalty costs which can be absorbed into the objective criterion.

Having mentioned value theory in the above context it is fitting to emphasise that D.P. plays an important conceptual role in the theory of value. It is, in a sense, the basis of a theory of value itself, for sequential processes. In Chapter 5 it is emphasised, particularly in the context of investment problems, that D.P. can play an important part in all forms of valuation, e.g. under certain conditions the appropriateness of 'present worth' forms of valuation can be established and a procedure for determining the appropriate interest factor determined.

One question remains, and that is: To what problems can D.P. be applied? The answer is that it can be applied to any problem, providing we allow single stage process, for ordinary optimisation problems then form a single stage problem.

Thus our standard optimisation problem can be formulated as D.P. as follows:

$$f_1(z_1, z_2, \ldots z_m) = \max_{\{[x_1, x_2, \ldots x_n] \, : \, \phi_i(x_1, x_2 \ldots x_n) = z_i\}} [\theta(x_1, x_2, \ldots x_n)]$$
$$z_i' = 0, \qquad i = 1, 2, \ldots m.$$

However, this answer is rather empty, and we really want to know to what class of problems it can be applied with advantage. Perhaps the following chapters, plus the present discussion, will help here.

There remains the important practical problem of formulating problems (particularly standard optimisation problems) as D.P. problems. This may require a change in the representation of the problem, for if we stick to the same variables they may not be able to be embedded in a sequential model, whereas a change of variables may be so embedded. Chapter 3 should shed some light on this problem. We cannot, as yet, provide a routine procedure for such, but this chapter in conjunction with succeeding analyses, has been written with this purpose in mind.

Chapter 2

THE OPTIMAL PATH PROBLEM

THE purpose of spending one chapter on this problem is that, in many ways, it typifies, apart from modifications of many kinds, the whole D.P. area, both conceptually and computationally. We can illustrate the combined use of the functional equation approach and the 'Principle of Optimality' to analyse sequential decision processes; we can use it to illustrate the three main computational algorithms used in general for D.P. situations; we can illustrate at least one dodge for simplifying the computations; we can illustrate the ideas of 'backward' and 'forward' formulations of a problem (where possible); and finally we can draw attention to one of the four main advantages of D.P. over other approaches.

2.1. Statement of Problem

Consider a set of points $\{P_i\}$, $i = 1, 2, \ldots N$, with an associated cost matrix $[c_{ij}]$, where c_{ij} is the cost of moving directly from P_i to P_j in one move, and we assume $0 \leqslant c_{ij} \leqslant \infty$. What is the minimal cost of moving from any point P_i to point P_N using as many moves as required, and what is the optimal sequence of moves?

2.2. Derivation of the Functional Equation

We note that we require, essentially, some decision rule which tells us to which point we move next if we are at point i now (we simply represent the point P_i by i from now on). This decision rule is termed a 'Policy', and is equivalent to some function $s(i)$ which states: if at point i, move next to point $s(i)$, which we will call the point j. The cost involved is c_{ij}, and, since this depends only on i and j, it is determined completely by our starting point i and the policy $s(i)$, which prescribes j. The same policy applied to the new starting point j brings us to k, and the new cost, c_{jk}, is likewise a function of the policy and the initial starting point i. Thus, for any given policy, we see that the cost of getting from i to N is determined completely by the policy and depends, for a fixed N, only on i. This applies in particular to the optimal policy, and we denote the associated cost by $f(i)$.

Suppose now that we decide to move from i to j. A direct cost c_{ij} will be incurred. Once we are at j our objective will now be to move to N in an optimal manner (this invokes the 'Principle of Optimality' described more fully in Chapter 3), and by definition this is equal to $f(j)$.

Thus the total cost of getting from i to N, first via j and then optimally to N is:

$$c_{ij} + f(j). \tag{2.1}$$

Since j can now be chosen to suit us best, we see that $f(i)$ satisfies the functional equation

$$f(i) = \min_j [c_{ij} + f(j)]. \tag{2.2}$$

This equation is termed a 'forward' functional equation (see White [45]). It is termed 'forward' since we are deciding which point to move 'to' in the next step, given our state now.

If our problem had been to find the optimal policy for getting from some fixed point, say 1, to any final point i, our functional equation would have been

$$f(i) = \min_j [f(j) + c_{ji}]. \tag{2.3}$$

This is termed a 'backward' functional equation, and $f(i)$ would be the minimal cost of getting from 1 to i. It is termed 'backward' since we are deciding which point to move 'from' given our required state at the end of a specific step.

We could generalise (2.2) and (2.3) if we are interested in obtaining the optimal policy for getting from any point i to any other point j and our functional equation would be

$$f(i,j) = \min_s [f(i,s) + f(s,j)], \tag{2.4}$$

where $f(i,j)$ is the minimal cost of getting from i to j, but in which any number of single steps may be required. It is not a 'one-step decision problem' in the sense of the above, although, mathematically, it is equivalent to one. In practice the one-step 'c_{ij}' figures may be an aggregation of several smaller links joining i and j.

This is both a forward and backward functional equation, and can be used to some advantage if the general policy is required.

2.3. Computational Algorithms

A. Method of Successive Approximations

By far and away the most used method of solving equation (2.2), is by Bellman's method [9] of successive approximations.

Define a function $f_1(i)$ as follows:

$$f_1(i) = c_{iN}. \tag{2.5}$$

Define a sequence of functions $\{f_n(i)\}$ inductively as follows:

$$f_n(i) = \min_j [c_{ij} + f_{n-1}(j)]. \tag{2.6}$$

For example, with $n = 2, 3$ we have

$$f_2(i) = \min_j[c_{ij} + f_1(j)],$$
$$f_3(i) = \min_j[c_{ij} + f_2(j)].$$

Physically speaking, $f_2(i)$ is equal to the minimal cost of getting from i to N in at most two steps, and $f_n(i)$ is equal to the minimal cost of getting from i to N using at most n steps.

At each stage we determine the optimal policy $s_n(i)$.

It can be shown that the sequence $\{f_n(i)\}$ converges monotonely to a unique solution of equation (2.2) among all those solutions with $f(N) = 0$. Convergence is guaranteed in $(N-1)$ steps (see Appendix to Chapter 2, p. 160).

Similar results apply to equation (2.3). If a solution to (2.4) is required, then we can considerably cut down the computations. Using a straightforward counterpart of (2.6) would simply result in relating $f_n(i,j)$ to $f_{n-1}(s,j)$ and would result in N separate cases of equation (2.2). We can see that $f_m(i,j)$ is physically equal to the minimal cost of getting from i to j using at most m steps. We can thus replace equation (2.4) by a sequence of equations

$$f_n(i,j) = \min_s[f_{n-m}(i,s) + f_m(s,j)]. \tag{2.7}$$

All we are saying is that we can divide the n possible steps from i to j into $(n-m)$ possible steps from i to a suitable s, and m possible steps from this s to the final point j.

Now let z be chosen so that $2^z \geqslant (N-1) > 2^{z-1}$. Thus we can subdivide the $(N-1)$ possible steps, from i to j, at most z times, but at least $(z-1)$ times, allowing for null steps (if we move from k to k in one step then this is a 'null' step). If $N-1 = 5$, then $z = 3$, and we can move from i to j in eight moves by suitable inclusion of null steps, allowing us to divide the eight steps from i to j into four from i to s and four from s to j, and allowing the four from i to s to be subdivided into two from i to k and two from k to s, and so on until we have three subdivisions, each one halving the previous number of steps by inserting a suitable intermediate point.

Since we do not need more than $(N-1)$ non-null steps, because of the ineffectiveness of any additional steps, we must have $f_{2^z}(i,j) = f_{N-1}(i,j)$ and we can replace equation (2.7) by a sequence of equations as follows, in which m has been appropriately chosen equal to 2_{r-1} at each stage

$$f_{2^r}(i,j) = \min_s[f_{2^{r-1}}(i,s) + f_{2^{r-1}}(s,j)]. \tag{2.8}$$

Thus if we have a system with 129 points, we need only compute, at most, $\log_2(128) = 7+1 = 8$ separate matrices, viz. $f_1(i,j)$, $f_2(i,j)$, $f_4(i,j)$, $f_8(i,j)$, $f_{16}(i,j)$, $f_{32}(i,j)$, $f_{64}(i,j)$, $f_{128}(i,j)$.

B. Method of Approximation in Policy Space

The second method which is applicable to some D.P. cases is, in this case, perhaps the simplest one to use. We choose an initial policy, $s_0(i)$ making sure that no loop exists. (A loop is a minimal set of points closed under a specific policy. Thus if $N = 5$, and $\{s_0(i)\}$ results in a sequence of moves 1–2–3–1–2–3 . . . then '1, 2, 3' constitute a minimal loop relative to $\{s^0(i)\}$, not containing the point 5.)

We can then solve the set of simultaneous equations

$$f_0(i) = c_{i,s_0(i)} + f_0(s_0(i)), \qquad i = 1, 2, 3, \ldots N \qquad (2.9)$$

with $f(N) = 0$.

This is illustrated in the example following later in the chapter.

Having determined $\{f_0(i)\}$ we find that policy $s_1(i)$ which minimises, for all i, *

$$c(i, s_1(i)) + f_0(s_1(i)) \qquad (2.10)$$

This policy $s_1(i)$ replaces $s_0(i)$ and the cycle continually repeated until a stationary policy is obtained. That this will occur is proved in the Appendix (p. 161).

C. Direct Method for Directed Sets

In some cases (see example to follow later in this chapter) the sets of points form a directed set in the sense that movements from one point can only be in the direction of the ordering of the points, viz., the points are ordered so that we can only go from 1 to 2, 3, . . . N; from 2 to 3, 4, . . . N; from 3 to 4, 5, . . . N; etc.

In this case the most efficient computational method is given directly by equation (2.2). We begin with $f(N) = 0$. We then compute $f(N-1)$, then $f(N-2)$ . . . and, ultimately, $f(1)$.

2.4. Some Advantages of Dynamic Programming for the Optimal Path Problem

D.P. is often criticised, quite rightly so, for its inefficient computational demands in situations usually characterised by the need for an answer to a 'one-off' type decision. It need hardly be stated that, in the case where answers to a class of similar and related problems are required, the D.P. approach is a 'natural' in many cases.

In the general application of D.P. several computational difficulties do arise, and, in the case of controlling, say, an inventory system over some time period, we are usually faced (except in simple cases, e.g. one product) with either trying to determine the best policy from a restricted set (e.g. the class of linear decision rules), but with fewer computational

---

* If $s_0(i)$ minimises (2.10) then we set $s_1(i) = s_0(i)$ even though other moves may produce the same minimum.

difficulties, or trying to apply D.P., with more computational difficulties but, if successful, resulting in a less restricted optimal solution. As is the case with most techniques, we face the inevitable battle of computational costs versus the quest for higher levels of optimality. This thus raises the question of measuring, in some sense, the computational efficiency of D.P. We can give no general answer to this, but we can, for the same level of optimality, compare the efficiency of method A with the crudest available (viz. considering every possible path between two specific points). Certainly, if analytic methods do not apply, and we do not wish to sub-optimise, we may, without D.P., be forced to use this crude method.

The total number of possible loopless paths between two points, if N is fairly large, is of the order of $(N-2)!e$. The application of method A would involve the computation of the order of N^3 path values, so that a crude measure of efficiency would be a ratio of the order of $(N-5)!e$ in paths considered; e.g. if $N = 10$, the ratio is of the order of 330; for $N = 20$ the ratio is of the order of $3\cdot7 \times 10^{12}$. If we required the solution for every pair, the crude method would involve immense computation.

The second method, B, has the distinct advantage that, if we have reason to believe that a certain policy is near optimal, then we can use this directly as a starting policy, and perhaps only a few interations will be needed; in some cases as little as one iteration has been needed.*

To get from point 1 to point N using method C, would require of the order of $N^2/2$ paths to be considered; the crude method would require 2^{N-2}, and hence the ratio would be of the order of $2^{N-1}/N^2$, e.g. $N = 10$ gives a ratio of only about 5; $N = 20$ gives a ratio of about 1300 and so on.

2.5. Example

Consider the cost matrix for $N = 5$ as follows:

$$c_{ij}$$

		j				
		1	2	3	4	5
	1	0	20	5	∞	∞
	2	20	0	10	8	20
i	3	5	10	0	∞	40
	4	∞	8	∞	0	6
	5	∞	20	40	6	0

* It has been recently established by the author and D. Davidson that convergence is guaranteed within $N-1$ steps as with method A.

Using method A we derive the following sequence:

	i				
	1	2	3	4	5
$f_1(i)$	∞	20	40	6	0
$s_1(i)$	5	5	5	5	5
$f_2(i)$	40	14	30	6	0
$s_2(i)$	2	4	2	$\left.\begin{matrix}4\\5\end{matrix}\right\}$	5
$f_3(i)$	34	14	24	6	0
$s_3(i)$	2	$\left.\begin{matrix}2\\4\end{matrix}\right\}$	2	$\left.\begin{matrix}4\\5\end{matrix}\right\}$	5
$f_4(i)$	29	14	24	6	0
$s_4(i)$	3	$\left.\begin{matrix}2\\4\end{matrix}\right\}$	$\left.\begin{matrix}2\\3\end{matrix}\right\}$	$\left.\begin{matrix}4\\5\end{matrix}\right\}$	5

Thus, suppose we wish to calculate $\{f_2(i)\}$, $\{f_1(i)\} \equiv \{d(i,5)\}$. Add row $\{f_1(j)\}$ row by row to the matrix $[c_{ij}]$ to obtain

$$c_{ij} + f_1(j)$$

			j		
	1	2	3	4	5
1	∞	*40*	45	∞	∞
2	∞	20	50	*14*	20
i 3	∞	*30*	40	∞	40
4	∞	28	∞	*6*	6
5	∞	40	80	12	*0*

For each i the minimal value of $c_{ij}+f_1(j)$, taken over j, is printed in italics, and we thus obtain $f_2(i)$, and the corresponding optimal value of $j(= s_2(i))$ is the column in which the minimal value occurs.

To calculate $\{f_3(i)\}$ we now add the row $\{f_2(j)\}$ to the matrix $[c_{ij}]$ to obtain

$$c_{ij}+f_2(j)$$

		j			
	1	2	3	4	5
1	40	*34*	35	∞	∞
2	60	*14*	40	*14*	20
3	45	*24*	30	∞	40
4	∞	22	∞	6	6
5	∞	34	70	12	0

(with i labelling the rows $1,2,3,4,5$)

The minimal entry in each row gives $f_3(i)$ and the column in which it occurs gives the optimal value of $j(= s_3(i))$.

The bracketed pairs indicate that two equally optimal decisions at the respective points existed, although one of each pair is the null decision; this arises only in the intermediate calculations where the number of steps is fixed.

Since the sequence converges in four steps, the optimal policy is

i	1	2	3	4	5
$s(i) \equiv s_4(i)$	3	4	2	5	5

e.g. to get from 1 to 5, the path is 1–3–2–4–5, and the total cost is 29.

All null moves are, of course, redundant in calculating the optimal path and have been excluded.

Using method B, let us choose an arbitrary policy:

i	1	2	3	4	5
$s_0(i)$	2	3	4	5	5

The equations then become

$$f_0(1) = 20+f_0(2),$$
$$f_0(2) = 10+f_0(3),$$
$$f_0(3) = \infty+f_0(4),$$
$$f_0(4) = 6.$$

Thus $\{f_0(i)\}$ is given as

i	1	2	3	4	5
$f_0(i)$	∞	∞	∞	6	0

Then $\{s_1(i)\}$ is obtained as follows:

i	1	2	3	4	5
$s_1(i)$	any	4	5	4⎱ 5⎰	5
choose	2	4	5	5	5

This is obtained in a manner identical to that by which $\{s_1(i)\}$ was obtained using method A, only different values of $\{f_0(i)\}$ are used. Thus we add row $\{f_0(j)\}$ to matrix $[c_{ij}]$ to obtain

$$c_{ij}+f_0(j)$$
$$j$$

i		1	2	3	4	5
	1	∞	∞	∞	∞	∞
	2	∞	∞	∞	*14*	*20*
	3	∞	∞	∞	∞	*40*
	4	∞	∞	∞	*6*	*6*
	5	∞	∞	∞	*12*	*0*

The minimising values of $j(= s_1(i))$ are then read off for each i. The equations become

$$f_1(1) = 20 + f_1(2)$$
$$f_1(2) = 8 + f_1(4)$$
$$f_1(4) = 6$$
$$f_1(3) = 40.$$

Then $\{f_1(i)\}$ is obtained as follows:

i	1	2	3	4	5
$f_1(i)$	34	14	40	6	0

$\{s_2(i)\}$ is then found as follows:

i	1	2	3	4	5
$s_2(i)$	1⎱2⎰	4	2	4⎱5⎰	5
choose	2	4	2	5	5

The equations become

$$f_2(1) = 20+f_2(2)$$
$$f_2(2) = 8+f_2(4)$$
$$f_2(4) = 6$$
$$f_2(3) = 10+f_2(2).$$

Then $\{f_2(i)\}$ is obtained as follows:

i	1	2	3	4	5
$f_2(i)$	34	14	24	6	0

$\{s_3(i)\}$ is then obtained as follows:

i	1	2	3	4	5
$s_3(i)$	3	4	2⎱3⎰	4⎱5⎰	5
choose	3	4	2	5	5

We then obtain $\{f_4(i)\}$:

i	1	2	3	4	5
$f_4(i)$	29	14	24	6	0

We can then show that $\{s_5(i)\} \equiv \{s_4(i)\}$ and that, therefore, $\{s_4(i)\}$ is the required optimal policy, and $\{f_4(i)\}$ is the corresponding minimal cost vector.

For an example where method C applies see White [45] where the problem of rolling metallic strip, at a minimal cost, is considered.

2.6. Some Interpretations of the Optimal Path Problem

As formulated, the problem was one of getting from point i to point N at minimal cost. It could equally well have been one of covering minimal distance, or one of minimising the time taken to get from i to N. The problem can be interpreted outside its spacial form given above, e.g. as pointed out, a 'point' may represent the gauge of strip at some tage of processing, or it might represent the state of a product at any stage of production; more generally it might represent the state of any system or object at any stage during a transition or transformation from some given initial state to some desired final state. Wherever we have a choice of intermediate transitions, we may use the Optimal Path representation of the problem as referred to in this chapter, providing the decisions involved are equivalent, in all aspects of the model, with the choice of the next state to move to. A more general 'Optimal Path' formulation than the one traditionally referred to as such allows a wider extension of applicability as seen in Chapter 3.

In order to illustrate the non-spacial nature of a point P_i, let us consider the following problem of operating equipment in an optimal manner.

A production manager has the choice of two machines to meet a known uniform demand for some product over n periods of time. Each machine has different cost characteristics, depending on the time worked (age) since last overhauled. When a machine is not in use it is overhauled, within a unit time period, at a certain cost. How should he sequence the use and overhauls of the machines to minimise the cost of satisfying the known product demand over n periods of time, using only one machine at a time? We assume that once a machine is taken off it is automatically overhauled.

Let our 'point' now be a pair of numbers (i,m) which are interpreted as:

'we are, at the end of the present period, using machine i which has been working m time units since last overhaul (i.e. is now of 'age' m in our terminology)'.

We thus see that we can describe the history of the production schedule by a series of transitions such as

$$(1,0) \rightarrow (1,1) \rightarrow (1,2) \rightarrow (2,1) \rightarrow \ldots \text{ etc.}$$

The costs of operation for each period depend only on our 'positions' at the beginning of two successive time periods, and the Optimal Route formulation applies as before, except in as much as the step number 'n' enters into the formulation directly and not as a means of getting a solution, as was the case previously.

As before, we note that, for any policy, the sequence of transitions is fully determined once the initial point (i,m), and (in this case) the number of steps allowed are specified. In particular, for the optimal policy, these are also determined, and the associated overall cost, which we, unambiguously, define by $f_n(i,m)$.

Let us now decide to move from point (i,m) with $n(>1)$ steps left, to point (j,l) (with $(n-1)$ steps left). This means that, for this period, we will operate machine j, with a commencing age $(l-1)$ and the associated cost for that period is

$$a(j,l-1)+c\delta_{ij},$$

where $a(i,m)$ is the operating cost of machine i now of age m, in the next time period; $\delta_{ij} = 1$ if $i \neq j$, $\delta_{ij} = 0$ if $i = j$; c is the overhaul cost. Of course, if $j \neq i$, then $l = 1$; if $j = i$, then $l = m+1$.

We now begin at a new point (j,l) and, using the Principle of Optimality over the remaining $(n-1)$ periods, the residual optimal cost is then

$$f_{n-1}(j,l).$$

Since (j,l) is open to optimal choice we now have, as the counterpart of equation (2.2), the equation

$$f_n(i,m) = \min_{\substack{(j,l)=(j,1)\ if\ i\neq j \\ =(i,m+1)\ if\ i=j}} [(aj,l-1)+c\delta_{ij}+f_{n-1}(j,l)]. \quad (2.11)$$

If $n = 1$, we get

$$f_1(i,m) = \min_{\substack{(j,l)=(j,1)\ if\ i\neq j \\ =(i,m+1)\ if\ i=j}} [a(j,l-1)+c\delta_{ij}].$$

We can, if we wish, put it in a form directly analogous to (2.2) by numbering the binary points (i,m) by single numbers $\{I\}$. Thus, consider the following data.

machine: i	age: $m \rightarrow$	Period operating cost $a(i,m)$				Overhaul cost
		0	1	2	3	
1		1·0	1·1	1·2	1·3	0·2
2		1·1	1·2	1·3	1·4	0·2

Any machine of age 3 or above is equivalent to one of age 3. Define the renumbering of the points (i,m) as follows:

(i,m)	I
(1,0)	1
(1,1)	2
(1,2)	3
(1,3)	4
(2,0)	5
(2,1)	6
(2,2)	7
(2,3)	8

We then get a cost matrix $c(I,J)$, as follows:

		1	2	3	4	5	6	7	8
					J				
I	1	∞	1·0	∞	∞	∞	1·3	∞	∞
	2	∞	∞	1·1	∞	∞	1·3	∞	∞
	3	∞	∞	∞	1·2	∞	1·3	∞	∞
	4	∞	∞	∞	1·3	∞	1·3	∞	∞
	5	∞	1·2	∞	∞	∞	1·1	∞	∞
	6	∞	1·2	∞	∞	∞	∞	1·2	∞
	7	∞	1·2	∞	∞	∞	∞	∞	1·3
	8	∞	1·2	∞	∞	∞	∞	∞	1·4

If we cannot get from I to J in one step, $c(I,J) = \infty$. Thus $c(3,2) = \infty$ since we cannot go from $i = 1$, $m = 2$ to $i = 1$, $m = 1$ in one step. $c(4,5) = \infty$ since we cannot end up at the end of a period with a machine, in use, of age 0. $c(4,6) = a(2,0)+c = 1·3$ since this means that we operate with a new machine of type 2 for this period having taken off a machine of age 1 which was of age 3. Remember that m refers to the age now of the machines we have just been operating for the previous period.

Equation (2.11) becomes

$$f_n(I) = \min_J[c(I,J)+f_{n-1}(J)]. \qquad (2.12)$$

The calculations proceed as follows. From the matrix $[c(I,J)]$, $f_1(I)$ is easily calculated.

I	1	2	3	4	5	6	7	8
$f_1(I)$	1	1·1	1·2	1·3	1·1	1·2	1·2	1·2
$s_1(I)$	2	3	4	(4;6)	6	(2;7)	2	2
physical action	(n.c)	(n.c)	(n.c)	(n.c;c)	(n.c)	(c;n.c)	(c)	(c)

(c) = change machine
(n.c) = do not change machine.

Adding $\{f_1(J)\}$ to the matrix $c(I,J)$ we obtain:

$$c(I,J)+f_1(J)$$
$$J$$

	1	2	3	4	5	6	7	8
1	∞	2·1	∞	∞	∞	2·5	∞	∞
2	∞	∞	2·3	∞	∞	2·5	∞	∞
3	∞	∞	∞	2·5	∞	2·5	∞	∞
4	∞	∞	∞	2·6	∞	2·5	∞	∞
5	∞	2·3	∞	∞	∞	2·3	∞	∞
6	∞	2·3	∞	∞	∞	∞	2·4	∞
7	∞	2·3	∞	∞	∞	∞	∞	2·5
8	∞	2·3	∞	∞	∞	∞	∞	2·6

(I labels the rows.)

For each value of I, the minimal value in each row gives $f_2(I)$, and the minimising column number, J, gives $s_2(I)$. Thus

I	1	2	3	4	5	6	7	8
$f_2(I)$	2·1	2·3	2·5	2·5	2·3	2·3	2·3	2·3
$s_2(I)$	2	3	(4;6)	6	(2;6)	2	2	2
Physical action	(n.c)	(n.c)	(n.c;c)	(n.c)	(c;n.c)	(c)	(c)	(c)

We now proceed to calculate $\{f_3(I)\}$ and $s_3(I)$ in the same way by adding $\{f_2(J)\}$ to the matrix $c(I,J)$ and by selecting the minimal values in each row and the corresponding minimising columns. As an exercise the interested student can now carry out the next sets of calculations, the answers to which are:

I	1	2	3	4	5	6	7	8
$f_3(I)$	3·4	3·6	3·6	3·6	3·4	3·5	3·5	3·5
$s_3(I)$	2	(3;6)	6	6	6	(7;2)	2	2
Physical action	(n.c)	(n.c;c)	(c)	(c)	(c)	(n.c;c)	(c)	(c)
$f_4(I)$	4·8	4·7	4·8	4·8	4·6	4·7	4·8	4·8
$s_4(I)$	2	3	(4;6)	6	6	7	(8;2)	2
Physical action	(n.c)	(n.c)	(n.c;c)	(c)	(n.c)	(n.c)	(n.c;c)	(c)

[continued

I	1	2	3	4	5	6	7	8
$f_5(I)$	5·7	5·9	6·0	6·0	5·8	5·9	5·9	5·9
$s_5(I)$	2	3	(4;6)	6	6	2	2	2
Physical action	(n.c)	(n.c)	(n.c;c)	(c)	(n.c)	(c)	(c)	(c)
$f_6(I)$	6·9	7·1	7·2	7·2	7·0	7·1	7·1	7·1
$s_6(I)$	2	3	(4;6)	6	2	(7;2)	2	2
Physical action	(n.c)	(n.c)	(n.c;c)	(c)	(c)	(n.c;c)	(c)	(c)

It is worth noting that the functional equation (2.12) is a forward functional equation. We know what state we are in now and wish to know 'to which state we should move'. If we knew the state I we wished to be in, n periods from now (previously n was defined as the number of periods remaining and was measured in the opposite direction to the direction in which we now measure it), then, if we wished to know 'the previous state J from which to move' we would have the backward functional equation

$$f_n(I) = \min_J[f_{n-1}(J) + c(J,I)]. \tag{2.13}$$

This is the counterpart of equation (2.3), I being the state we wish to end up in n periods from now and J the state prior to this one period before.

As we shall see in Chapters 4 and 5, the notions of 'forward' and 'backward' play important roles in the use of D.P.

It is hoped that this chapter will serve as an adequate introduction to the underlying concepts and methods of computation relevant to D.P. Chapter 3 will consider the more general abstract nature of D.P. Further work on the Optimal Path problem can be found in Parikh,[36] Bellman,[10] Pollock,[37] Norahari Pandit.[35]

The Appendix on pp. 157–159 deals with some of the proofs required in this chapter. These are not to be treated as of purely academic interest, for contemplation of computer programming can be made only if we know our procedure is going to be valid. Thus convergence needs to be ascertained, and some idea of the number of steps required is essential in general applications; the uniqueness of the solution is another essential, since, should there be several possible solutions (for the $\{f(i)\}$, that is, for we can easily get several optimal policies) we would not know which one was correct; this usually arises when the problem has been insufficiently defined.

Chapter 3

THE NATURE OF DYNAMIC PROGRAMMING

THE purpose of this chapter is to give some idea of the underlying ideas in the construction of D.P. models for a wide variety of different situations. We begin with the concept of a sequentially controlled system, and some concepts essential to the development of a D.P. model.

3.1. Sequentially Controlled Systems

Let us first consider a standard inventory system. We can describe the behaviour of this system over time by a sequence of stock levels, say at daily or weekly intervals, together with the sequence of re-ordering decisions made at the beginning of each time period. We could thus adequately represent the behaviour of the system as a *path* whose *nodes* are the stock levels (or *states*) of the system at any time (or *stages*) and whose *links* are ordered triples (x_k, d_k, x_{k+1}) where x_k, x_{k+1} are successive stock levels, and d_κ is the separating re-order decision. The re-order decision *transforms* x_k into x_{k+1}. In such a standard inventory system a measure of performance depends only on the states realised and on the decisions made, and gives rise therefore to a *path value*. An objective for such a system would be one of maximising (or minimising) the measure of performance given. To achieve this, some decision rule is required, which will determine the re-order quantity, dependent only on the stock level at the specific time concerned. Such a decision rule is called a *policy*.

Let us consider a system defined by the quantity of a particular equity a person holds, the quantity of cash he has, and the selling price (equals purchasing price, for our purposes) of the equity. If these are denoted by variables x, y, z respectively, we can adequately represent the behaviour of the system as a path, whose node at time k is $(x_k, y_k, z_k) \equiv s_k$, whose links are complex triples, (s_k, d_k, s_{k+1}), where d_k represents the decision to buy or sell some of the stock. d_k determines x_{k+1}, y_{k+1} once x_k, y_k, z_k are given, but z_{k+1} is a random variable dependent only on z_k (in our example). The measure of performance would be the net cash value at some predetermined time (stage) T, viz. $y_T + x_T z_T$. In this case the decision rule would tell us how to buy or sell at a given price at a given time depending on cash available and stock held.

These systems are time ordered, in that they pass from one state to another over time, and are essentially the same system at each point in time. Let us consider now a multi-stage production process, say the rolling of steel strip in a series of rolling operations in a multi-stand mill. In this case our system is a mixture of machines and steel strip. The decisions made are essentially concerned with setting the operating mode of each stand, and these are all set (apart from minor automatic controls) before the production cycle is commenced. The stage therefore has no time element in it, only indirectly in as much as strip passes from one stage to another over time, and yet we can still describe the system by a path in which the decisions are a sequence of stand settings, and in which the state at any stage is the gauge of the strip at entry to a specific stand, and hence our nodes would be 'gauge of strip' and our links would be an ordered triple (x_k, d_k, x_{k+1}), the x_k's being gauges and d_k being the setting at the kth stand.

The stand-setting decision transforms the system from one state to another by changing the gauge of the strip. A path value would be induced by the measure of performance relevant to the process, e.g. minimum power consumption (depending on input gauges at each stand setting) etc. A policy in this case would be a decision rule which determines the setting at the stand when the incoming gauge is given.

We have thus exhibited three systems whose behaviour may be represented by a path in some sense, and whose measure of performance induces a path value on the describing path, and which are vastly different in nature. In each of these systems control is implemented by a sequence of decisions, each decision occurring at a specific stage of the system's operations. Such systems may be termed *sequentially controlled*, and the class of systems with which we shall be concerned in D.P. is a sub-class of these. For our purposes a 'sequentially controlled system' must be describable by a *path* consisting of *links* and *nodes*, the nodes being identified with the *state* of the system at any *stage* and the *links* being ordered triples (x_k, d_k, x_{k+1}), where x_k, x_{k+1} are successive *states*, and d_k is a decision made at the kth stage; the decisions result in a *transformation* of the *state* at one *stage* to another *state* at the next *stage*; *path values* will be induced by the *measure of performance* given for the real system; a decision rule, termed a *policy*, is required, according to which the decision will depend only on the *state* of the system at any *stage*, and which will optimise *system performance* and hence *path value*.

The above pre-requisites are not sufficient, by any means, for a D.P. model to be able to be constructed. Before discussing the D.P. model, it is worth while, in order that an appreciation of the breadth of coverage by sequentially controlled system be obtained, to say a few words about variability in such a class, and to identify some of the characteristics needed for D.P. to be relevant.

3.2. Variations in the Nature of Sequentially Controlled Systems

The concepts which have been used to describe such a class are: state, decision, transformation, stage, measure of performance (or path value), policy. These will be discussed in this order.

(i) State

In the inventory problem the state of the system at any time will be the stock level. Should the stock consist of components of some kind, then the state would be of the *discrete* type, i.e. an integral number of units. In theory there is no reason why the variables in the second and third problems should not assume any specific value, and in this case we would term the state to be of the *continuous* type. In all real cases, because of limitations on the form of measurements, all states are discrete, but from an analytical point of view sometimes advantages occur if the state is treated as continuous (see Bellman [9] on inventory control).

In both cases considered, the states at any stage are all measurable cardinally and are of the same type at each stage. We may have situations where the state description is ordinal (e.g. if we describe the system by whether a piece of equipment is working or not) and we may have situations where succeeding states may be of a different nature (e.g. in a production sequence in which raw material is transformed through several stages to a final product, and in which the intermediate stage products are dissimilar). We may have states having several components, and hence being represented by a vector. Such a vector may have a mixture of ordinal and cardinal variables. The vectors at each stage may have different dimensions.

Finally one point is worth mentioning, viz. the state of a system at any stage can include information about previous events. In 'adaptive D.P.' we allow for the state description at any stage to include past observational data.

(ii) Decision

The decision variable can take the variety of forms mentioned in the discussion of state variable. One point needs to be made, for D.P. to be applicable, and that is that the state of the system must include all information which is required to identify the set of allowable decisions at that stage, e.g. if a past event precludes certain actions at some stage, the state description should cater for this; thus production decisions are constrained by labour and equipment availability; portfolio change decisions are constrained by cash available, etc.

3

(iii) Transformation

In the steel strip problem, if we are given the input gauge at any stage, the consequence of a decision (in this case stand setting) is that the input gauge will be transformed into some pre-determined output gauge (at least within fine limits of error) which becomes the new state of the system at the next stage. The type of transformation inherent in this system is said to be *deterministic*, otherwise, of *level 0* (see Bellman [11]). It is of course possible that the transformation operator has a particularly simple deterministic nature (see Chapter 2).

In the case where we do not know the outcome of a decision deterministically, but can associate with the state and decision at each stage a known probability distribution for the state at the next stage, we say that the system is of *level 1* (see Bellman [11]) otherwise *stochastic*. Howard [27] considers Markov type systems in this class. The inventory problem will belong to this class if the demand can only be described in a probabilistic manner. Parikh [36] considers the case where the system is of level 0 but the costs arising at each stage are stochastic. This arises for example in a stochastic version of the optimal path problem and it is not in general possible to classify this under level 0 processes, since the functional equation derived would, for more general forms of path values require probability distributions and not just expectations. See, for example, the Appendix to Chapter 3 on pp. 163–164, in which path values are the minimum value of link values and in which, although, under one representation, the transformed states could be deterministic, the use of expected link values is not valid. It is better, for the sake of consistency, to make Parikh's example a degenerate case of level 1. Thus if, in the optimal path problem of Chapter 2, c_{ij} is replaced by $c_{ij}+\varepsilon_{ij}$, replace this by c_{iju} where $c_{iju} = c_{ij}+\varepsilon_u$, so that the new binary states (i,u) form a closed stochastic set, analysable by Howard's method. In Parikh's problem this state description is redundant, but not in general problems. In any case, one has to begin this way before one can establish redundancy in relation to specific value functions.

There are cases where the system is known to behave in a stochastic manner, in which the precise form of this behaviour is unknown but about which we can learn something by observation. Such systems are said to be *adaptive* and of *level 2* (see Bellman [11]). Essentially, this class of system is identical with class 1, at least as far as formal models are concerned, the only, essentially superficial, difference being that the transformation probabilities at each stage depend on past observations. Bellman [12] has a chapter on such processes. Bellman and Kalaba [13, 14] investigate certain communication processes of this type. Aoki [1-4] considers control systems in a noisy environment. Bellman [15] considers a problem in ths sequential design of experiments.

The remaining systems are classified by Bellman [11] into systems of *level 3*, for want of a better method. Essentially any such classification must depend on what we know about the system. It may be that we know that the system behaves in a probabilistic manner, but that we cannot learn anything about this behaviour. This may arise if the probability distributions change from time to time in an unknown manner, and in such a case the sequential game type approach appears appropriate (see Bellman [9]), where it is assumed that the successive states are chosen by an adversary; it is conceivable, at least in abstraction, that situations may exist in which stable statistical behaviour may be assumed, again without the ability to learn anything about this, and, in such a case, we would have to find an optimal policy for each possible probability description and then choose the policy to be used from this set in some manner. There are no doubt many situations where the idea of a probability distribution is not acceptable. In this case we may know only that the transformed states belong to one of a set of possible states, with no way of attaching probabilities to them, and in such cases we may wish to choose a policy on a minimax (or maximin) basis (see Bellman,[12] on Sequential Machines).

Other characteristics of the transformation operator may exist which may influence the computational algorithm used for getting a solution, e.g. the transformation may be such that it is *directed*, i.e. all transformed states are ordered. This happens in the strip rolling problem and in any similar problem where each decision results in a *shrinking* of the state variable, e.g. in allocation problems, where the state is the resource available at each stage and this is being used up bit by bit at each stage. Another type is *projective* in nature. Thus, in the example at the end of Chapter 3 on p. 33, the state $[u_1, u_2, \ldots u_{k+1}]$ in $(1+k)$-dimensional Euclidean space, E_{k+1}, is projected into a state $[u_1, u_2, \ldots u_k]$ in k-dimensional Euclidean space, E_k.

(iv) Stage

The stage concept is needed so that decisions can be ordered, and this is achieved by the stage index variable. In most cases, as in the two examples quoted, the stage variable is *discrete*, i.e. is a member of the set of integers (in this context, if a D.P. process is referred to as discrete, it is meant with respect to the stage structure, and not with respect to the state structure). However, there are cases where the stage variable is considered to be of a *continuous* nature; this occurs in time oriented decision situations where, in theory, a decision can be made at any point in time, allowing an infinity of decisions between any two distinct points in time (see Howard [27]). It also occurs in purely mathematical problems in the class of the 'Calculus of Variations' type (see Bellman [9]), where, from the point of view of the equation derived, whether we consider it as a stage or a state variable does not matter, but from the point of view of ordering the decisions, it is called a stage variable.

There is one other important characteristic of the stage structure of a system, viz. *duration* of system. This is some measure of the difference between the first and last stage of the sequence of stages over which the system is operating in terms of the number of decisions made (we shall assume, as is the case in most cases, that a first and last stages exist, without going into the theory of ordered sets; a good axiomatic treatment of D.P. dealing with generalities of this kind, for *final value* systems only, can be found in Ellis [24]). In the inventory system this would be 365 if we were optimising over a year and decisions were made day by day; in the rolling problem, it would be 5 for a 5-stand mill. However, in general we may not know the duration over which we are optimising, for several reasons. Thus it is possible to classify a sequential system with respect to its duration as follows, in the discrete case.

(*a*) *Finite, known.* The duration has a finite known value in advance of the decisions. Thus, if we specify, in advance, that we are optimising over a definite number of stages, this applies to the inventory problem. It automatically applies to the rolling problem discussed in Chapter 4.

(*b*) *Finite, unknown, deterministic.* If we know beforehand that it is finite and can be determined, but do not know what the value is until the optimal policy has been obtained. This applies in the optimal path problem where we do not know how many steps will be required, until we have found the optimal policy. A characteristic of this sort of system is that the stage variable does not enter explicitly into the functional equation.

(*c*) *Unknown, stochastic.* If the duration is a stochastic variable depending on the policy used and/or external events. This occurs in one of the problems discussed in Chapter 5, and, again, no stage variable occurs explicitly in the equation.

(*d*) *Unknown.* If we know little or nothing about the duration, even in a probabilistic sense. In such cases we cannot formulate any problem. It is the case in many long term decision processes that the life of a firm for example creeps into the analysis, and this is unknown (except perhaps to say at least 10 years, etc.), and the best we can do is to analyse the sensitivity of the solutions to differing duration lengths, hoping that some stability of solution is found for differing values.

(*e*) *Infinite.* If the duration of the system is infinite (or in practice very large). It is sometimes advantageous in a situation with a large number of stages to consider the limiting infinite case.

For systems with a continuous stage structure, the number of decisions becomes meaningless, and the measure of the duration becomes simply the normal real variable cardinal measure.

(v) *Measure of Performance* (*or Path Values*)

Two main distinctions can be drawn at this stage, viz. between *final value* and *non-final value* systems (see Aoki [1-4] and Ellis [24] for final value systems). In the final value system, the system performance depends only on the final condition of the system, e.g. on how close we get to some target at the end of the year, or, in the rolling problem, on the final output rate, which may be a function of the input gauge at the final stage (the output gauge being fixed in advance). Non-final value systems have measures of performance dependent directly on intermediate behaviour, prior to the final stage, e.g. in the inventory problem, the total operating cost is the sum of individual operating costs for each period.

So far the only restriction we have placed on the sequentially controlled systems relevant to D.P. is on the allowable actions, i.e. we said that these should only depend on the stage and the state of the system. However, it is in the nature of the measure of performance, or path value, that we find the severest restrictions. In the following we shall deal solely with discrete D.P. processes, although analogous remarks apply to continuous processes.

Let us number the stage 1 to n. Denote the state of the system at stage r by x_r and the decision taken at the rth stage by d_r. For purposes of expediency, we shall consider path values to exist for any sequential sub-path, i.e. beginning and ending at any two stages. For many cases this is not essential, but for many cases in which D.P. is applicable, it holds. In any case if a particular sub-path is not used in the equation, it does not matter whether it exists or not or what its value is.

Thus we denote the path value between any two stages r,s by:

$$_sV_r(x_r,d_r,x_{r+1},d_{r+1},\ldots x_s).$$

Consider now a sub-path beginnning at stage 1 and ending at stage r. This is called a *backward contraction* of any sub-path beginning at stage 1 and ending at stage s for $s \geqslant r$. Similarly we define a sub-path beginning at stage r and ending at stage n to be a *forward contraction* of sub-paths beginning at any stage s, with $s \leqslant r$, and ending at stage n.

Let us now only consider forward contractions, for similar remarks apply to backward contractions. A postulate which is essential for the application of D.P. is that we can express the value of a path as some function of the first link and the value of the contracted path resulting from removal of this link, i.e.

$$_sV_r(x_r,d_r,x_{r+1}, \ldots x_s) = {_s}\phi_r[x_r,d_r,x_{r+1},{_s}V_{r+1}(x_{r+1},d_{r+1}, \ldots x_s)]. \quad (3.1)$$

This we may call the *first postulate* needed for the application of D.P., and two others follow in the next section.

As examples of such path structure we may consider:

(*a*) The case in which the path values are the sum of the link costs, i.e.

$$_sV_r(x_r,d_r, \ldots x_s) = c_r(x_r,d_r,x_{r+1}) + c_{r+1}(x_{r+1},d_{r+1},x_{r+2}) + \ldots$$
$$+ c_{s-1}(x_{s-1},d_{s-1},x_s).$$

We then obtain

$$_sV_r(x_r,d_r, \ldots x_s) = c_r(x_r,d_r,x_{r+1}) + {_s}V_{r+1}(x_{r+1},d_{r+1}, \ldots x_s),$$

(*b*) The case in which path values are the product of link costs, i.e.

$$_sV_r(x_r,d_r, \ldots x_s) = \prod_{t=0}^{s-1-r} c_{r+t}(x_{r+t},d_{r+t},x_{r+t+1}).$$

We then obtain

$$_sV_r(x_r,d_r, \ldots x_s) = c_r(x_r,d_r,x_{r+1}){_s}V_{r+1}(x_{r+1},d_{r+1}, \ldots x_s).$$

(*c*) The case in which the path value is the minimum of some function of the link variables, i.e.

$$_sV_r(x_r,d_r, \ldots x_s) = \min_t[c_{r+t}(x_{r+t},d_{r+t},x_{r+t+1})].$$

We then obtain

$$_sV_r(x_r,d_r, \ldots x_s) = \min[c_r(x_r,d_r,x_{r+1}); {_s}V_{r+1}(x_{r+1},d_{r+1}, \ldots x_s)].$$

It will be seen in Chapter 4 that the rolling process satisfies an equation similar to (*c*).

Bellman [9] (see p. 145) derives a more complicated functional relationship for an example of multi-stage racket in which his path values satisfy the equation,

$$_nV_r(x_r,d_r,x_{r+1}, \ldots x_n) = {_n}V_{r+1}(x_{r+1}, \ldots x_n) + w({_n}V_{r+1}(x_{r+1}, \ldots x_n),$$
$$x_{r+1} - x_r),$$

where

$$d_r \equiv x_{r+1} - x_r.$$

The above equations are forward functional equations. We could equally well derive backward functional equations. Parikh [36] considers backward functional equations. The idea of forward and backward functional equations arose in a paper by Kimball.[28]

(vi) Policy

A policy was described as a set of decision rules for making a decision at any stage, dependent only on the stage and state of the system at that stage. Two types of policy exist, one of which is, in reality, a special case of the other, viz. *pure* and *mixed*.

A pure policy determines at each stage, for any state, a unique action to be taken from among the allowable actions. A mixed policy on the other hand determines for each state, at each stage, a unique chance mechanism by which the ultimate action will be chosen, e.g. the toss of a coin may be the rule by which one of two alternatives may be chosen. It is easily seen that a pure policy is a special case of a mixed policy. Bellman [9] discusses multi-stage games in which such policies are used.

Having defined contracted paths, it is perhaps appropriate to define a *contracted policy* as the contraction of the overall policy, which includes decision rules at each stage, to the stages corresponding to the contracted path. This will be used in the next section. For the sake of generality it is worth noting that decision rules may vary from stage to stage, and hence the need for the definition of a general policy.

3.3. Dynamic Programming, Functional Equations, and the Principal of Optimality

Having discussed the basic concepts needed in D.P. and the variety which these may exhibit, we are now in a position to develop the D.P. model. We have mentioned one essential postulate concerning path values (in Chapter 3, § 3.2), and shall shortly mention two others, one of which is not required for deterministic systems. Let us now consider for the time being only such systems, also of the discrete type.

Consider, again, only forward contractions and a system with an n stage duration. Let us assume a fixed policy $\pi(\cdot)$ of the pure type, and let $\pi_r(\cdot)$ be the contraction of this policy to stages r to n inclusive. Let x_r be the state of the system at the rth stage. We make the observation that, given x_r and $\pi_r(\cdot)$, the path the system will follow is completely determined. Hence we may unambiguously define the value of being in state x_r at stage r using policy $\pi_r(\cdot)$ to be equal to the value of the path followed from the rth stage onwards, viz.

$$_nv_r[x_r,\pi_r(\cdot)] = {}_nV_r(x_r,d_r,x_{r+1}, \ldots x_n),$$

where

$$x_{r+s} = T_{r+s-1}(d_{r+s-1}).\, x_{r+s-1},$$
$$d_{r+s-1} = \pi_{r+s-1}(x_{r+s-1}).$$

$T_m(d)$ is the transformation operator acting on the state x_m at the mth stage, when decision d is taken, to produce the state x_{m+1} at the next stage.

Returning to equation (3.1), we now see that our general equation, resulting from the first postulate, relating sub-path values, can be written:

$$_nv_r[x_r,\pi_r(\cdot)] = {}_n\phi_r[x_r,\pi_r(x_r),T_r(\pi_r(x_r).x_r,{}_nv_{r+1}[T_r(\pi_r(x_r)).x_r,\pi_{r+1}(\cdot)]]].$$

We can re-write this in a purely functional form, as follows, in which a general function of a variable t is henceforth denoted by $v(\cdot)$, $f(\cdot)$, etc., in which a specific t is not specified; this is done to avoid the danger of ambiguity since $v(t)$ is not, in general, a function; it is the value of the function $v(\cdot)$ at a particular argument t.

$$_nv_r[x_r,\pi_r(\cdot)] = {}_n\theta_r[x_r,\pi_r(x_r),T_r(\cdot),{}_nv_{r+1}[\cdot,{}_,\pi_{r+1}(\cdot)]]. \qquad (3.2)$$

This is used to denote that the state value at the rth stage depends, in *some* manner, on the state, x_r, at the stage, on the decision made according to policy $\pi_r(\cdot)$, on the transformation operator, $T_r(\cdot)$, on the form of the value function, $[{}_nv_{r+1}(\cdot)]$, for the transformed state, and on the contraction of the policy $\pi_r(\cdot)$ to the remaining stages. It is essential to use this form of the value function since, as we shall see in the next paragraph, we must cater for stochastic transformations, in which case one of many states may result. Equation (3.2) is the general form of the *functional equation* encountered in D.P.*

Let us now turn to systems of level 1, i.e. stochastic systems. Because the system is stochastic, there is more than one path which the system can trace under the policy $\pi_r(\cdot)$ and hence we have no analogous unambiguous definition of state value in the same sense as the deterministic case. We thus resort to the definition of state value as the *expectation* over all path values which the system may follow from its given condition at the rth stage, viz.

$$_nv_r[x_r,\pi_r(\cdot)] = E_{x_{r+1},x_{r+2}\ldots x_n/\pi_r(\cdot),x_r}\{{}_nV_r(x_r,\pi_r(x_r),x_{r+1},\ldots x_n)\}$$

$$= E_{x_{r+1},x_{r+2}\ldots x_n/\pi_r(\cdot),x_r}\{{}_n\phi_r[x_r,\pi_r(x_r),x_{r+1},{}_nV_{r+1}(x_{r+1},$$

$$\pi_{r+1}(x_{r+1}),\ldots x_n)]\}. \qquad (3.3)$$

The essential characteristic of D.P. is that of the use of the functional equation technique to relate state values at successive stages, the point being that the state value is sufficient to describe future performance without having to give a detailed picture of the paths travelled, this being implicit in the policy used. In general equation (3.3) is not reducible to

---

* Providing decisions are made at successive stages. Modifications are needed when the decisions are taken at varying intervals. See, for example, Chapter 4, § 4.2.

an equation of type (3.2). We therefore introduce our *second postulate*, viz. equation (3.3) shall be reducible to one of type (3.2). There are examples where this is possible and there are examples where, under one form of state description, this is impossible and, under another form, it does apply. Quite obviously the second postulate is redundant for deterministic systems, and postulates 1 and 2 are equivalent. The reason for giving two postulates is that, in general, postulate 1 is weaker than postulate 2 and, in the deterministic case, it would be inappropriate to use a postulate less physically meaningful and implied by a more meaningful postulate.

It is easy to see that the example (*a*) given in Chapter 3, § 3.2, with additive path values, is admissible, and, in fact

$$_nv_r[x_r,\pi_r(\cdot)] = E_{x_{r+1}/x_r,\pi_r(\cdot)}\{c_r(x_r,\pi_r(x_r),x_{r+1})\} +$$
$$E_{x_{r+1}/x_r,\pi_r(\cdot)}\{_nv_{r+1}[x_{r+1},\pi_{r+1}(\cdot)]\}.$$

In case (*b*), the multiplicative case, we see that

$$_nv_r[x_r,\pi_r(\cdot)] = E_{x_{r+1}/x_r,\pi_r(\cdot)}\{c_r(x_r,\pi_r(x_r),x_{r+1})_nv_{r+1}[x_{r+1},\pi_{r+1}(\cdot)]\}.$$

In the Appendix in Chapter 3, we show for example (*c*), given previously, no equation of the form of equation (3.2) exists in terms of the original state variable. By modifying the state description, it does fall into line however (Bellman, private communication).

So far it has been assumed that the number of stages is fixed. We can now also allow for systems of uncertain duration. In such cases, by defining the state appropriately, termination occurs when certain states are realised (e.g. a machine cycle terminates when a desired state of achievement has been reached, etc.). In the cases where expected path values are bounded, the state variable n is not explicit in the equations, and we find that equation (3.2) is replaced by

$$v_r[x_r,\pi_r(\cdot)] = \theta_r[x_r,\pi_r(x_r),T_r(\cdot),v_{r+1}[\cdot,\pi_{r+1}(\cdot)]].$$

In many cases we find that neither the state values, nor the policy, nor the functional operator θ depend on the stage number, and we derive completely stationary equations of the form

$$v[x,\pi(\cdot)] = \theta[x,\pi(x),T(\cdot),v[\cdot,\pi(\cdot)]].$$

This latter applies, in particular, to the optimal path problem of Chapter 2 and to the optimal lot size problem in Chapter 5.

Our final prerequisite is that the *Principle of Optimality* should hold, and we call this our *third postulate*. It is seen in the inventory problem, that, at any point in time, providing the state has been adequately defined, our future decisions are all optimal decisions for the residual duration of the system, and only present stock levels influence these decisions. In the rolling problem, the stand settings are all optimal for the residual processing to be carried out at each stage, and depend only on the incoming gauge. Bellman [9] states his principal as follows

'An optimal policy has the property that, whatever the initial state and decision are, the remaining decisions must constitute an optimal policy with regard to the state resulting from the first decision.'

In terms of contracted policy, we say that 'an optimal policy has the property that all its contractions are optimal'.

It is essential that some care be taken here in its interpretation. It does not mean that past events do not influence the future decision at any stage. It does mean that, if this is the case, the state description must cater for it, i.e. if certain events have happened prior to a specific decision epoch which have a bearing on the decision to be made, then the state description must record this.

If then the optimality principle is held to be valid, and in equation (3.2) we now define $\pi_r(\cdot)$ to be our optimal policy we obtain, dropping the policy as an explicit variable,

$$_nv_r(x_r) = \mathrm{Opt}_{d_r}\{_n\theta_r[x_r,d_r,T_r(\cdot),_nv_{r+1}(\cdot)]\}. \tag{3.4}$$

Even for systems which satisfy the second postulate, and hence give rise to equations of type (3.2), the optimality principle may not hold. For an example of this see the Appendix to this Chapter, p. 164.

D.P. therefore centres around functional equations of type (3.4). There are many different forms even here, and it would be an exhausting task to iterate them. From a computational point of view this would be desirable, and perhaps in due time this will be accomplished, giving rise to a list of appropriate algorithms or analytic solutions for each type. It is hoped that the remainder of the book will illustrate this variety, together with appropriate methods of solution.

3.4. Dynamic Programming and Classical Optimisation Problems

It is perhaps worth giving an example of how one might formulate the general mathematical problem of maximising a function of several variables subject to constaints. This is only an interest item, and its usefulness depends on the precise form of the function and its constraints, but it does illustrate the conceptual power of the approach; in particular it illustrates the occurrence of situations where the dimension of the state variable may change from stage to stage.

The problem is: maximise a function $\phi(u_1,u_2,\ldots u_n)$ subject to m constraints: $g_i(u_1,\ldots u_n)\leqslant 0$, $i = 1, 2, \ldots m$.

Define the state variables $\{x_r\}$ as follows

$$x_r = [u_1, u_2, \ldots u_r].$$

The restrictions $g_i(u_1, u_2, \ldots u_n) \leqslant 0$ can be replaced by a sequence of inclusion relationships

$$u_1 \in R_1, \, u_2 \in R_2(u_1), \ldots u_k \in R_k(u_1, u_2, \ldots u_{k-1}), \ldots u_n \in R_n(u_1, u_2, \ldots$$
$$u_{n-1})$$

where $R_k(u_1, u_2, \ldots u_{k-1})$ is some region in which u_k must lie, subject only to $u_1, u_2, \ldots u_{k-1}$ being specified.

To illustrate this, let $n = 2$ and

$$g_1(u_1, u_2) \equiv \alpha_1 u_1 + \alpha_2 u_2 - \alpha_0$$
$$g_2(u_1, u_2) \equiv \beta_1 u_1 + \beta_2 u_2 - \beta_0$$
$$\alpha_i, \beta_i \geqslant 0.$$

Then

$$R_1 \equiv \{u_1 : \alpha_1 u_1 + \alpha_2 u_2 \leqslant \alpha_0, \beta_1 u_1 + \beta_2 u_2 \leqslant \beta_0, \text{ for some } u_2\}$$

i.e.

$$R_1 \equiv \{\text{all } u_1\}.$$

Then

$$R_2(u_1) \equiv \{u_2 : u_2 \leqslant \min[(\alpha_0 - \alpha_1 u_1)/\alpha_2 ; \, (\beta_0 - \beta_1 u_1)/\beta_2]\}.$$

In terms of the state variables, $\{x_k\}$, these become

$$x_1 \in \Omega_1, \, x_2 \in \Omega_2(x_1), \ldots x_k \in \Omega_k(x_{k-1}), \ldots x_n \in \Omega_n(x_{n-1}).$$

This allows us to write x_k instead of $[u_1, u_2, \ldots u_k]$ each time, but it is not essential for the analysis.

We can then formulate our problem as a dynamic programming problem thus:

$$v_{n-1}(x_{n-1}) = \max_{x_n \in \Omega_n(x_{n-1})} [\phi(x_n)],$$

$$v_{n-2}(x_{n-2}) = \max_{x_{n-1} \in \Omega_{n-1}(x_{n-2})} [v_{n-1}(x_{n-1})],$$

$$\cdot$$
$$\cdot$$
$$\cdot$$

$$v_k(x_k) \quad = \max_{x_{k+1} \in \Omega_{k+1}(x_k)} [v_{k+1}(x_{k+1})],$$

$$\cdot$$
$$\cdot$$
$$\cdot$$

$$v_1(x_1) \quad = \max_{x_2 \ \Omega_2(x_1)} [v_2(x_2)].$$

Then

$$\max_{u_1,u_2\ldots u_n \,:\, g_i(u_1,\ldots\,u_n)\leqslant 0, \ \ i=1,2,\ldots m}\left[\phi(u_1,u_2,\ldots u_n)\right] =$$

$$\max_{x_1 \in \Omega_1}\left[v_1(x_1)\right] = v, \text{ say.}$$

Let us consider the following problem.

Maximise $\displaystyle\prod_{i=1}^{N} u_i$ subject to $u_i \geqslant 0, \ \ \displaystyle\sum_{1}^{N} u_i = a.$

With $x_k \equiv [u_1, u_2, \ldots u_k]$ we obtain

$$R_1 \equiv \{u_1 : 0 \leqslant u_1 \leqslant a\} \equiv \Omega_1,$$

$$R_2(u_1) \equiv \{u_2 : 0 \leqslant u_2 \leqslant a - u_1\} \equiv \Omega_2(x_1),$$

$$\begin{array}{cc} \cdot & \cdot \\ \cdot & \cdot \\ \cdot & \cdot \end{array}$$

$$R_k(u_1,u_2,\ldots u_{k-1}) \equiv \left\{u_k : 0 \leqslant u_k \leqslant a - \sum_{1}^{k-1} u_s\right\} \equiv \Omega_k(x_{k-1}),$$

$$\begin{array}{cc} \cdot & \cdot \\ \cdot & \cdot \\ \cdot & \cdot \end{array}$$

$$R_N(u_1,u_2,\ldots u_{N-1}) \equiv \left\{u_N : 0 \leqslant u_N \leqslant a - \sum_{1}^{N-1} u_s\right\} \equiv \Omega_N(x_{N-1}).$$

Then

$$v_{N-1}(x_{N-1}) = \max_{x_N \in \Omega_N(x_{N-1})}\left[\prod_{s=1}^{N} u_s\right].$$

$$= \left(\prod_{s=1}^{N-1} u_s\right)\max_{x_N \in \Omega_N(x_{N-1})}[u_N]$$

$$= \left(\prod_{s=1}^{N-1} u_s\right)\left(a - \sum_{1}^{N-1} u_s\right).$$

Now suppose

$$v_{N-k}(x_{N-k}) = \left(\prod_{s=1}^{N-k} u_s\right)\left(\frac{a - \sum_{1}^{N-k} u_s}{k}\right)^{k}.$$

Then

$$v_{N-k-1}(x_{N-k-1}) = \max_{x_{N-k} \in \Omega_{N-k}(x_{N-k-1})}\left[v_{N-k}(x_{N-k})\right]$$

$$= \left(\prod_{s=1}^{N-k-1} u_s\right)\max_{x_{N-k} \in \Omega_{N-k}(x_{N-k-1})}\left[u_{N-k}\left(\frac{a - \sum_{1}^{N-k-1} u_s - u_{N-k}}{k}\right)^{k}\right].$$

Now

$$\max_{0 \leqslant z \leqslant l}\left[z\left(\frac{l-z}{k}\right)^k\right] = \left(\frac{l}{k+1}\right)^{k+1}$$

and

$$z(\text{optimal}) = \frac{l}{(k+1)}.$$

Hence

$$v_{N-k-1}(x_{N-k-1}) = \left(\prod_{s=1}^{N-k-1} u_s\right)\left(\frac{a - \sum_1^{N-k-1} u_s}{k+1}\right)^{k+1}.$$

Since the result is true for $k = 1$, it is true for all k. Hence

$$v = \max_{0 \leqslant u_1 \leqslant a}[v_1(x_1)]$$

$$= \max_{0 \leqslant u_1 \leqslant a}\left[u_1\left(\frac{a-u_1}{N-1}\right)^{N-1}\right]$$

$$= (a/N)^N.$$

By tracing backwards we see that the optimal solution is

$$u_1 = a/N; \quad u_2 = (a - a/N)/(N-1) = a/N$$

$$\ldots u_{k+1} = (a - ka/N)/(N-k) = a/N$$

$$\ldots u_N = (a - (N-1)a/N)/1 = a/N.$$

Bellman (reference 9, p. 40), has a much simpler way of obtaining this result and quite obviously one would not advocate the above approach when Bellman's alternative exists. However, the point to be made is that the above approach is general, irrespective of its practicability, whereas Bellman's approach, to this problem, relies on the separability of the objective function and on the particular form of the constraints given.

It is hoped that this chapter has served as a useful guide to the general nature of D.P. The following chapter will deal with some of the classes of D.P. situation which may arise, together with the presentation of solutions or methods of solution. The chapters will deal successively with systems of levels 0, 1, and 2, i.e. deterministic, stochastic (known) and adaptive. For those interested in multi-stage games perhaps I can refer to Bellman,[9] this exposition being, at the moment, the only existing one. It is perhaps worth noting that in the minimax (or maximin) type situation, for pure policies only, the system is, in a sense, deterministic, in that the result of a decision is known beforehand. The difference of course is that the transformation is implicit in the behaviour of the adversary and hence, although deterministic, is not known until the complete solution has been found.

Chapter 4

DETERMINISTIC PROCESSES

DETERMINISTIC processes are characterised by the fact that, once the decision rule has been selected, the outcomes are known in advance. For naturally sequential processes it means that the change of state at any stage is completely determined by the action at the preceding stage and by the state at that stage. As a consequence, for naturally sequential deterministic processes, one can either treat the decisions one by one or all together.

It is, of course, the characteristic of D.P. to treat them one by one, but, as a consequence of the previous remark, the converse proposition of embedding non-sequential type processes within a sequential process becomes possible.

It is, of course, a property of the D.P. approach that solutions are computed for a very large number of states, which, in a deterministic system, are definitely not entered into, and herein lies the main criticism against D.P., which, undoubtedly, has its least firm footing in the deterministic area. There are, of course, the situations in which the answer to a class of problems may be wanted, in which case no redundancy occurs. Such a problem is the optimal path problem of Chapter 2. Another such case may occur for systems which are likely to be disturbed, although infrequently, which are deterministic except for this possibility. Thus we may have a forecast of the precise demand for a product over the next couple of years, such a forecast known to be influenced by the possibility of a state of war. Alternatively, the demand is known except for the very infrequent occurrence of certain orders. Such situations require little need to justify D.P. However, where possibilities of redundancies do arise, the D.P. approach may still be a rational choice in the face of difficulties with other methods and may still yield less computational time. The following notes will discuss various problems from the point of view of the possible advantages of D.P.

We shall first of all present some advantages of using D.P. for processes which are not naturally sequential in any sense, since this must be the weakest link of D.P. Next we shall examine some problems which are naturally sequential, but which, by virtue of our introductory remarks, must also be formalisable in non-sequential terms, for surely, if a certain characteristic is possessed by a process, one ought to exploit it? These problems will be of the discrete (stage) type. Finally there is a whole area of problems which come traditionally within the realm of Calculus of Variations, or, some such approach, to which D.P. can contribute. These problems involve, in their solution, partial differential equations of various degrees of complexity, which are usually extremely difficult to solve. Many of these problems come within the general framework of optimal control processes operating over a time period, and are naturally sequential. Others involve the determination of functions of a variable with optimal properties, in some sense, over the range of the variable (e.g. the isoperimetric problem discussed later on) and can be embedded in a sequential model. We shall discuss the possibilities of using D.P. in these areas.

4.1. Dynamic Programming and Non-Sequential Discrete Optimisation Problems

We shall deal, in this section, with two specific classes of non-dynamic discrete optimisation problems, which should serve our purpose. Further examples can be found in Bellman.[9, 16] These come under the headings of Allocation and Assortment Problems, respectively.

A. Allocation Problems

The simplest form of this problem is

maximise $\sum_{i=1}^{n} g_i(x_i)$ subject to $\sum_{1}^{n} \alpha_i x_i = c$, and $x_i \geqslant 0$, $i = 1, 2, \ldots n$.

The standard approach is to consider the Lagrangian function

$$\phi(x, \lambda) = \Sigma_i g_i(x_i) - \lambda \Sigma \alpha_i x_i = \Sigma_i (g_i(x_i) - \lambda \alpha_i x_i). \qquad (4.1)$$

If all the $\{g_i\}$ are differentiable, if $\{x_i\}$ can take any real value, and if, fortuitously, no boundary solutions occur, then the solution is given by finding $\{x_i\}$ and λ which satisfy

$$g_i'(x_i) = \lambda \alpha_i, \ \Sigma \alpha_i x_i = c, \ i = 1, 2, \ldots n. \qquad (4.2)$$

If the conditions all hold, except for the possibility of boundary solutions (e.g. $x_i = 0$), then we can still solve the problem but with some difficulty (see Koopman [29] and White[54]). These equations are replaced by

$$g_i'(x_i) = \lambda \alpha_i, x_i > 0$$
$$\leqslant \lambda \alpha_i, x_i = 0$$
$$\Sigma \alpha_i x_i = c. \qquad (4.3)$$

If we only want integer solutions, then the problem becomes vastly more difficult. Finally if the $\{g_i\}$ are not differentiable we cannot use the calculus method.

The D.P. approach overcomes all of these difficulties, although it *may* increase the computational time. The word *may* is stressed, for problems, which have all these difficulties, may require more computational time using other methods. The functional equation would be

$$f_m(z) = \max_{0 \leqslant x_m \leqslant z/\alpha_m}[g_m(x_m) + f_{m-1}(z - \alpha_m x_m)], \qquad (4.4)$$

where $f_m(z)$ is defined as equal to the overall return obtained when the available resource is z, we are allocating to the activities $1 = 1, 2, \ldots m$ and we are using an optimal allocation policy. $f_0(z) \equiv 0$ by definition.

This is explained as follows. We allocate x_m to activity m. The new state (residual resource) is then $z - \alpha_m x_m$. The return from the original allocation, is $g_m(x_m)$, and, using the Principle of Optimality, the residual return over the next $(m-1)$ activities (stages) is $f_{m-1}(z - \alpha_m x_m)$. Since x_m is free, subject only to upper and lower bounds, as indicated, we therefore choose it optimally and thus derive equation (4.4.).

Consider the following problem. A barge owner has a fixed capacity c, and a set of packages of different types. Package type i weighs w_i and has value v_i. How should he load the barge to maximise the value of the packages loaded?

Number the packages $1, 2, \ldots n$.

Defining $f_m(w)$ as the value obtained with a capacity w, using any mixture of packages type $1, 2, \ldots m$, and using an optimal policy, we derive the following functional equation:

if $m \geqslant 1$,

$$f_m(w) = \max_{0 \leqslant r \leqslant [z/w_m]}[rv_m + f_{m-1}(w - rw_m)], \qquad (4.5)$$

* $f_0(w) \equiv 0$,

where $[z/w_m]$ is the largest integer less than or equal to z/w_m.

Table 1 gives details of calculations carried out for specific values of $\{v_i\}$, $\{w_i\}$. This problem is simple enough to be solved by other means but it can be appreciated just how difficult the task would be with, say, 10 types of package. Whatever else the D.P. method is, at least it is computationally simple.

To calculate $f_1(w)$, for each value of w, we see that we cannot use more than two packages, if $w \leqslant 100$. For each number of packages, $r = 0, 1, 2$, we tabulate, for each w, the total value obtainable. Thus, for $w = 100$, the values for $r = 0, 1, 2$, are, respectively, 0, 40, 80. The maximum value is 80, which we print in italics, and arises with $r = 2$. Thus $f_1(100) = 80$. To calculate $f_1(55)$, we let $r = 0, 1, 2$, and get values

---

* We introduce a dummy variable x_0 with $v_0 = 0$.

0, 40 and an inadmissible value, giving $f_1(55) = 40$, which we italicise, and an optimising value of r equal to 1.

With $n = 2$, we note that we never use more than two packages of this type, in an optimal policy, since three such packages have a value of 75 and a weight of 90, and this can be improved on with two packages of

TABLE 1

Package No.	Weight	Value
1	40	40
2	30	25
3	15	10
4	8	5

Residual weight, w	$f_1(w)$	$f_2(w)$	$f_3(w)$	$f_4(w)$
No. of Packages	0. 1. 2	0. 1. 2	0. 1	0. 1. 2. 3.
100	0.40.*80*	80.65.*90*	90.*90*	90.85.*90*.80
95	0.40.*80*	80.65.50	80.*90*	90.85.75.80
90	0.40.*80*	80.65.50	80.75	80.85.75.65
85	0.40.*80*	80.65.50	80.75	80.70.60.65
80	0.40.*80*	80.65.50	80.60	80.70.60.65
75	0.*40*. *x*	40.*65*.50	65.60	65.55.60.55
70	0.*40*. *x*	40.*65*.50	65.50	65.55.50.55
65	0.*40*. *x*	40.25.*50*	50.50	50.55.50.55
60	0.*40*. *x*	40.25.*50*	50.50	50.45.50.40
55	0.*40*. *x*	40.25. *x*	40.50	50.45.35.40
50	0.*40*. *x*	40.25. *x*	40.35	40.45.35.25
45	0.*40*. *x*	40.25. *x*	40.35	40.30.20.25
40	0.*40*. *x*	40.25. *x*	40.10	40.30.20.25
35	*0. x. x*	0.25. *x*	25.10	25.15.20.15
30	*0. x. x*	0.25. *x*	25.10	25.15.10.15
25	*0. x. x*	*0. x. x*	0.10	10.*15*.10.*15*
20	*0. x. x*	*0. x. x*	0·10	*10*. 5.*10*. *x*
15	*0. x. x*	*0. x. x*	0.10	*10*. 5. *x*. *x*
10	*0. x. x*	*0. x. x*	*0. x*	0. 5. *x*. *x*
5	*0. x. x*	*0. x. x*	*0. x*	*0. x. x. x*
0	*0. x. x*	*0. x. x*	*0. x*	*0. x. x. x*

type 1 with a value 80. Similarly we can exclude $r \geqslant 2$ when $n = 3$. Let us now calculate $f_4(100)$ assuming $\{f_n(w)\}$ has been calculated for $n \leqslant 3$, $w \leqslant 100$. Letting $r = 0, 1, 2, 3$ we obtain

$$f_4(100) = \max \begin{cases} r = 0: & 0 + f_3(100) = & 0 + 90 = 90 \\ r = 1: & 5 + f_3(92) = & 5 + 80 = 85 \\ r = 2: & 10 + f_3(84) = & 10 + 80 = 90 \\ r = 3: & 15 + f_3(76) = & 15 + 65 = 80 \end{cases}$$

4

This takes its maximum value when $r = 0$ or $r = 2$ and is printed in italic in the appropriate columns.

The optimal policy is given by the columns in which the values are italicised. Thus if $r_n(w)$ is the optimal number of packages of type n when packages up to type n are allowed and capacity w exists, we have, for example:

$$r_1(85) = 2$$
$$r_2(90) = 0$$
$$r_3(65) = 0, 1$$
$$r_4(80) = 0.$$

The optimal package numbers when $n = 4$, $w = 100$ are then obtained as follows:

$r_4(100) = 0$	Leaving residual capacity			100
$= 2$	,,	,,	,,	84
$r_3(100) = 0$	,,	,,	,,	100
$= 1$	,,	,,	,,	85
$r_3(84) = 0$	,,	,,	,,	84
$r_2(100) = 2$	,,	,,	,,	40
$r_2(85) = 0$	,,	,,	,,	85
$r_2(84) = 0$	,,	,,	,,	84
$r_1(40) = 1$	,,	,,	,,	0
$r_1(85) = 2$	,,	,,	,,	5
$r_1(84) = 2$	,,	,,	,,	4

Optimal solutions:

r_4	0	0	2
r_3	0	1	0
r_2	2	0	0
r_1	1	2	2

Other examples of this type of problem occur which are a little more realistic, e.g. in the design of electronic systems where reliability is required but resources are limited. The reliability of the system is given by a function $R = \prod_{i=1}^{n} (1 - q_i^{N_i})$, where q_i is the probability that an ith stage component will fail when called upon and we use N_i components in parallel, at the ith stage.

If c_i is the cost of the component type i, and if c is the allowable budget, we get the functional equation

$$f_m(c) = \max_{0 \leqslant N_m \leqslant [c/c_m]} [(1 - q_m^{N_m}) f_{m-1}(c - c_m N_m)], \qquad (4.6)$$

where $f_m(c)$ is the optimal reliability attainable over the first m stages with a given budget c, and $[c/c_m]$ is the integral part of c/c_m.

Further examples can be found in Bellman.[9, 16]

The problems we have dealt with so far are of the single resource type. The general problem is of the multiple resource type and can be stated thus:

maximise $\sum_{i=1}^{n} g_i(x_i)$ subject to:

$$\sum_{s=1}^{n} \alpha_{ks} x_s = c_k, \; k = 1, 2, \ldots l$$

$$x_s \geqslant 0, \, s = 1, 2, \ldots n.$$

The D.P. approach results in the following functional equation (derived in a fashion similar to (4.4)).

$$f_m(c_1, c_2, \ldots c_l) = \max_{0 \leqslant x_m \leqslant \min_k [c_k/\alpha_{km}]} [g_m(x_m) + f_{m-1}(c_1^* c_2^* \ldots c_l^*)],$$
$$(4.7)$$

where

$$c_k^* = c_k - \alpha_{km} x_m, \; k = 1, 2, \ldots l.$$

$f_m(c_1, c_2, \ldots c_l)$ is the total return from given resource $(c_1, c_2, \ldots c_l)$, using activities $1, 2, \ldots m$ and using an optimal policy.

Of course computational difficulties arise in using (4.7) if l is large, but these are purely computational as distinct from problems of procedure in other methods. Later on we shall discuss a method of simplifying such computations, which is applicable to a much wider class of problems than those at present being discussed. We consider the Lagrangian function

$$\phi(x, \lambda) = \sum_{i=1}^{n} g_i(x_i) - \sum_{k=1}^{l'} \sum_{i=1}^{n} \lambda_k \alpha_{ki} x_i.$$

We then use the D.P. approach to maximise ϕ subject to the restrictions

$$\sum_{s=1}^{n} \alpha_{ks} x_s = c_k, \, k = l'+1, \ldots l.$$

The parameters $\lambda_1 \lambda_2 \ldots \lambda_{l'}$ are varied until constraints $1-l'$ are satisfied. The proof that such a procedure will give an optimal solution to the original problem is included in the appendix for convenience. This is true, however, only if we know that eventually, by varying $\{\lambda_i\}$, we shall enter the constraint area. In the Appendix to this Chapter (p. 165) we given an example where this is not the case. As a consequence we need to take care in using this approach.

The Lagrange parameter method reduces the problem from one of storing functions of l variables to one of storing functions of $(l-l')$

variables. However the l' variables $\lambda_1 \lambda_2, \ldots \lambda_{l'}$ also enter into the calculations for only by observing how the first l' constraints are broken or otherwise, for each set of $\lambda_1, \lambda_2, \ldots \lambda_{l'}$, can we decide how to alter the $\{\lambda_k\}$ to reach a satisfactory solution. Nevertheless the solution of the D.P. only requires storage of functions of $(l-l')$ variables and the relationships between the manner in which the first l' constraints are broken and the l' parameters $\lambda_1, \lambda_2, \ldots \lambda_{l'}$ requires only vector functions of l' variables.

Thus, if $l = 5$, the D.P. approach, using the full dimension of 5, would be almost impossible if a fine division of the range of each variable is called for. Taking $l' = 2$, we can reduce the problem to a D.P. problem in three variables (c_3, c_4, c_5), conditional on specified values of λ_1, λ_2. For each λ_1, λ_2 we calculate $f_n(c_3, c_4, c_5 \mid \lambda_1, \lambda_2)$ where $g_i(x_i)$ is replaced by

$$g_i(x_i) - \lambda_1 \alpha_{1i} x_i - \lambda_2 \alpha_{2i} x_i.$$

We then check that the optimum solution, $x_1, x_2, \ldots x_n$ satisfies the constraints

$$\Sigma_i \alpha_{ki} x_i = c_k, \quad k = 1, 2.$$

If not, we vary λ_1, λ_2 until such a solution is obtained.

If we knew more about how to change the parameters $\lambda_1, \lambda_2, \ldots \lambda_{l'}$, after each D.P. step, then, without a doubt, this approach would, in spite of the amount of computation, have a lot to recommend it. Unfortunately we do not. Bellman [16] shows that certain monotone properties exist for problems in which one Lagrange parameter is involved. To be more specific, if we wish to maximise $J(x_1, x_2, \ldots x_n)$ subject to $H(x_1, x_2, \ldots x_n) = 0$ and if the Lagrangian function is $X(x, \lambda) = J - \lambda H$, then, if $x(\lambda)$ maximises $X(x, \lambda)$, Bellman shows that $H[x(\lambda)]$ decreases with λ (and so also does $J[x(\lambda)]$, but this is not of great significance).

Extending Bellman's analysis to the problem of maximising J subject to r restrictions $H_s(x) = 0$, we consider the Lagrangian

$$X(x, \lambda) = J - \sum_{s=1}^{r} \lambda_s H_s.$$

We can show (see Appendix, p. 166) that, if λ, λ' are two sets of λ parameters, then

$$\Sigma_s(\lambda'_s - \lambda_s)\{H_s[x(\lambda)] - H_s[x(\lambda')]\} \geqslant 0. \tag{4.8}$$

If λ' is such that $H_s[x(\lambda')] = 0$. $s = 1, 2, \ldots r$ then

$$\Sigma_s(\lambda'_s - \lambda_s)H_s[x(\lambda) \geqslant 0].$$

This seems to suggest that if we have just computed a solution for a specific λ, then any change $\Delta\lambda$, for the next iteration, should satisfy

$$\Sigma_s\Delta\lambda_s H_s[x(\lambda)] \geqslant 0. \qquad (4.9)$$

This helps a little, but in general further work is needed to rationally guide our choice of changes in λ from one iteration to the next.

Before proceeding to the next class of problems it ought perhaps to be mentioned that there is no increase in complexity, using D.P. if neither the constraints nor the objective function are linear, but remain separable. This is all in keeping with the points made in Chapter Three, about general functional relations between path values and sub-path values.

As an example, suppose our objective function satisfies the relation

$$\theta_n(x_1, x_2, \ldots x_n) = F_n[x_n, \theta_{n-1}(x_1, x_2, \ldots x_{n-1})],$$

and in general,

$$\theta_m(x_1, x_2, \ldots x_m) = F_m[x_m, \theta_{m-1}(x_1, x_2, \ldots x_{m-1})].$$

Suppose also we have one restriction
$\phi_n(x_1, x_2, \ldots x_n) = c$ which can, as above, be separated into

$$\phi_m(x_1, x_2, \ldots x_m) = H_m[x_m, \phi_{m-1}(x_1, x_2, \ldots x_{m-1})], \quad m = 1, 2, \ldots n.$$

If $H_{m-1}^{-1}(x_m, c)$ is the inverse function for ϕ_{m-1} in terms of x_m, c we derive the following functional equation

$$f_m(c) = \max_{x_m \in R_m(c)}[F_m\{x_m, f_{m-1}[H_m^{-1}(x_m, c)]\}]. \qquad (4.10)$$

This holds only if the Principle of Optimality holds of course, which it need not do, as pointed out in Chapter 3. $R_m(c)$ is the allowable region for x_m when c is given.

B. Assortment Problems

There are many situations in which a manufacturer either produces a product in various sizes and/or purchases a specific raw material (or components of some kind) in various sizes required to produce the products. Since, for a variety of reasons, the number of different sizes is limited, the inevitable question of the appropriate sizes to use arises. Too large a variety of sizes causes difficulties (e.g. production scheduling, etc.). Too few sizes also causes diseconomies (e.g. the manufacturer may have to provide the customer with a size (which will do the job) at a premium, since, had he produced a different size this might have been within the customer's requirements and might have cost less to produce). Sadowski [40] discusses the problem of determining the optimum variety of sizes of steel beams to produce. The customer requires a specified strength in his beams. This is related to cross section and hence to beam weight. He must be supplied with a beam of at least the strength he wants, but he can only be charged for a beam of precisely the strength he wants. What beam sizes should be produced, bearing in mind that these determine the equipment to install? A similar problem is discussed in White,[45] this time concerned with the determination of ingot mould sizes so as to minimise the deviation of total tonnage actually supplied from total tonnage requested. The following problem is taken from White.[45]

A manufacturer supplies plastic sheet in fixed widths. This sheet is laminated with a foil purchased from the supplier in a limited number of sizes. Obviously any foil width used must be at least as wide as the sheet it laminates. Which foil widths shall be used to minimise the cost of satisfying the customer's orders (assumed known) for laminated sheet over the next year? We would want to know the answer for any allowable number of widths to begin with.

Let $\phi(w,z)$ be the minimal cost of laminating all widths in the range $w \leqslant s \leqslant z$ using one foil width only. This is obtained by finding the cost of making all orders in this range from the one smallest possible foil width.

Let $f_m(w)$ be the cost of satisfying all orders for widths greater than or equal to w using at most m different foil widths and using an optimal policy. We then derive

if $\qquad\qquad m \geqslant 1$

$$f_m(w) = \min_{z \geqslant w}[\phi(w,z) + f_{m-1}(z^+)]$$
$$f_0(w) \equiv 0 \text{ if } w > 41$$
$$\qquad = \infty \text{ if } w \leqslant 41 \qquad\qquad (4.11)$$

z^+ is the next sheet width required above z.

Equation (4.11) is explained as follows. We wish to cover the range w to 41. We let our smallest foil width be used for the range w to z (inclusive), the associated cost being $\phi(w,z)$. This leaves us $(m-1)$ possible foil widths to cover the range above z, i.e. from z^+ to 41, which we do, in an optimal manner at a cost of $f_{m-1}(z^+)$. The reason z^+ was used is that it is pointless to cater for widths not demanded.

Table 2 indicates how the calculations were carried out for a specific example. As well as computing the optimal value, we need to compute the optimal policy at each stage, viz. $z_s(w)$.

TABLE 2: RAW MATERIAL WIDTHS ASSORTMENT PROBLEM

w / z	41	40	38	36	35	34	33	32	31	30	29	28	27	26	25	24	22	21	$f_1(z^+)$	$f_2(z^+)$	$f_3(z^+)$
41	50	91	101	124	270	218	243	357	384	479	689	718	764	920	1262	1500	1518	1576	50	50	50
40		41	51	74	120	168	194	308	334	429	639	669	714	871	1212	1450	1468	1527	91	91	91
38			11	33	79	127	152	265	291	385	594	623	668	824	1163	1399	1417	1475	101	101	101
36				22	68	115	139	251	277	370	577	605	650	803	1138	1371	1389	1446	124	123	123
35					45	93	117	229	255	348	554	583	627	781	1116	1349	1367	1421	170	169	168
34						46	70	180	206	297	500	528	572	722	1052	1281	1298	1354	218	216	215
33							24	133	158	248	449	477	520	669	995	1222	1239	1295	243	240	239
32								108	133	232	421	449	491	639	962	1186	1203	1258	357	350	348
31									25	113	309	336	378	524	843	1064	1081	1135	384	376	373
30										88	284	311	353	498	816	1036	1053	1107	479	466	463
29											195	223	265	410	728	948	965	1019	689	664	659
28												27	68	210	520	735	752	804	718	692	686
27													41	183	493	708	725	778	764	734	728
26														141	450	664	680	733	920	881	874
25															304	515	532	583	1262	1200	1184
24																208	224	275	1500	1420	1396
22																	16	66	1518	1437	1413
21																		50			

w	41	40	38	36	35	34	33	32	31	30	29	28	27	26	25	24	22	21
$f_2(w)$	50	91	101	123	169	216	240	350	376	466	664	692	734	881	1200	1420	1437	1492
$z_2(w)$	41	41 40	41 40	36	35 36	36 34	36 34	34	32 33 34	33	32	32	32	31	30 31	30	30	31
$f_3(w)$	50	91	101	123	168	215	239	348	373	463	659	686	728	874	1184	1396	1413	1464
$z_3(w)$	41	41 40	41 40	36	35	34	34	32	32	31	31	31	31	28 30 31	26 28	25	25	25
$f_4(w)$	50	91	101	123	168	214	238	347	372	461	657	684	726	869	1178	1389	1406	1457
$z_4(w)$	41	41 40	41 40	36	35	34	34	32	32	30 31	30 31	30 31	30 31	26 27 28	25 26	25	25	25

Suppose we have calculated $f_1(w)$ for all w, and suppose we wish to calculate $f_2(30)$

$$f_2(30) = \min_{z \geqslant 30}[\phi(30,z)+f_1(z^+)],$$

$$= \min \begin{bmatrix} \overset{z}{30} & 31 & 32 & 33 & 34 & 35 & 36 & 38 & 40 & 41 \\ \overline{88} & \overline{113} & \overline{232} & \overline{248} & \overline{297} & \overline{348} & \overline{370} & \overline{385} & \overline{429} & 479 \\ +384 & +357 & +243 & +218 & +170 & +124 & +101 & +91 & +50 & +0 \\ \overline{472} & \overline{470} & \overline{475} & \overline{466} & \overline{467} & \overline{472} & \overline{471} & \overline{476} & \overline{479} & \overline{479} \end{bmatrix},$$

$$= 466,$$

$z_2(30)$ (= highest width to be covered in next group) is 33.

When we have calculated $f_m(w)$, $z_m(w)$ for all w, and $m = 1, 2, 3, 4$ we can then find the optimal solution to cover the range $w = 21$ to $w = 41$.

Thus

$$f_4(21) = 1457 \qquad z_4(21) = 25 \qquad z^+ = 26$$
$$z_3(26) = 28 \qquad z^+ = 29$$
$$30 \qquad z^+ = 31$$
$$31 \qquad z^+ = 32$$
$$z_2(29) = 32 \qquad z^+ = 33$$
$$z_2(31) = 32 \qquad z^+ = 33$$
$$33 \qquad z^+ = 34$$
$$34 \qquad z^+ = 35$$
$$z_2(32) = 34 \qquad z^+ = 35$$
$$z_1(w) = 41.$$

Thus we have many possible solutions, e.g.

$$(25, 28, 32, 41)$$
or $$(25, 30, 32, 41), \text{ etc.}$$

Let us now look at an alternative formulation, viz. choose $x_1 \leqslant x_2 \leqslant x_3 \ldots \leqslant x_4$ (= 41) to minimize

$$\phi(21,x_1)+\phi(x_1+1,x_2)+\phi(x_2+1,x_3)+\phi(x_3+1,x_4). \qquad (4.12)$$

It is obvious that for general forms of $\phi(w,z)$ this could provide difficulties. The ϕ may not, in general, be particularly well behaved, and there is nothing to prevent some of the $\{x_i\}$ coinciding. Even such a simple problem can provide severe difficulties without D.P.

There is, in addition, one other very important advantage in using D.P. If it were not for some form of costs arising from producing a large number of widths, we would use a different foil width for each sheet width. Nevertheless the choice of the number of widths is, itself, free and must be made against the background costs associated with each degree of variety. We are therefore, in general, interested in the solution for any reasonable n. D.P. provides this quite naturally, whereas other approaches do not. As we shall see later, this point applies to sequential planning problems as well.

For this problem we might reason thus. The supplier will only supply us with four widths because of certain economic considerations. Suppose that, if we had five widths, we could make a further significant saving, we might, by offering more money to the supplier, induce him to provide five widths. How much can we save, at present prices, by having the fifth width? Immediately we calculate

$$f_5(21) = \min_{z \geqslant 21}[\phi(21,z) + f_4(z^+)]. \tag{4.13}$$

It does not take long to solve this and find out that $f_5(21) = 1452$. Thus only 5 units can be gained by allowing a further width. On the other hand, since $f_3(21) = 1461$, only 7 units are added by using three widths, and the supplier might gladly reduce the total cost by this amount if he could get away with three widths. In short, D.P. provides information which other methods do not, without complete recomputation at least.

4.2. Dynamic Programming and Sequential Discrete Optimisation Problems

In Chapter 4, Section 1 we tried to point out the advantage of using D.P. for some non-sequential optimisation problems. There are also problems of justifying the use of D.P. for some sequential problems for which other approaches exist. In this section several problems will be discussed which we may break up into two classes, viz. long term planning problems and multi-stage production processes; the first class being sequential through its time orientation, and the second because of the sequential nature of the production processes.

A. Long Term Planning Problems

There is a whole class of problems involving high cost repetitive decisions over a long time period which falls naturally within the D.P. area. Such problems may centre on the long term minimisation of costs to meet specified demands for products or service, and involve a variety of decisions. These decisions may be of the replacement-of-equipment type, overhaul-of-equipment type, and expansion-of-capacity type, etc. There are, of course, planning problems centering on some concept of long term income (or profit) maximisation, and these can be treated in a similar manner, although the idea of profit maximisation is not easy to define. For the present, we shall stick to cost minimisation, and refer the reader to Chapter 5 for a discussion of a stochastic problem of long term investment planning.

(a) *Optimal Equipment Replacement Policies*. Before proceeding to the mathematics it is perhaps worth emphasising a conceptual advantage of D.P. taken up again in Chapter 5. It is traditional among some diehards to take the attitude that what matters to some extent when deciding when to replace a piece of equipment is the amount of use we have got out of it so far. They are loth to replace a piece of equipment for the sole reason that 'we have only recently paid £5,000 for it and must get some use out of it before we replace it'. This point of view is retrospective and conflicts most strikingly with the governing Principle of Optimality, which states that 'it is future performance that matters', and if, economically speaking, a replacement is justified, since it will minimise the future operating costs, then what we have already paid for it should not matter in the least.

This attitude exists in the context of depreciation policies, which write off the equipment in a more or less arbitrary manner and inject a correspondingly arbitrary value of the equipment to the company at any point in time. Apart from the tax reasons, such a procedure is more concerned with setting aside money for replacing the equipment rather than with the economic values, to the company, of replacing it at any specific time. D.P. provides a natural way of deducing such values (in keeping with Chapter 3) which are derived from optimal future economic behaviour prerequisites.

A fair amount of research into economic replacement intervals has been carried out, previously by the Machinery and Allied Products Institute (M.A.P.I. for short) and later by Terborgh.[42] Although an effort is made to take account of the effect of present decisions on future decisions, and also to take account of technological changes, nevertheless these analyses are not based on the principle of optimising long term economic behaviour. Bellman [17] is, to my knowledge, the first one to attempt to do so. Starbuck [41] attempts to generalise Terborgh's work to the long-term optimisation case, and provides the non-sequential optimisation technique which we shall mention later, his objective being to simplify the results in the face of the computational difficulties inherent in this approach.

Although the following models omit many factors, not the least of which is the limited supply of cash for replacement, due to other competing activities, it is, we hope, at least a step in the right direction. It would be of interest to extend these models to take account of such contingencies, perhaps in a manner similar to the treatment of the stochastic investment problem of Chapter 5, but, for the purpose of exposition, we must keep to simple situations.

First of all let us consider the case where no technological change takes place. We shall make the following assumptions:

(*i*) Each piece of equipment will be identical in every characteristic.

(*ii*) A new piece of equipment costs p.

(*iii*) The cost of operating a piece of equipment of age t for one period of time is $c(t)$.

(*iv*) The trade-in value of a piece of equipment of age t is $s(t)$.

(*v*) The objective criterion will be to minimise overall operating costs over n periods of time, these costs being reduced to their present worth (see Chapter 6 for a discussion of this point) using a discount factor α.

Define $v_n(t)$ to be the cost of operating over the next n periods of time, beginning with equipment of age t and using an optimal policy. Then, if the decision is to keep the equipment for a further m units of time, before trading it in for a new one, we have:

if $n \geqslant 1$

$$v_n(t) = \min_{0 \leqslant m \leqslant n} \left[\sum_{k=0}^{m-1} \alpha^k c(t+k) + [p - s(t+m)]\alpha^m + \alpha^m v_{n-m}(0) \right],$$

$$v_0(t) \equiv 0. \tag{4.14}$$

The first two terms represent the operating cost plus purchase cost less trade-in price over the next m periods of time. The final term expresses, via the Principle of Optimality, the residual cost of beginning with new equipment and having $(n-m)$ time units left over which to operate.

In particular, for $t = 0$,

$$v_n(0) = \min_{0 \leqslant m \leqslant n} \left[\sum_{k=0}^{m-1} \alpha^k c(k) + \alpha^m [p - s(m)] + \alpha^m v_{n-m}(0) \right]. \tag{4.15}$$

If $\alpha < 1$, we can show (see Appendix, pp. 166–167), if $m \geqslant 1$, that $\{v_n(0)\}$ converges to a limit v satisfying:

$$v = \min_{m \geqslant 1} \left[\left\{ \sum_{k=0}^{m-1} \alpha^k c(k) + \alpha^m [p - s(m)] \right\} \middle/ (1 - \alpha^m) \right]. \tag{4.16}$$

Then (4.14) becomes, in the limit,

$$v(t) = \min_{m \geqslant 0} \left[\sum_{k=0}^{m-1} \alpha^k c(k+t) + \alpha^m [p - s(t+m)] + \alpha^m v \right]. \tag{4.17}$$

If the cost functions are given analytically the minimum can be determined using conventional calculus methods. Where these are not applicable then a straight tabulation for a range of likely m values is needed.

We settle down to a regular replacement period given by (4.16) and from (4.17) we can determine what to do if we at present possess a piece of equipment of age t.

When $\alpha = 1$, we can determine the optimal solution from (4.16) by letting $\alpha \to 1$, and substituting in (4.16). We see then that m minimises

$$\sum_{k=0}^{m-1} [c(k)+p-s(m)]/m. \qquad (4.18)$$

This expression is, of course, the average cost per unit time for a regular replacement period policy. It appears to be singularly difficult to determine this result direct from the original equations rigorously, although assuming $v_n(t) = ng + r_n(t)$ where $r_n(t)$ is uniformly bounded, for any replacement policy, gives the result heuristically. It may be, as is pointed out for stochastic systems in Chapter 5, that optimal policies may oscillate although the costs per unit time for steady state policies will be arbitrarily close to those for true optimal policies.

In reality, of course, technological change is taking place, and we ought to modify the functions involved to take account of this. This raises problems since not only costs change but so also does output capacity, and even quality of product or service. If we are replacing batches of equipment, all of the same age, at the same time, then the first point does not matter much providing we keep the total output capacity the same. Otherwise the problem ought really to be re-examined to see what use is made of changes in capacity of equipment. In principle precisely the same approach can be taken whatever the case, and we shall, again for expository reasons, assume that the capacity is the same for all replacements.

The changes we shall make are:

(i) A new piece of equipment costs $p(T)$ at calendar time T.

(ii) The cost of operating a piece of equipment of age t at calendar time T is $c(t,T)$.

(iii) The trade-in value of a piece of equipment of age t at calendar time T is $s(t,T)$.

(iv) The objective criterion will be as before, except that we begin at calendar time T, this being an essential part of the state description.

Defining $v_n(t,T)$ to be the cost of operating over the next n periods of time, beginning at calendar time T with equipment of age t and using an optimal policy, we see that, again using present worth values, if $n \geqslant 1$

$$v_n(t,T) = \min_{0 \leqslant m \leqslant n}\left[\sum_{k=0}^{m-1} \alpha^k c(t+k,T+k) + \alpha^m[p(T+m) - s(t+m,T+m)]\right.$$

$$\left. + \alpha^m v_{n-m}(0,T+m)\right], \qquad (4.19)$$

$$v_0(t,T) \equiv 0.$$

If

$$\sum_{r=0}^{\infty} \{\alpha^r c(0,r) + \alpha^{r+1}[p(T+r) - s(1,T+r)]\},$$

is uniformly convergent for all T, we can show (see Appendix, p. 167) that $\{v_n(t,T)\}$ tends uniformly to a function $v(t,T)$, satisfying

$$v(t,T) = \min_{0 \leqslant m \leqslant n}\left[\sum_{k=0}^{m-1} \alpha^k c(t+k,T+k) + \alpha^m[p(T+m) - s(t+m,T+m)]\right.$$

$$\left. + \alpha^m v(0,T+m)\right]. \qquad (4.20)$$

In particular, for $t = 0$, putting $v(0,T)$ equal to $u(T)$ we get, since we must have $m \geqslant 1$ for new equipment,

$$u(T) = \min_{m \geqslant 1}\left[\sum_{k=0}^{m-1} \alpha^k c(k,T+k) + \alpha^m[p(T+m) - s(m,T+m)] + \right.$$

$$\left. \alpha^m u(T+m)\right]. \qquad (4.21)$$

This can be rewritten:

$$u(T) = \min_{m \geqslant 1}[\theta(T,m) + \alpha^m u(T+m)], \qquad (4.22)$$

where

$$\theta(T,m) = \sum_{k=0}^{m-1} \alpha^k c(k,T+k) + \alpha^m[p(T+m) - s(m,T+m)].$$

Obviously $u(T)$ is monotone decreasing in T and $u(T) \geqslant 0$ for all T. Hence the sequence $\{u(T)\}$ converges to a limit u as $T \to \infty$. This limit satisfies the equation

$$u = \min_{m \geqslant 1}[\theta(m) + \alpha^m u], \qquad (4.23)$$

where $\theta(m) = Lt_{T \to \infty}\theta(T,m)$, which we assume exists. This becomes

$$u = \min_{m \geqslant 1}[\theta(m)/(1 - \alpha^m)]. \qquad (4.24)$$

This equation is identical with equation (4.16) in form, and, indeed, if $\theta(T,m)$ is independent of T, they are identical.

Having computed u, the problem is to choose a T such that $u(T)$ is approximately equal to u. This can be achieved by computing $u^*(T)$ from

$$u^*(T) = \min_{m \geqslant 1}[\theta(T,m)+\alpha^m u]$$
$$= \min_{m \geqslant 1}[\phi(T,m)], \text{ say}. \qquad (4.25)$$

We then choose T^* so that $u^*(T^*) = (1+\varepsilon)u$ for some small ε. Then since the states in (4.22) form a directed set, we can compute approximate values for $u(T)$ from this, viz.

$$u(T^*-1) = \min_{m \geqslant 1}[\theta(T^*-1,m)+\alpha^m u^*(T^*)]$$
$$u(T^*-2) = \min_{m \geqslant 1}[\theta(T^*-2,m)+\alpha^m u(T^*-1)]$$

and so on.

Let us now consider an example. Let $m(T)$ be the minimising m for $\phi(T,m)$. We then have

$$\phi[T,m(T)] \leqslant u(T) \leqslant \theta[T,m(T)]+\alpha^{m(T)}u(T+m(T)). \qquad (4.26)$$

We thus find $m(T)$ and $\theta(T,m(T))$ first of all.
Let

$$c(t,T) = c\lambda^t \mu^{T-t},$$
$$s(t,T) = s\delta^t,$$
$$p(T) = p.$$

Then

$$\theta(T,m) = c\mu^T \sum_{k=0}^{m-1} (\alpha\lambda)^k + \alpha^m(p-s\delta^m).$$

Let $\alpha\lambda = 1$, $\alpha = 0.9$, $\mu = 0.8$, $c = 0.1$, $\delta = 0.9$, $p = 1$, $s = 0.5$

Then

$$\theta(T,m) = 0.1m(0.8)^T + (0.9)^m[1 - 0.5 \times (0.9)^m].$$

It is easily seen that u (in equation (4.24)) $= 0$. We need therefore to find T^* such that $u(T^*)$ is 'approximately' 0. The word 'approximate' is used since it depends on the scale of costs. We need to calculate $u(1)$ to assess the relative smallness.

We see easily that

$$u(1) \geqslant \theta(1,m(1)) = 0.575.$$

Also
$$\theta(19,m(19)) = \text{(approximately) } 0.07,$$
$$m(19) = \text{(approximately) } 41.2.$$

Thus since $u(T) \leqslant \theta(T,m(T))/(1-\alpha^{m(T)})$
we have $u(19) \leqslant \text{(approximately) } 0.07$.

Hence, compared with $u(1)$, $u(19)$ is very small. If we put $u(T) = 0$, $T \geqslant 20$, say, and compute $u(T)$, $T \leqslant 19$ from equation (4.22), we should get a satisfactory result.

In fact, this is a little stronger than is needed. All we need to find is a T^* such that $\alpha^{m(T^*)}u(T^* + m(T^*))$ is small as compared with $\theta(T^*, m(T^*))$. We find that

$$\theta(10, m(10)) = (\text{approximately}) \ 0{\cdot}34,$$
$$m(10) = (\text{approximately}) \ 21{\cdot}6.$$

This follows since $u(31{\cdot}6) \leqslant u(20) \leqslant \theta(20, m(20)) + \alpha^{m(20)}u(20)$ and hence $u(31{\cdot}6) \leqslant u(20) \leqslant \theta(20, m(20))/(1 - \alpha^{m(20)})$.

TABLE 3

T	$m(\text{optimal}) \sim m(T)$	$u(T) \sim \theta(T, m(T))$
10	21·7	0·338
11	23·8	0·286
12	25·9	0·244
13	28·1	0·207
14	30·2	0·175
15	32·3	0·147
16	34·4	0·123
17	36·5	0·104
18	38·7	0·087
19	40·8	0·073
20	42·9	0·063
21	45·0	0·051
22	47·1	0·042
23	49·3	0·034
24	51·4	0·029
25	53·5	0·024
26	55·6	0·020
27	57·7	0·016
28	59·9	0·013
29	62·0	0·011
30	64·1	0·009
31	66·2	0·007
32	68·3	0·006
33	70·5	0·005

Hence, for $T \geqslant 10 = T^*$, we can take

$$u(T) = \theta(T, m(T)),$$

and $m(T)$ to be the optimal policy.

The tabulations for $T \geqslant 10$ are given in Table 3. We shall now calculate $u(T)$ for $T \leqslant 9$ using equation (4.22).

Let $X(T,m) = \theta(T,m)+\alpha^m u(T+m)$. Then in Table 4 we calculate $X(T,m)$, $T\leqslant 9$, $m\leqslant 24$, the latter limit being chosen by virtue of the nature of the behaviour of m (optimal) for $T\geqslant 10$. In fact we could have taken $T\leqslant 22$ without any risk. The italicised figures are the minimal costs for a given value of T and the optimal value of m is given by the

TABLE 4

					T					
	0	1	2	3	4	5	6	7	8	9
1.	1·620	1·475	1·339	1·178	1·136	1·048	0·978	0·916	0·856	0·813
2.	1·488	1·341	1·122	1·123	1·033	0·959	0·903	0·841	0·789	0·741
3.	1·395	1·255	1·140	1·038	0·958	0·889	0·827	0·772	0·723	0·683
4.	1·341	1·199	1·080	0·979	0·898	0·830	0·767	0·713	0·669	0·633
5.	1·313	1·161	1·037	0·936	0·855	0·782	0·716	0·667	0·625	0·591
6.	*1·300*	1·142	1·013	0·907	0·818	0·742	0·678	0·628	0·587	0·549
7.	1·309	*1·139*	1·002	0·885	0·790	0·714	0·647	0·597	0·555	0·523
8.	1·333	1·150	*0·998*	0·871	0·773	0·693	0·623	0·571	0·529	0·497
9.	1·385	1·164	1·000	*0·867*	0·762	0·678	0·604	0·550	0·506	0·473
10.	1·405	1·187	1·012	0·869	*0·758*	0·668	0·590	0·533	0·487	0·452
11.	1·456	1·223	1·035	0·883	0·763	*0·668*	0·585	0·524	0·476	0·440
m 12.	1·511	1·262	1·061	0·897	0·770	*0·668*	*0·580*	0·516	0·465	0·425
13.	1·576	1·308	1·092	0·921	0·783	0·674	*0·580*	0·512	0·457	0·416
14.	1·642	1·356	1·126	0·940	0·796	0·681	*0·580*	*0·508*	0·450	0·406
15.	1·715	1·410	1·166	0·968	0·815	0·693	0·585	0·509	0·447	0·401
16.	1·792	1·468	1·209	0·999	0·837	0·707	0·593	0·511	*0·446*	0·397
17.	1·870	1·528	1·253	1·030	0·859	0·721	0·601	0·515	*0·446*	0·394
18.	1·952	1·590	1·301	1·065	0·883	0·738	0·611	0·521	0·448	*0·393*
19.	2·036	1·655	1·347	1·101	0·910	0·757	0·623	0·528	0·451	0·394
20.	2·123	1·721	1·400	1·139	0·939	0·778	0·637	0·537	0·457	0·369
21.	2·209	1·788	1·451	1·177	0·967	0·798	0·651	0·546	0·461	0·398
22.	2·298	1·857	1·505	1·218	0·998	0·822	0·667	0·557	0·469	0·403
23.	2·388	1·928	1·559	1·260	1·029	0·845	0·684	0·569	0·477	0·408
24.	2·479	1·999	1·615	1·302	1·162	0·870	0·702	0·582	0·485	0·413

row number in which it occurs. Thus the complete table for m (optimal) and the $u(T)$ is given in Table 5 where we have taken m to be the best integer value.

As an exercise, the optimal (integer) value of m, if we have initially a machine of age 3 at absolute time 10, is 11, and $v(3,10) = 0·613$ (equation (4.20)).

This gives only an approximate solution but should be adequate for all practical purposes. The computational algorithm is of the directed type as mentioned in Chapter 2. We could, if we wished, use the method of successive approximations, which is valid for this problem also, under the conditions placed on the uniform convergence of

$$\sum_{r=0}^{\infty} \alpha^r \{c(0,T+r)+\alpha[p(T+r)-s(1,T+r)]\} \text{ viz.}$$

$$\text{if } r \geqslant 1$$
$$u_r(T) = \min_{m \geqslant 1}[\theta(T,m)+\alpha^m u_{r-1}(T+m)],$$
$$\theta_0(T) \equiv 0. \tag{4.27}$$

The case when $\alpha = 1$ remains to be solved, but we can approximate to it by letting α be close to 1.

TABLE 5

T	m (optimal)	$u(T)$
0	6	1·300
1	7	1·139
2	8	0·998
3	9	0·867
4	10	0·758
5	10, 11, 12	0·668
6	12, 13, 14	0·580
7	14	0·508
8	16, 17	0·446
9	18	0·393

What now of any alternative procedure for solving, say, the problem with technological change? The obvious approach, and one adopted by Starbuck,[41] is to allow for replacements at times $T_1, T_2, \ldots T_k$ beginning with a new piece of equipment at time $T_0 = 0$ (chosen for convenience). The long term objective criterion is then, if $T_0 = 0$,

$$\phi(T_1, T_2, \ldots T_k \ldots) = \sum_{k=1}^{\infty} \alpha^{T_{k-1}}\theta(T_{k-1}, T_k - T_{k-1})$$

$$= \sum_{k=1}^{\infty} \alpha^{T_{k-1}} R(T_{k-1}, T_k). \tag{4.28}$$

Even if we could use calculus methods, and differentiate, we would have an infinite number of equations for the infinite time period. Unless the function R takes a particularly easy form, it will be very difficult to solve. If we try to treat a finite duration problem this way, we do not know how many replacement points, T_k, will be required for each n, and would have to carry out computations for various possible numbers of replacements.

Thus we see that, if we can treat n as infinite, the D.P. method is extremely easy, but the other method virtually impossible in general. If n is quite small, the D.P. approach not only overcomes the difficulty

5

arising from the, initially, unknown number of replacements, but we can also, as with the optimal widths problem of Section 4.1, provide ourselves with an analysis of the sensitivity of the solution to changes in *n*, a very important point in long term planning problems.

It must be noted that it is not the sensitivity of policy to changes in *n* which is important. The correct sensitivity analysis is to find the difference in the cost over a specific period $n+\Delta n$, using the optimal policy pertaining to an *n* period duration, and the optimal cost for an $n+\Delta n$ period duration. An analysis of this kind, for a similar type of problem, has been carried out by Norman.[33]

(*b*) *Optimal Capacity Expansion Policies.* As pointed out previously, there is a whole class of problems in which demand for a service, or product, is increasing over time, and for which problems of meeting this demand in a most economical manner exist. We shall analyse a relatively simple one, from the D.P. point of view, but for which other analyses again meet difficulties. McDowell[31] discusses the following problem from the conventional point of view.

Apart from the numerical computational side of the problem, we shall show that D.P. provides a basis for carrying out certain convergence and sensitivity analyses which other methods fail to have.

The assumptions we shall make are:

(*i*) The demand for service is assumed to be exponential with time (viz. e^{kt}), although any demand function can be analysed similarly.

(*ii*) Capacity to meet an increase in demand, *x*, costs $(b+ax)$ where *b* is a fixed set up cost.

(*iii*) Such capacity can be provided relatively quickly although we could extend the analysis to account for installation time if need be.

(*iv*) The objective will be to minimise costs of meeting demand over some time period, again using the present worth valuation of such costs.

If the far time horizon is fixed, *N*, and *f*(*s*) is the cost of meeting demand from time *s* to *N*, assuming that capacity equals demand at time *s*, and hence an expansion decision is needed at *s*, and we use an optimal policy, we get

$$f(s) = \min_{s \leqslant r \leqslant N}[b + a(e^{kr} - e^{ks}) + e^{-c(r-s)}f(r)], \qquad (4.29)$$

where $e^{-c} = \alpha =$ discount factor.

Equation (4.29) is explained as follows. The decision is the point *r* at which we next install further capacity. The cost of covering the period *s* to *r* is the sum of the first two terms in the bracket. Using the Principle of Optimality, the residual discounted cost is equal to the final term in the bracket. Since r is open to choice, subject only to $s \leqslant r \leqslant N$, we choose it optimally and derive equation (4.29).

This can obviously be solved by computing $f(N)(= 0)$ then $f(N-1)$, and so on until we compute $f(0)$, (choosing 0 as our time origin). This however involves a great deal of computing time, although, again, the alternative calculus approach is also time consuming and far less simple in procedure.

Equation (4.29) is the forward contraction (see Chapter 3) formulation of the problem, involving backward computations.

Since we know our commencing point in time, and may not know the final time horizon with any degree of precision, a more logical formulation would be the backward formulation. Defining $f(s)$ as the cost of meeting demand from now to time s (so that at time s capacity matches demand) and using an optimal policy, we see that:

$$f(s) = \min_r \{ f(r) + e^{-cr} [b + a(e^{ks} - e^{kr})] \}. \tag{4.30}$$

We begin with $f(0) = 0$, then compute $f(1)$ and so on.

The advantage of the backward formulation is that the sensitivity of decisions to changes in time horizon can easily be ascertained, whereas the forward formulation, as it stands, does not do this. The advantage of the forward formulation lies in the fact that demands are uncertain, and hence, although we install enough initially to get up to year r, we may need more before year r or we may still have excess at year r. Assuming that the demand is $e^{kt} + \varepsilon$, where ε is a random variable with small variance, the deterministic version may yet give an adequate approximation, and we will need to cater for the variability in r (assuming that once we have made our choice we wait until demand catches up with capacity) for the next installation. The forward formulation does just this.

Of course a more complete formulation with two variable end points, would be to minimise the cost of operating from year s to year N, giving rise to:

$$f_N(s) = \min_{s \leqslant r \leqslant N} [b + a(e^{kr} - e^{ks}) + e^{-c(r-s)} f_N(r)],$$
$$= \min_{s \leqslant r \leqslant N} \{ f_r(s) + e^{-c(r-s)} [b + a(e^{kN} - e^{kr})] \}. \tag{4.31}$$

* If the problem of solving either (4.29) or (4.30) appears to be difficult, we can obtain reasonable approximating answers with an

---

* From here to page 64 we shall be concerned with analytic considerations which either aid the computations in (4.29), (4.30), (4.31), or provide approximate solutions. These pages can be omitted without significant loss except to specialists in the field.

analysis, part of which depends on equation (4.31), and part of which does not.

First of all we can establish the existence of a monotone increasing sequence of functions $\{m_t(s)\}$ (see White [45] (pp. 224–60) such that an optimal policy, beginning with an installation at time s, has the property that if m is the tth installation point (not including s), then $m \leqslant m_t(s)$. The sequence $\{m_t(s)\}$ satisfies the following backward and forward functional equations:

$$m_t(s) = m_1[m_{t-1}(s)] \qquad (4.32)$$

$$= m_{t-1}[m_1(s)]. \qquad (4.33)$$

The manner of achieving this is to show that if we consider the cost of covering the period s to m with one instalment only ('capacity $\equiv$ demand' at time s), then if m is increased enough it becomes profitable to introduce a second installation, at some point in the interval $s < r < m$. The largest value of m, for a given value of s, is then equal to $m_1(s)$. We can show that $m_1(s)$ increases monotonically with s.

Now suppose we have established the existence of $m_2(s), \ldots m_{k-1}(s)$. Let us consider a period, s to m, which is covered optimally by $(k+1)$ installations, including the one at s. If the second one is at r, then the period r to m is covered by $(k-1)$ further installations. We thus have

$$r \leqslant m_1(s)$$

$$m \leqslant m_{k-1}(r)$$

$$\leqslant m_{k-1}[m_1(s)].$$

Hence $m_{k-1}[m_1(s)]$ is defined as $m_k(s)$. Note that this only means that if $m > m_k(s)$ then an optimal policy involves at least $(k+1)$ installations including the one at s. It does not mean that if $m < m_k(s)$ then an optimal policy exists containing only k installations. This may be true but we do not prove or use it.

Quite obviously

$$m_k(s) = m_{k-1}(m_1(s)) = m_{k-2}(m_1(m_1(s)))$$

$$= m_{k-2}(m_2(s)) = m_{k-3}(m_1(m_2(s))) = m_{k-3}(m_3(s))$$

$$= \ldots m_1(m_{k-1}(s)).$$

Straight away we can reduce the search region in (4.29) giving rise to

$$f(s) = \min_{s \leqslant r \leqslant m_1(s)}[b + a(e^{kr} - e^{ks}) + e^{-c(r-s)}f(r)]. \qquad (4.34)$$

This aid to computation must be emphasised, for further progress in the use of D.P. will depend, to some extent, on the ability to use analytic characteristics to reduce search procedures wherever possible.

Let us now suppose that N is large, but uncertain. We must know something about how $\{f_N(s)\}$ behaves for N increasingly large, for, otherwise, our initial decisions may be virtually meaningless, especially if a larger and larger proportion of the (present value) costs occur towards the time horizon.

For $k < c$, $\{f_N(s)\}$ can be shown to converge with N uniformly for all s, and hence, providing we choose N sufficiently large, we may use equation (4.34) without any fear of our initial decisions being sensitive to N. Equation (4.31) is needed in this proof, which follows similar lines used in other convergence analyses in this book.

For $k \geqslant c$, $\{f_N(s)\}$ diverges, but it is still possible that annual contributions to cost form a smaller and smaller proportion of the costs, and this can again be analysed via (4.31).

For a specific value of $N(>s)$, defining $m_0(s) \equiv s$, we can find l such that:

$$m_l(s) < N \leqslant m_{l+1}(s), \qquad l = l(N). \tag{4.35}$$

We cannot have more than two installation points between each pair $[m_t(s), m_{t+1}(s)]$, $t = 1, 2, \ldots (l-1)$ (this follows from properties of $\{m_t(s)\}$) and more than one installation point between pairs $[s, m_1(s)]$, $[m_l(s), N]$. Hence, in all, including the installation at s, we do not need more than $(2l+1)$ installation points. On the other hand we need at least $(l+1)$ instalments. Therefore the number of instalments, $n(N)$, satisfies

$$l(N) + 1 \leqslant n(N) \leqslant 2l(N) + 1. \tag{4.36}$$

Now an optimal 'l instalment' policy for the period $[s, m_l(s)]$ must have installations at points $s, m_1(s), \ldots m_{l-1}(s)$. If now

(i) such a policy is approximately optimal for $[s, m_l(s)]$

(ii) $(f_N(s) - f_{m_l(s)}) / f_N(s)$, and $(b + a(e^{kN} - e^{km_l(s)})) / f_N(s)$ are small, then the policy $m_0(s)(= s)$, $m_1(s), \ldots m_l(s), \ldots$ would be approximately optimal for the period (s, N).

We can show, using (4.31) that

$$0 \leqslant (f_N(s) - f_{m_l(s)}) / f_N(s) \leqslant e^{-c(m_{l-1}(s) - 1)}(e^{kN} - e^{km_l(s)})(e^{(k-c)} - 1)/(e^k - 1)$$
$$(e^{(k-c)N} - e^{(k-c)s}). \tag{4.37}$$

$$(b + a(e^{kN} - e^{km_l(s)})) / f_N(s) \leqslant (b + a(e^{kN} - e^{km_l(s)}))(e^{(k-c)} - 1)/ae^{c(s-1)}$$
$$(e^k - 1)(e^{(k-c)N} - e^{(k-c)s}). \tag{4.38}$$

From (4.36) and the usual flatness characteristics at optimal points, using the $(l+1)$ installation policy may not be too far off the mark. Similar results apply for more general demand functions (see White [50]) and in order to test the above proposals, a case, in which the exact answer was known, was taken, viz,

$$G(t) \equiv kt. \qquad (4.39)$$

The equations from which $m_1(s)$ (and $r(s)$) are to be computed, for general $G(t)$, with derivative $g(t)$, are

$$g(r)(e^{c(r-s)}-1) = (bc/a)+c[G(m)-G(r)] \qquad (4.40)$$

$$b/a = (e^{c(r-s)}-1)[G(m)-G(r)]. \qquad (4.41)$$

The sequence $\{m_k(s)\}$ can then be computed from (4.32) or (4.33). The counterpart of (4.29) is

$$f(s) = \min_{s \leqslant r \leqslant N}[b+ak(r-s)+e^{-c(r-s)}f(r)]. \qquad (4.42)$$

As $N \to \infty$, $f(s) \to f$ satisfying

$$f = \min_{T \geqslant 0}[(b+akT)/(1-e^{-cT})]. \qquad (4.43)$$

Thus the optimal solution involves a repetitive installation period I(opt). The approximate solution gives rise, again, to a repetitive installation period, given by

$$k(e^{-cu}-1) = -(b/a)\log(e^{-c})-k(T-u)\log(e^{-c}) \qquad (4.44)$$

$$(b/a) = (e^{-cu}-1)k(T-u). \qquad (4.45)$$

These are two equations in T and u.
Several calculations were carried out as follows:

$\gamma = b/ak$	e^{-c}	T(approx)	T(opt)	akf(approx)	akf(opt)	% diff
1	0·5	1·98	1·46	4·02	3·92	2·5
10	0·9	15·27	11·1	31·6	30·6	3·3
100	0·8	18·4	14·7	120·5	119·0	1·3

In actual fact, we can prove the following remarkable result for this example:

$$1 \geqslant f_{T(\text{opt})}/f_{T(\text{approx})} \geqslant 0.856 \qquad (4.46)$$

Returning to the exponential case, since this is perhaps a little more realistic in some cases, tables have been computed from which the approximate optimal policies can be read off for various values of $\lambda(= k/c)$ and $q(= bc/ak)$. The entries in Table 6 have to be divided by c to give the actual period in years. This table gives only the results begining at time $s = 0$, but can be used to get approximate results for $m_1(s)$ (and hence $m_k(s)$), since each column entry is the m_1 value for the previous entry, e.g. for $\lambda = 0.5$, $q = 0.1$,

$$m_1(0) = 0.54, \ m_1(0.54) = 1.02, \ m_1(1.02) = 1.45$$

and so on, and these can be used to interpolate $m_1(s)$ for any s.

TABLE 6

| λ | 0·5 | 0·5 | 0·5 | 0·5 | 0·5 | 0·5 | 0·5 | 0·5 | 0·5 | 0·5 |
q	0·1	0·2	0·5	1·0	1·5	2·0	2·5	5·0	10	20
1.	0·00	0·00	0·00	0·00	0·00	0·00	0·00	0·00	0·00	0·00
2.	0·54	0·70	0·96	1·25	1·41	1·60	1·80	2·10	2·55	2·90
3.	1·02	1·31	1·78	2·28	2·54	2·83	3·05	3·65	4·30	4·95
4.	1·45	1·85	2·49	3·16	3·48	3·81	4·05	4·83	5·65	6·48
5.	1·84	2·33	3·11	3·85	4·26	4·63	4·88	5·77	6·70	7·66
6.	2·19	2·76	3·65	4·47	4·93	5·33	5·60	6·56	7·56	8·61
7.	2·51	3·16	4·13	5·01	5·52	5·94	6·23	7·24	8·30	9·41
8.	2·81	3·52	4·56	5·49	6·04	6·48	6·78	7·84	8·94	10·09
9.	3·09	3·86	4·96	5·92	6·50	6·96	7·26	8·36	9·50	10·69
10.	3·35	4·17	5·32	6·32	6·92	7·39	7·70	8·83	9·99	11·21
11.	3·60	4·46	5·65	6·69	7·30	7·79	8·10	9·25	10·43	11·67
12.	3·84	4·73	5·96	7·02	7·64	8·15	8·46	9·64	10·84	12·09
13.	4·06	4·98	6·25	7·34	7·96	8·48	8·81	10·00	11·21	12·47
14.	4·27	5·22	6·52	7·63	8·26	8·78	9·10	10·33	11·55	12·82
15.	4·47	5·46	6·78	7·90	8·54	9·17	9·40	10·64	11·87	13·14
16.	4·66	5·66	7·02	8·15	8·80	9·43	9·66	10·92	12·17	13·44
17.	4·85	5·86	7·23	8·39	9·05	9·67	9·92	11·19	12·44	13·72
18.	5·03	6·06	7·46	8·62	9·29	9·90	10·16	11·44	12·70	13·99
19.	5·20	6·24	7·65	8·84	9·52	10·12	10·38	11·67	12·95	14·24
20.	5·36	6·42	7·84	9·04	9·73	10·33	10·59	11·89	13·18	14·47

TABLE 6 (cont.)

| λ | 1·0 | 1·0 | 1·0 | 1·0 | 1·0 | 1·0 | 1·0 | 1·0 | 1·0 | 1·0 |
q	0·1	0·2	0·5	1·0	1·5	2·0	2·5	5	10	20
1.	0·00	0·00	0·00	0·00	0·00	0·00	0·00	0·00	0·00	0·00
2.	0·48	0·64	0·88	1·10	1·20	1·32	1·42	1·70	1·95	2·30
3.	0·90	1·14	1·52	1·87	2·05	2·22	2·36	2·75	3·15	3·65
4.	1·23	1·56	2·03	2·44	2·67	2·88	3·03	3·51	3·97	4·53
5.	1·52	1·90	2·44	2·90	3·17	3·38	3·55	4·08	4·58	5·19
6.	1·78	2·19	2·78	3·29	3·58	3·80	3·98	4·54	5·07	5·71
7.	2·01	2·45	3·08	3·62	3·93	4·15	4·33	4·92	5·47	6·12
8.	2·21	2·68	3·34	3·90	4·22	4·45	4·63	5·25	5·81	6·47
9.	2·40	2·89	3·57	4·15	4·48	4·71	4·89	5·53	6·11	6·77
10.	2·58	3·08	3·78	4·37	4·71	4·95	5·13	5·78	6·37	7·03
11.	2·74	3·25	3·97	4·57	4·92	5·16	5·35	6·00	6·60	7·27
12.	2·89	3·41	4·15	4·76	5·11	5·36	5·55	6·20	6·81	7·48
13.	3·03	3·56	4·31	4·93	5·29	5·54	5·73	6·39	7·00	7·67
14.	3·16	3·70	4·46	5·09	5·45	5·71	5·89	6·56	7·17	7·84
15.	3·28	3·84	4·60	5·23	5·60	5·86	6·05	6·71	7·33	8·00
16.	3·40	3·96	4·73	5·37	5·74	6·00	6·19	6·86	7·48	8·15
17.	3·51	4·08	4·85	5·49	5·87	6·13	6·32	6·99	7·62	8·29
18.	3·61	4·19	4·97	5·61	5·99	6·25	6·44	7·12	7·75	8·43
19.	3·71	4·30	5·08	5·73	6·11	6·37	6·56	7·24	7·87	8·55
20.	3·81	4·40	5·19	5·84	6·23	6·48	6·67	7·35	7·99	8·68

TABLE 6 (cont.)

λ	2·0	2·0	2·0	2·0	2·0	2·0	2·0	2·0	2·0	2·0
q	0·1	0·2	0·5	1·0	1·5	2·0	2·5	5	10	20
1.	0·00	0·00	0·00	0·00	0·00	0·00	0·00	0·00	0·00	0·00
2.	0·41	0·52	0·70	0·85	0·96	1·00	1·05	1·25	1·40	1·65
3.	0·71	0·90	1·25	1·37	1·42	1·60	1·67	1·93	2·16	2·45
4.	0·95	1·18	1·55	1·74	1·80	2·00	2·07	2·37	2·64	2·94
5.	1·15	1·41	1·78	2·01	2·12	2·29	2·37	2·68	2·97	3·28
6.	1·32	1·60	1·98	2·22	2·36	2·52	2·61	2·92	3·22	3·54
7.	1·47	1·76	2·15	2·40	2·56	2·72	2·81	3·12	3·43	3·75
8.	1·60	1·91	2·30	2·56	2·73	2·89	2·97	3·29	3·60	3·93
9.	1·72	2·03	2·42	2·70	2·88	3·03	3·11	3·44	3·75	4·08
10.	1·82	2·11	2·53	2·82	3·00	3·15	3·24	3·57	3·88	4·21
11.	1·91	2·21	2·64	2·92	3·12	3·26	3·36	3·68	4·00	4·33
12.	2·00	2·31	2·73	3·01	3·22	3·36	3·46	3·79	4·10	4·43
13.	2·08	2·40	2·82	3·09	3·32	3·46	3·56	3·88	4·20	4·53
14.	2·15	2·49	2·90	3·17	3·40	3·54	3·65	3·97	4·29	4·62
15.	2·22	2·56	2·97	3·24	3·48	3·62	3·73	4·05	4·37	4·70
16.	2·29	2·63	3·04	3·31	3·55	3·69	3·80	4·12	4·44	4·78
17.	2·35	2·71	3·10	3·37	3·62	3·76	3·87	4·19	4·51	4·85
18.	2·41	2·77	3·16	3·43	3·69	3·83	3·94	4·26	4·57	4·92
19.	2·46	2·83	3·22	3·48	3·75	3·89	4·00	4·32	4·63	4·98
20.	2·51	2·89	3·28	3·53	3·80	3·94	4·06	4·38	4·69	5·04

Let us now consider the alternative calculus formulation, as given by McDowell. If we install equipment at years $n_1 n_2, \ldots n_{T-1}$ to optimise over the period 0 to n_T, the overall cost is, for the general case, with $e^{-c} = \alpha$,

$$f_{N_T}(0) = b + a[G(n_1)-1] + \sum_{s=1}^{T-1} \alpha^{n_s}\{b + a[G(n_{s+1})-G(n_s)]\}. \quad (4.47)$$

Assuming we can differentiate (if we cannot then (4.29) or (4.30) must have distinct advantages) we obtain the differential equations

$$ag(n_1) + \alpha^{n_1}\{\log(\alpha)(b + a[G(n_2)-G(n_1)]) - ag(n_1)\} = 0 \quad (4.48)$$

$$\alpha^{n_r-1}ag(n_r) + \alpha^{n_r}\{\log(\alpha)(b + a[G(n_{r+1})-G(n_r)]) - ag(n_r)\} = 0 \quad (4.49)$$

for $r = 2, 3, \ldots T-1$.
These reduce to

$$n_2 = \theta(n_1) \quad (4.50)$$

$$n_{r+1} = \phi(n_r, n_{r+1}), \quad r = 2, 3, \ldots T-1 \quad (4.51)$$

for suitable functions $\theta, \phi, \ldots$.

The solution procedure is to choose n_1, compute n_2 and so on. If the computed n_T agrees with the given value we have at least a local optimum.

There will in general be several sets of $\{n_r\}$ which satisfy the equations, and hence not only do we have to vary n_1, until we get a solution of the equations, but also until we have determined all local optima. This double procedure can prove quite tedious.

In general n_T will not be known with any degree of accuracy and we will have the problems of not only analysing the sensitivity of the solutions to changes in n_T but also the behaviour of $f_{n_T}(0)$ in terms of n_T, something only possible numerically with the above method, but to which analytic answers can be given using the D.P. method which gives rise to the inequalities

$$ae^{cs}e^{-cr_{N+1}(s)}[G(N+1)-G(N)] \leqslant f_{N+1}(s)-f_N(s) \leqslant ae^{cs}e^{-cr_N(s)}$$

$$[G(N+1)-G(N)], \qquad (4.52)$$

where $r_N(s)$ is the last installation point in an optimal policy for the period s to N, and where, from the definition of $m_1(s)$, we have

$$0 < N - r_N(s) \leqslant m_1[r_N(s)]. \qquad (4.53)$$

Equation (4.52) was used to deduce, for the exponential case, that $\{f_N(s)\}$ converged uniformly if $k < c$, in which case little sensitivity of $n_1, n_2, \ldots n_T \ldots$ to changes in N would be expected and were found. It was also possible to deduce that, if $k < 2c$, $f_{N+1}(s) - f_N(s)$ was bounded but $f_{N+1}(s)$ diverged, and again little sensitivity was expected and found.

With a great deal of uncertainty in N and with severe long term divergence it matters little what the initial decision is.

Let us now put a case for the use of the approximating sequence $\{m_t(s)\}$. In general not only is N uncertain, but so are a, b, c, and certainly the form of G. A general sensitivity analysis for all these possibilities is out of the question, whereas a sensitivity analysis for the approximating sequence is quite feasible.

As a point of general interest as to the validity of the sequence $\{m_t(0)\}$ as an approximating sequence, some results obtained this way were compared with those given by McDowell [31] for long duration systems, although these were read off from his graphs and are subject to slight error. These are given in Table 7 and are very encouraging considering the likely flatness of the cost behaviour in the region of the optimal solution.

We could, quite obviously, have carried out a convergence analysis with respect to the backward form (4.30), but this would have been specific in relation to one fixed time origin and hence of no general validity. Equation (4.31) is of general use for convergence analysis since the initial and final points are variable. Equation (4.31), therefore, carries both the virtue of its generality in convergence analysis, with respect to the time horizon, and the virtue of its ability to be useful in stochastic cases when the use of expectations affords an initial approximation.

TABLE 7

λ	q	c	Optimal				Approximate			
			n_1	n_2	n_3	n_4	n_1	n_2	n_3	n_4
2·0	5	0·025	42	64	81	95	50	77	95	107
1·0	10	0·050	33	54	70	83	39	63	79	92
0·5	20	0·100	22	42	53	65	29	50	65	77
0·5	20	0·050	50	80	105	132	58	99	130	153
2·0	5	0·050	20	33	40	48	25	39	47	54
1·0	0·1	0·050	7	14	20	25	10	18	25	30
1·0	1	0·050	17	31	41	50	22	37	49	58
1·0	10	0·050	32	53	69	82	39	63	79	92

B. Multi-stage Production Processes

In Section A we dealt with processes which were sequential because of their time orientation. There are problems whose sequential nature derives more from the order of operations than from the time factor. Such a class of problems arise from general multi-stage production processes, in which an interest is arising in the use of D.P. Aris,[5] for example, devotes a whole volume to the application of D.P. to problems in the design of optimal chemical reactors. There are also problems in the steel industry very much of the multi-stage type, and the author would like to discuss now a simple problem of this class dealt with more fully in White[45] (suggested originally to him by M. G. Simpson * in a private communication) and then make a few remarks about the problem in the area of counter current flow processes in general (see Dranoff[22]).

(a) *Optimal Operation of a Multi-stand Rolling Mill.* The production process we shall consider is a multi-stand rolling mill consisting of N independent stands, each stand reducing the strip by a certain amount and the steel having to be transported from mill to mill, with negligible time. The reasons for having a sequence of stands are that only a limited reduction can be taken in one reducing operation, and also, by taking a series of smaller reductions rather than one large one, we can increase the rate of production and, finally, if we tried to do the same with a single mill, valuable time would be lost in refeeding the strip back into the mill for each reduction. As we shall see, in the course of the analysis,

* Now at the University of Lancaster, Department of Operational Research.

there remains the problem of choosing an optimal N as well as the problems of determining the reduction to make at each stand.

Let us assume that we are interested in maximising the total through-put rate for a large number of coils for a strip of a given width. Let us assume that for any stand the maximum throughput rate with an input gauge y and an output gauge x is a known function $t(y,x)$.

If we assume a fixed input gauge, p, to the first stand, and define $T_r(x)$ to be the output rate at the rth stand, when the output gauge at this stand is x, and we use an optimal reduction policy, then we derive the functional equation:

$$T_r(x) = \max_{p \geqslant y \geqslant x}[\min[T_{r-1}(y); t(y,x)]]. \qquad (4.54)$$

$$T_1(x) = t(p,x). \qquad (4.55)$$

Equation (4.54) is derived as follows. We consider the decision to be the last but one state of the system, i.e. the imput gauge y to the rth stand. The rate of throughput through the last stand has a maximum value of $t(y,x)$. Using the Principle of Optimality, the maximum throughput rate through the first $(r-1)$ stands, to finish with gauge y after these $(r-1)$ stands, is, by definition, $T_{r-1}(y)$. Since the throughput rate through any two parts of a serial system cannot be greater than the smaller rate in each part, for decision y, the maximum throughput rate is the minimum of $T_{r-1}(y)$ and $t(y,x)$. Since y is now open to choice, subject only to $p \geqslant y \geqslant x$, we choose y to maximise this minimum and thus derive equation (4.54).

It is noted that no mention of strip speed is made in this equation. This is not necessary since the input and output speeds at any stand are determined by throughput rate and input and output gauges respectively.

As an example consider the following problem in which only ten discrete values of x are considered. Table 8 gives the value of $t(y,x)$.

TABLE 8

					x					
	10	9	8	7	6	5	4	3	2	1
10	1·00	0·95	0·89	0·84	0·77	0·71	0·63	0·55	0·45	0·32
9		1·00	0·95	0·88	0·82	0·74	0·67	0·57	0·47	0·33
8			1·00	0·94	0·87	0·79	0·71	0·61	0·50	0·35
7				1·00	0·93	0·84	0·76	0·66	0·55	0·37
y 6					1·00	0·91	0·82	0·71	0·58	0·41
5						1·00	0·89	0·77	0·63	0·45
4							1·00	0·87	0·71	0·50
3								1·00	0·82	0·57
2									1·00	0·71
1										1·00

Let $p = 10$. Then $T_1(x) = t(1,x)$ and this is put down in Table 9. Quite obviously $\mu_1(x)$ is not meaningful. Then

$$T_2(10) = \max_{10 \geqslant y \geqslant 10} \min \left[T_1(y);t(y,10) \right] = T_1(10) = 1{\cdot}00$$

$$T_2(9) = \max_{10 \geqslant y \geqslant 9} \min \left[T_1(y);t(y,9) \right]$$

$$= \max \begin{bmatrix} \min[T_1(10);t(10,9)] \\ \min [T_1(9);t(9,9)] \end{bmatrix}$$

$$= \max \begin{bmatrix} \min [1{\cdot}00;0{\cdot}95] \\ \min [0{\cdot}95;1{\cdot}00] \end{bmatrix} = 0{\cdot}95$$

$$\mu_2(9) = 10 \text{ or } 9.$$

TABLE 9

x	10	9	8	7	6	5	4	3	2	1
$T_1(x)$	1·00	0·95	0·89	0·84	0·77	0·71	0·63	0·55	0·45	0·32
$\mu_1(x)$	—	—	—	—	—	—	—	—	—	—
$T_2(x)$	1·00	0·95	0·95	0·89	0·87	0·84	0·77	0·71	0·63	0·55
$\mu_2(x)$	10	10/9	9	8	8	7	6	5/6	4/5	3
$T_3(x)$	1·00	0·95	0·95	0·94	0·89	0·87	0·84	0·77	0·71	0·63
$\mu_3(x)$	10	10/9	8/9	8	7	6	5	5/4	3/4	2
$T_4(x)$	1·00	0·95	0·95	0·94	0·93	0·89	0·87	0·84	0·77	0·71
$\mu_4(x)$	10	10/9	8/9	7/8	7	6	5	4	3	2
$T_5(x)$	1·00	0·95	0·95	0·94	0·93	0·91	0·89	0·87	0·82	0·71
$\mu_5(x)$	10	10/9	8/9	7/8	7/6	6	5	4	3	2/1

The general procedure is quite easy. To get $T_r(x)$ we pair off elements in the xth column of Table 8 with the corresponding elements in the row $T_{r-1}(x)$, the first elements going together, the second elements going together, and so on. The minimum of each pair is calculated and then the maximum of these minima gives the value of $T_r(x)$, the point at which it occurs giving the optimal choice, $\mu_r(x)$. Thus to get $T_2(3)$ we pair off and calculate as follows:

y	Column 3 of Table 8	row T_1	Min	Solutions
10	0·55	1·00	0·55	
9	0·57	0·95	0·57	
8	0·61	0·89	0·61	
7	0·66	0·84	0·66	
6	0·71	0·77	0·71	6
5	0·77	0·71	0·71	5
4	0·87	0·63	0·63	
3	1·00	0·55	0·55	

This gives $T_2(3) = 0.71$, $\mu_2(3) = 6$ or 5.

The complete table for $r = 1, 2, 3, 4, 5$ is given for anyone wishing to carry out exercises.

This is the backward functional form (see Chapter 3). If the problem had been one with a fixed final gauge q, and a variable input gauge we would use the forward formulation given below, where $T_r(x)$ is the output rate at the last stand when the input gauge to the rth stand from the end $[(N-r+1)$th] stand is x and we use an optimal policy to produce gauge q.

If $r > 1$, $$T_r(x) = \max_{x \geqslant y \geqslant q}[\min [t(x,y);T_{r-1}(y)]]. \tag{4.56}$$

$$T_1(x) = t(x,q). \tag{4.57}$$

If we want the answer for any initial gauge u, and any final gauge v, and if we define $T_r(u,v)$ to be the output rate over the first r stands beginning with gauge u and ending with gauge v, using an optimal policy, we get the functional equation

$$T_r(u,v) = \max_{u \geqslant s \geqslant v}[T_{r-1}(u,s);t(s,v)]. \tag{4.58}$$

The solution to (4.54) is also easily obtained graphically, for let us suppose that we have plotted the family of curves $z = t(y,x)$ for the range of parameters of x. Let us suppose that we have computed $z = T_{r-1}(y)$. Superimposing $z = T_{r-1}(y)$ on the family $z = t(y,x)$ we obtain Fig. 1.

We would expect $t(y,x)$ to decrease as y increases and increase as x increases, and $T_{r-1}(y)$ to increase as y increases (but this need not be true, and similar results hold even if this is so). We see easily that if $t(y,x) = z$ and $T_{r-1}(y) = z$ intersect at $y = \mu_r(x)$ we have

$$T_r(x) = t[\mu_r(x),x]. \tag{4.59}$$

Equation (4.59) may be useful if $t(y,x)$ is known analytically, e.g. if each stand is fully efficient in changing the input speed to the output speed and no heat losses are incurred anywhere, $t(y,x)$ is a decreasing function of the ratio (y/x) only and we can easily show (see Appendix, pp. 167, 168) that, if $t(y,x) = \rho(y/x)$,

$$\mu_r(x) = (px^{r-1})^{1/r}. \tag{4.60}$$

$$T_r(x) = \rho[(p/x)^{1/r}]. \tag{4.61}$$

We have assumed that each stand has its own independent power supply. However it may be that the total power supply is fixed and we may wish to solve the problem subject to any distribution of this fixed power over the stands. Letting $T_r(x,w)$ be the throughput rate through the first r stands with final gauge x, power resources w and using an optimal policy, we get:

if $\qquad\qquad r>1$

$$T_r(x,w) = \max_{\substack{p \geqslant y \geqslant x \\ w \geqslant u \geqslant 0}}[\min [T_{r-1}(y,u);t(y,x,w-u)]]. \qquad (4.62)$$

$$T_1(x,w) = t(p,x,w), \qquad\qquad\qquad (4.63)$$

where $t(y,x,w)$ is the maximum single stand throughput rate with input gauge y, output gauge x, and power resource w. Again no explicit mention of speed is needed.

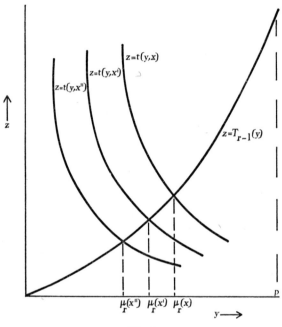

Fig. 1

The only difference between this and previous formulations is that we have an allocation of resources problem as well as having to decide how much to reduce the strip at each stand. The initial state (x,w) is transformed into the new state $(y,w-u)$ by the choice of last but one gauge, y, and the power u, allocated to the first $(r-1)$ stands.

Let us now consider an alternative approach to the simplest equation (4.54). Let R be the output rate for any policy. We then have

$$R = ps = x_1s_1 = x_2s_2 = \ldots x_Ns_N, \qquad (4.64)$$

where s is the input speed to the first stage and s_r is the output speed at the rth stage.

At each stage, technological and power restrictions require that

$$(x_r, x_{r+1}, R) \in \Omega, \tag{4.65}$$

where Ω is some allowable region for the specified triple, e.g. if only power limitations, w, are the determining elements, then we might have

$$\phi(x_r, x_{r+1}, R) \leqslant w. \tag{4.66}$$

The problem is to maximise R subject to (4.65) with $x_0 = p$, $x_N = x$, $x_r \geqslant x_{r+1}$, for all r. In general this can be quite complicated. The other two main disadvantages are that we would find it very tedious to carry out a sensitivity analysis for N using the second approach, and this may be an essential design feature of the mill, and also that we cannot determine the answer to the class of problems requiring reductions from p to every gauge x, whereas D.P. does just this. Equation (4.62) gives much more difficulty of course.

(b) *Multi-stage Chemical Processes.** As was pointed out previously, Aris [5] has produced a volume on the use of D.P. for multi-stage chemical processes, to which the reader is referred for detailed analysis. We shall follow Dranoff [22] who deals specifically with counter current flow processes.

A counter-current flow process is a multi-stage process with a two-way flow of production from stage to stage, and with possible external feeds and takeoffs at each stage. The processes which Dranoff deals with allow only flows between successive units, and not between separated units. A typical unit representation would be:

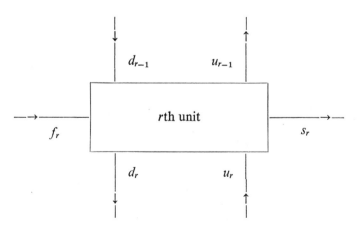

* This section is a very specialised practical application and can be omitted without any loss except to the specialist reader.

where d_r is the downstream flow from the rth unit,
   u_r is the upstream flow into the rth unit,
   f_r is the feed into the rth unit, and
   s_r is the take-off from the rth unit.

The notation is changed slightly from Dranoff's purely for convenience. In general d, u, f, s will be vectors.

Let us now suppose that the gain from the rth stage is a function, p_r, of the variables d, u, f, s.

Let the decision, δ, which can be made at the rth stage, be a general vector restricted to some region $\Omega_r(u,d)$, e.g. δ may simply be the choice of s and/or f. δ must be sufficient to determine u and d.

Defining $v_n(d,u)$ to be the return over n stages, beginning with downstream and upstream flows, d, u, respectively, at the nth stage, and using an optimal policy, we derive

$$v_n(d,u) = \max_{\delta \in \Omega_n(u,d)} \{p_n(u,d,f,s) + v_{n-1}(T_{n-1}(d,u,\delta))\}, \quad (4.67)$$

where $T_{n-1}(d,u,\delta)$ is the vector state at the $(n-1)$th stage when δ, u, d are given.

There will, of course, be some technological relationships given, e.g. if F, U, D, S are flow rates (components of f, u, d, s) we have a flow rate conservation equation, viz.

$$F_r + U_r + D_{r-1} = S_r + U_{r-1} + D_r. \quad (4.68)$$

The number of fixed relations will obviously reduce the freedom of choice. However care must be taken in any relations used in the formulation particularly with a view to reducing dimensionality difficulties. Dranoff's examples treat s, and f, as the free variables at each stage, and assume that u suffices to describe system state, and that d_{r-1} is obtained either from technological restrictions or from u_{r-1} directly as a function of optimal behaviour over $(r-1)$ stages. This is, of course, erroneous and has been corrected by Dranoff in a note in a later reference.[23]

A direct approach would give rise to the standard mathematical, non-sequential, optimisation problem of

$$\text{maximise } \Sigma p_r(u_r,d_r,f_r,s_r) \text{ subject to}$$
$$\theta_{ir}(u_r,d_r,f_r,s_s) = 0, \qquad i = 1, 2, \ldots n_r$$
$$u_n = d_n = 0,$$

plus restrictions on the signs of some of the components of u, f, d, s. . . .

Even with the simplest cases this approach can be very difficult to use. Perhaps, even more important, as with other multi-stage problems, we do not acquire the relationship between the optimal solution and the number of stages very easily, and have to carry through the procedure from scratch for each value of N.

We have discussed only two classes of multi-stage production processes, but there are many more. The approach applies even when the product is changing form (e.g. in the steel industry we begin with crude iron ore and finish with one of a variety of finished steel products).

C. Sequencing Problems

Many problems involving selection of a sequence of operations to achieve a desired objective can be given a D.P. formulation. In Chapter 6 we discuss a stochastic search problem of the sequential type. In this section we shall discuss a problem of sequencing machine operations, taken from Bellman.[9] Consider the problem of sequencing a set of jobs on two machines, each job being operated on first by machine 1 and then by machine 2. What sequence will minimise overall time to complete the jobs?

It can be proved that there is an optimal solution which maintains the same sequence on each machine and we shall confine our attention to such solutions.

If we had 10 jobs there would be $10! = 3\ 628\ 800$ possible sequences. The direct evaluation of each would be a mammoth task even for a computer. A calculus approach is obviously inapplicable, at least directly. D.P. provides us with a fruitful attack and a simple algorithm.

Let S, U be sets of jobs. Let $S - U$ be the set of jobs in S, not in U.

Define $f(S, t)$ to be the overall production time to complete the set of jobs, S, starting in a state when the second machine is loaded a time t ahead and we use an optimal sequence from S.

Define $f_i(S, t)$ as for $f(S, t)$ but with the condition that job i is put on machine 1 first, and an optimal sequence used thereafter.

Let $\{a_i\}$, $\{b_i\}$ be the process times on machines 1 and 2 respectively. Now consider the two cases.

(i) $t \geqslant a_t$, (ii) $t \leqslant a_i$

(i) $t \geqslant a_i$ end of last job on machine 1

When job i is completed on machine 1, it has to wait a time $(t-a_i)$ before machine 2 is ready to take it. Hence, when it is finished on machine 1, we are in a new state $(S-i, t-a_i+b_i)$, having jobs $S-i$ yet to sequence, with machine 2 committed ahead a time $(t-a_i+b_i)$. The minimal time to completion of the set $S-i$ is then, using the Principle of Optimality, $f(S-i, t-a_i+b_i)$. Thus

$$f_i(S,t) = a_i + f(S-i, t-a_i+b_i)$$

(ii) $t \leqslant a_i$ end of last job on machine 1

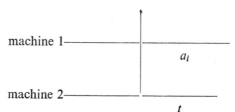

Quite obviously when job i is finished on machine 1 the new state is $(S-i, b_i)$ (since machine 2 no longer has to wait for job i). Thus, as above,

$$f_i(S,t) = a_i + f(S-i, b_i).$$

If we now define $z_i(t) = \max [t-a_i, 0] + b_i$ the above two conditions can be combined to give

$$f_i(S,t) = a_i + f[S-i, z_i(t)].$$

Now define $f_{ij}(S,t)$ as for $f_i(S,t)$ with the proviso that job i is put on machine 1 first, then job j and then an optimal sequence from $(S-i-j)$.
Then

$$f_{ij}(S,t) = a_i + f_j[S-i, z_i(t)]$$
$$= a_i + a_j + f[S-i-j, z_{ij}(t)],$$

where

$$z_{ij}(t) = \max [z_i(t)-a_j; 0] + b_j$$
$$= \max [\max [t-a_i; 0] + b_i - a_j; 0] + b_j$$
$$= \max [t-a_i-a_j+b_i+b_j; b_i+b_j-a_j; b_j].$$

Similarly

$$f_{ji}(S,t) = a_i + a_j + f[S-i-j, z_{ji}(t)],$$

where

$$z_{ji}(t) = \max [t-a_j-a_i+b_j+b_i; b_j+b_i-a_i; b_i].$$

Quite obviously $f(S,t)$ increases with t, and we therefore see that

$$f_{ij}(S,t) \leqslant f_{ji}(S,t) \text{ if } z_{ij}(t) \leqslant z_{ji}(t),$$

i.e. if

$$\max [b_i + b_j - a_j; b_j] \leqslant \max [b_j + b_i - a_i; b_i],$$

i.e.

$$\max [-a_j; -b_i] \leqslant \max [-a_i; -b_j],$$

i.e.

$$\min [a_i; b_j] \leqslant \min [a_j; b_i].$$

This condition for job i to precede job j is independent of S and t and hence is a sufficient condition for i to precede j anywhere in the sequence if they are adjacent.

Now consider the following procedure:

(i) find $\min [a_1; a_2, \ldots a_n; b_1; b_2, \ldots b_n]$,

(ii) if the minimum equals a_i, then put job i first, and delete it from the set of jobs,

(iii) if the minimum equals b_i, then put job i last, and delete it from the set of jobs,

(iv) repeat cycle at (i), using depleted set of jobs, until the set is empty.

Now if (ii) is true, we have:

$$\min [a_i, b_s] \leqslant \min [a_s, b_i] \text{ for all } s,$$

and hence putting job i first is optimal for the problem.

If (iii) is true, we have

$$\min [a_s, b_i] \leqslant \min [a_i, b_s] \text{ for all } s,$$

and putting job i last is optimal for the sequence. Thus the procedure gives an optimal sequence.

The following example is self-explanatory.

Job No.	a_i	b_i	Removal order	a or $b = \min$	Optimal sequence
1	4	5	3	a	2
2	4	1	1	b	5
3	30	4	4	b	4
4	6	30	5	a	3
5	2	5	2	a	1

In principle the same approach can be applied to many sequencing problems including the celebrated 'travelling salesman' problem, although one will not obtain such simple algorithms as in the above.

Routine computation would be much too heavy for even the simplest travelling salesman problem or for the above problem with more than two machines, bearing in mind that for more than three machines the order of processing may not (in the optimal solution) be the same for all machines. Work going on at the Centre for Business Research, Manchester (see Norman [33]), may help reduce such computations and it is hoped to include some of this work in a later edition.

4.3. * The Calculus of Variations and Pontryagin's Maximum Principle

There is a whole class of problems in which it is required to determine optimal functions, $x(t)$, of some continuous variable t, rather than, as in Section 4.1 the determination of a set of discrete variables $x_1, x_2, \ldots x_n$. Sometimes the continuous form is taken as a limiting form of the discrete case, the advantage being, in some cases, that the differential equations obtained can easily be solved whereas the discrete case computations may be rather more difficult. We shall look at some of the approaches to deriving differential equations for some problems and show how the D.P. approach may, computationally, be easier. We shall, in fact, be reversing the process, i.e. suggesting that the discrete form plus D.P. may be better than the continuous form. Begging a little of what follows the reason is this: the Calculus of Variations approach tries to avoid heavy calculations which would arise with a discrete optimisation formulation, by deriving differential equations, which, it is hoped, can be solved analytically, or, even if not, can be solved reasonably easily, using discrete approximations to the final differential equations found. However, in general, and also with Pontryagin's extensions, this is not the case, and severe difficulties often being procedural as distinct from the time factor. D.P. has no procedural difficulties and is very feasible for the smaller dimension problem, with which the other approaches may yet have difficulties.

To this we can add that, for either the Calculus of Variations approach or Pontryagin's approach to be valid, certain conditions must hold (discussed in the following) which are not essential to a D.P. approach.

In case any confusion arises in the next few pages the basic points covered are:

(*i*) Where the Calculus of Variations approach deduces the Euler equations, so can the D.P. approach (equation (4.70)).

---

* The section on Pontryagin's Maximum Principle is included by request, since it relates to a relatively new Principle of Optimality and hence is relevant to the theme of the book. The whole of this section can be omitted except by special readers.

(*ii*) It may not be known how to solve these equations, in which case the discrete D.P. approach provides a feasible computational procedure in many cases (equation (4.72)).

(*iii*) A special case in which the Calculus of Variations approach does not apply is discussed, and an alternative procedure, due to Bellman, resulting in necessary conditions (4.89), (4.90), is outlined. This is the continuous equivalent to the standard discrete Linear Programming form, and is not, in general, solvable routinely. Again the discrete D.P. formulation provides a feasible procedure (equation (4.95)).

(*iv*) Sometimes an analytic solution is possible and Bellman deduces one from the differential (D.P.) equations (4.97) in a small dimensional case.

(*v*) An alternative approach to a class of problems (which class includes those to which the Calculus of Variations approach) is embedded in Pontryagin's 'Maximum Principle' and is discussed on page 82 onwards. The solution procedure is expressed in equations (4.100), (4.101), (4.102), and (4.103). The same results can be obtained using the D.P. approach which is, again, a much stronger procedure. However, except in certain simple situations (one of which is analysed) analytic solutions (and numerical solutions) of the equations expressing optimality of solution are not routine (as yet).

(*vi*) The discrete D.P. approach to the Pontryagin class of problems provides a feasible computational approach, at least for low dimension problems, for which the other approaches are still not routine (as yet). (See equation (4.104).)

Let us begin with the simplest problem treated in the area of Calculus of Variations, viz. find a function $x(t)$ which minimises the functional

$$J(x(\cdot)) = \int_a^b F(x(t),\dot{x}(t),t)dt. \qquad (4.69)$$

One example might be where we have a demand function, $r(t)$, per unit time, for a product at time t, and require to find the optimal production rate, $x(t)$ with costs depending, not only on production rate, but also on rate of change of production, $\dot{x}(t)$. Such a model would be a continuous approximation to the real discrete case.

The normal Calculus of Variations approach (see Bellman [16]) gives rise, formally, to the Euler equation

$$\partial F/\partial x = d/dt(\partial F/\partial \dot{x}). \qquad (4.70)$$

As Bellman points out, not only is an analytic solution usually out of the question, but so also do numerical approaches to solving this equation give rise to difficulties, especially with two point boundary conditions $x(a) = \alpha$, $x(b) = \beta$. There are, however, two further difficulties, the second one being quite serious. Firstly F may not be differentiable, with respect to x or $\dot{x}$, at all points; e.g. we might have a term max $[\alpha\dot{x},\beta\dot{x}]$, $\alpha > 0 > \beta$, (costs of changing production rate), and then $\partial F/\partial\dot{x}$ does not exist at $\dot{x} = 0$. However, (4.70) may still apply to all points except on a set of measure zero, and the problem would be one of matching up the segments within which it did apply. Secondly (4.70) only applies to those positions of the path properly within the allowable area of the $x,\dot{x}$; i.e. it assumes such regions are open. Hence if part of the optimal solution required $x(t) = 0$, $t_0 \leqslant t \leqslant t_1$, and negative $x(t)$ are excluded, (4.67) would not apply on this segment. This becomes a serious difficulty with higher dimensional problems. We should also observe that such an approach would only give stationary points, and we still need to determine which points give a global minimum (Bellman [18] gives the conditions for such minima).

Let us now consider the D.P. approach, and let us consider discrete intervals of time, of size δ. Let $(b-a) = N\delta$. Define $f(m\delta,c)$ as the minimum value of $\delta \sum\limits_{r=m}^{N-1} F(x_r,u_r,r\delta)$, subject to

$$x_{r+1} = x_r + \delta u_r, x_m = c. \qquad (4.71)$$

We have, if $m \leqslant N-2$

$$f(m\delta,c) = \min_u [\delta F(c,u,m\delta) + f((m+1)\delta,c+u\delta)]. \qquad (4.72)$$

$$f((N-1)\delta,c) = \min_u[\delta F(c,u,(N-1)\delta)]. \qquad (4.73)$$

The manner in which (4.72) is obtained is as follows. The initial state is: $x = c$ at time $m\delta$. The decision concerns the value of u and gives an immediate cost $\delta F(c,u,m\delta)$ and a new state: $x = c+u\delta$ at time $(m+1)\delta$. The Principle of Optimality gives a residual optimal cost

$$f((m+1)\delta,c+u\delta).$$

Since u is free (within certain restrictions) we derive the equation (4.72). Note that the usual 'stage' variable, m, has been treated as a state variable for the purpose of taking ratio limits later on.

If, formally, we let $\delta \to 0$ and expand

$$f[(m+1)\delta,c+u\delta] = f(m\delta,c) + \delta(u(\partial f/\partial c) + \partial f/\partial m\delta) + 0(\delta), \qquad (4.74)$$

we get, if $m\delta = t$,

$$-\partial f/\partial t = \min_u[F(c,u,t) + u(\partial f/\partial c)]. \qquad (4.75)$$

It can easily be seen (see Bellman [18]) that this equation gives rise to Euler's equation (4.70).

An interesting example, within the realm of calculus of variations, is the 'iso-perimetric' problem, viz. given two points A,B (see Fig. 2), with a continuous simple arc of known length, S, joining them, what form of curve will maximise the area between the curve and the line AB?

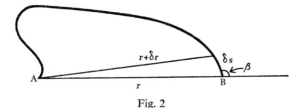

Fig. 2

The classical formulation is to maximise

$$J(r(\cdot)) = \int_{s=0}^{S} \tfrac{1}{2} \cdot r(s) \sin (\beta(s)) ds$$

where S is the curve length, and $\beta(s)$ is the angle between the tangent to the curve and the radius, at a given distance S along the curve, measured from B.

$$\sin (\beta(s)) = \{1 - [\dot{r}(s)]^2\}^{\frac{1}{2}}.$$

This is quite obviously of the same form as (4.69) with $x(t)$, $\dot{x}(t)$ being replaced by $r(s)$, $\dot{r}(s)$ respectively. Letting β be the control variable (instead of $\dot{r}(= \cos (\beta))$) equation (4.75) becomes

$$-\partial f/\partial s = \max_{\beta}[\tfrac{1}{2} \cdot r \sin (\beta) + \cos (\beta) \partial f/\partial r].$$

This gives rise to

$$\partial f/\partial r = (r/2) \cot (\beta)$$
$$\partial f/\partial s = -(r/2) \operatorname{cosec} (\beta).$$

These give rise, by differentiating respectively with respect to s,r and equating $\partial^2 f/\partial r \partial s$ in each case,

$$r \partial \beta/\partial s + r \cos (\beta) \partial \beta/\partial r = \sin (\beta).$$

Putting kr, ks in place of r,s respectively, does not alter this equation, and hence we conclude that the equation is of the form $(r/s) = z(\beta)$ or $\beta = g(r/s)$.

$z(\beta)$ then satisfies:

$$z(\cos (\beta) - z) = \dot{z} \sin (\beta).$$

Putting $z = u \sin (\beta)$, we have

$$\dot{u} = -u^2.$$

This gives $u = (\beta + c)^{-1}$ for some constant c.

Thus $r/s = \sin(\beta)/(\beta + c)$.

When $r = \overline{AB}$, $s = 0$ and we must have $c = -\beta_0$ (the initial tangential angle at B).

Therefore

$$r/s = \sin(\beta)/(\beta_0 - \beta) = \sin(\gamma)/(\gamma - \gamma_0)$$

where $\gamma = \pi - \beta$.

Letting $r(s) = R(s) \sin(\gamma(s))$, we have

$$s = [\gamma_0 - \gamma(s)]R(s).$$

This gives, $1 = (\gamma_0 - \gamma)\dot{R} - \dot{\gamma}R$.

But
$$\dot{r} = \cos(\beta) = -\cos(\gamma),$$
$$= R\cos(\gamma)\dot{\gamma} + \dot{R}\sin(\gamma).$$

Thus $(1 + \dot{\gamma}R) = (\gamma_0 - \gamma)\dot{R}$ and $\cos(\gamma)(1 + \dot{\gamma}R) = -\dot{R}\sin(\gamma)$ whence

$$\dot{R}(\cos(\gamma)(\gamma_0 - \gamma) + \sin(\gamma)) = 0.$$

This gives $\dot{R} \equiv 0$ (since only a denumerable number of γ's satisfy $\cos(\gamma)(\gamma_0 - \gamma) + \cos(\gamma) = 0$).

Whence $R \equiv$ constant.

Hence the solution is

$$r = R\sin(\gamma(s)).$$

This is the equation to a circle of diameter R passing through A, B, which is the answer obtained using the classical method.

The usefulness of D.P. here lies in the discrete form (4.72) which offers a routine solution to a variety of such problems, and it needs to be noted that u can be conditionally restricted quite easily without any trouble.

A further extension is to consider the minimisation of (4.69) subject to

$$\int_a^b G(x,\dot{x},t) = k. \qquad (4.76)$$

The variational approach would need the introduction of a Lagrange parameter, λ, and given rise to the solution of

$$\partial/\partial x(F + \lambda G) = d/dt[\partial/\partial \dot{x}(F + \lambda G)]. \qquad (4.77)$$

λ would need to be varied until $x(t)$ satisfies (4.76).

The discrete D.P. approach would give the equation

$$f(m\delta,c,k) = \min_u[\delta F(c,u,m\delta) + f((m+1)\delta,c + u\delta,k - \delta G(c,u,m\delta))] \qquad (4.78)$$

The variable, k, is a resource type restriction as used in equation (4.4), equivalent to

$$\int_{m\delta}^{b} G(x,\dot{x},t)dt = k. \tag{4.79}$$

The type of problem discussed above involves an integral objective function and, possibly integral constraints. There are a class of control problems which involve integral objective functions and point constraints. Bellman [9, 18] considers a class of these under the heading of 'bottleneck' problems. The physical problem concerns a closed set of industries, in that each produces a product needed by the other industries to produce their own products. The example he takes consists of a closed group of three industries, viz. auto, steel and tool industries. Let us number the industries $1, 2, \ldots n$. Let

$x_i(t)$ be the stockpile of product i at time t.

$y_i(t)$ be the capacity of industry i at time t.

$z_{sj}(t)$ be the amount of product s allocated to industry j for increasing capacity, at time t.

$u_{sj}(t)$ be the amount of product s allocated to industry j to produce product j at time t.

a_{ij} be the number of units of product j required to produce one unit of product i.

b_{ij} be the number of units of product j required to expand capacity output of industry i by one unit.

We then get

$$x_i(t+1) = x_i(t) - \Sigma_j z_{ij}(t) - \Sigma_j u_{ij}(t) + \min \{y_i(t), \min_{j \in R_i}[a_{ij}^{-1} u_{ji}(t)]\} \tag{4.80}$$

$$y_i(t+1) = y_i(t) + \min_{j \in S_i}[b_{ij}^{-1} z_{ij}(t)] \tag{4.81}$$

$$x_i(t) \geqslant \Sigma_j z_{ij}(t) + \Sigma_j u_{ij}(t) \tag{4.82}$$

R_i is the set of all industries whose output is needed to produce product i.

S_i is the set of all industries whose output is needed to increase the expansion of industry i.

If R_i or S_i are empty then the right hand bracket of (4.80) is replaced by $y_i(t)$ and the right hand bracket of (4.81) by 0, respectively.

The objective criterion is one of maximising the total number of autos produced up to time T, and no intermediary costs are included. It is cost free but can be modified to include, say, stock holding costs. We easily see that, in this case, we have therefore the auxiliary relations (to be strictly correct we can only say that there exists an optimal path in which these relations are true):

$$a_{ij}^{-1}u_{ji}(t) = a_{ij'}^{-1}u_{j'i}(t) \leqslant y_i(t), \qquad j,j' \in S_i \qquad (4.83)$$

$$b_{ij}^{-1}z_{ji}(t) = b_{ij'}^{-1}z_{j'i}(t) \qquad\qquad j,j' \in S_i \qquad (4.84)$$

Using these relations, and eliminating some of the variables, by a change of notation (i.e. extending the x vector to include the y vector, and the z vector to include the u vector) we derive the equations

$$x(t+1) = x(t) + A_1 x(t) + A_2 z(t), \qquad A_1 \geqslant 0. \qquad (4.85)$$

$$Bz(t) \leqslant x(t), \quad x(t), z(t) \geqslant 0. \qquad\qquad (4.86)$$

The continuous counterpart of these is:

$$\dot{x}(t) = A_1 x(t) + A_2 z(t), \; A_1 \geqslant 0 \qquad\qquad (4.87)$$

$$Bz(t) \leqslant x(t), \quad x(t), \; z(t) \geqslant 0. \qquad\qquad (4.88)$$

$z(t)$ will now be a vector rate of allocation, and $x(t)$ will be a vector stock level.

The problem, in general, is to maximise

$$\sum_{i=1}^{N} \alpha_i x_i(T) \text{ subject to } x(0) = c.$$

Bellman shows that a necessary condition $u(t)$ be a solution to the optimisation problem is that there exist a vector $w(t) \geqslant 0$ satisfying:

$$w_i(t) = 0 \text{ if } c_i > \Sigma_j q_{ij} z_j(t) - \int_0^t [\Sigma_j p_{ij} u_j(t)] dt, \qquad (4.89)$$

$$u_i(t) = 0 \text{ if } \Sigma_j p_{ji}\alpha_j < \Sigma_j q_{ij} w_j(t) + \int_0^t [\Sigma_j p_{ji} w_j(t)] dt. \qquad (4.90)$$

These conditions only serve to verify if indeed $u(t)$ is an optimal solution. They are of no direct help in getting a solution. They are in fact the continuous counterpart of the primal and dual sets of equations one would get if the problem were treated as a discrete linear programme, and, indeed linear programming provides one means of solution, although, from equations (4.80)–(4.82), if $n = 10$ and $T = 10$, we get a matrix of the order of 300×1300.

By replacing in (4.87), (4.88) z by

$$v = \begin{bmatrix} x \\ z \end{bmatrix} \qquad\qquad (4.91)$$

and setting

$$Q = [0, I], \quad R = [I, 0], \qquad\qquad (4.92)$$

these equations can be reduced to the form

$$\dot{x} = Pv \text{ (dropping the } t), \tag{4.93}$$

$$Qv \leqslant x, \quad Rv = x, \quad v,x \geqslant 0. \tag{4.94}$$

Let us look at the D.P. approach to the canonical form (4.93), (4.94). Define $f(m\delta,c)$ to be the maximum value of $x'(M\delta)$. α subject to $x = c$ at time $m\delta$. We derive:
if $m \leqslant M - 1$

$$f(m\delta,c) = \max_{v \geqslant 0}[f((m+1)\delta,c+\delta Pv)] \tag{4.95}$$
$$v \geqslant 0$$
$$Qv \leqslant c$$
$$Rv = c$$
$$f(M\delta,c) = c'\alpha. \tag{4.96}$$

At this point the reader may find it useful to compare equations (4.95), (4.72), (4.7) and (4.4), each of which differs in a certain way from the others.

The limiting continuous form of this is

$$0 = \max_{\substack{0 \leqslant v \\ Qv \leqslant c, Rv = c}} [\partial f/\partial t + \sum_{i=1}^{N} \sum_{j=1}^{K} \partial f/\partial c_i p_{ij} v_j]. \tag{4.97}$$

The equation will hold at all points except a set of measure zero, where f may not be differentiable. The advantage of (4.97) is that if the dimension of c is small, an analytic solution can be given to the problem (see Bellman [9, 18]) and this helps in that a sensitivity analysis with respect to parameter values can be carried out. This equation cannot be deduced using the calculus of variations approach since the allowable region of x is not open (completely) and neither is the allowable region of v for a given x. Although the solution to (4.95) is straightforward, in principle, we still need to use functional approximation to solve it.

Let us now turn to a new approach to determining optimal policies for control systems of a special kind. This is due to Pontryagin.[38]

The simplest control problem he considers is defined as follows. The state variables $x_1 x_2, \dots x_n$ satisfy the equations

$$\dot{x}_i = f_i(x,u), \quad i = 1, 2, \dots n, \tag{4.98}$$

where u is the control vector for the process.

The objective is to find a control function $u(t)$ which optimises the integral

$$\int_{t_0}^{t_1} f_0(x,u)dt. \tag{4.99}$$

The system begins at x_0 at time t_0 and t_1 is determined by the time the system reaches a fixed point given in advance. We are thus minimising some cost, say, of getting from one point to another.

The control vectors are limited in some manner.

The $\{u\}$ are assumed to belong to a specified region U, given in advance. A class of admissible controls is only restricted in as much as the following properties must hold, viz.

(i) All controls $u(t)$, $t_0 \leqslant t \leqslant t_1$, which belong to the admissible class D, are measurable and bounded.

(ii) If $u(t) \in D$, $t_0 \leqslant t \leqslant t_1$, $v \in U$, and $t_0 \leqslant t' \leqslant t'' \leqslant t_1$, the control $u_1(t)$, $t_0 \leqslant t \leqslant t_1$, defined by the formula given below, is also in D:

$$u_1(t) = \left\{ \begin{array}{l} v \text{ if } t' \leqslant t \leqslant t'' \\ u(t) \text{ if } t_0 \leqslant t \leqslant t' \text{ or } t'' \leqslant t \leqslant t_1 \end{array} \right\}.$$

(iii) If the interval, $t_0 \leqslant t \leqslant t_1$, is broken up by means of a subdivision of points into a finite number of subintervals, on each of which the control, $u(t)$, is admissible, then this control is also admissible on the entire interval.

(iv) An admissible control considered on a subinterval is also admissible. A control obtained from an admissible control by a translation in time is also admissible.

For such a system Pontryagin's main result is contained in his Maximum Principle, viz:

'Let $u(t)$, $t_0 \leqslant t \leqslant t_1$, be an admissible control such that the corresponding trajectory, $x(t)$, which begins at the point x_0 at time t_0, passes at some time t_1 through x_1. In order that $u(t)$, $x(t)$ be optimal, it is necessary that there exist a non-zero continuous vector function $X(t) \equiv [X_0(t), X_1(t), \ldots X_n(t)]$ corresponding to $u(t)$ and $x(t)$ such that:

1. For every t, $t_0 \leqslant t \leqslant t_1$, the function $H(X(t), x(t), u)$ of the variable $u \in U$ attains its maximum at the point $u = u(t)$ where H is defined as follows:

$$H(X, x, u) = \sum_{\alpha=0}^{n} X_\alpha f_\alpha(x, u). \tag{4.100}$$

2. If $M(X(t), x(t)) = H(X(t), x(t), u(t))$, then

$$X_0(t_1) \leqslant 0, \quad M(X(t), x(t_1)) = 0. \tag{4.101}$$

Furthermore it turns out that, if

$$\dot{x}_i = \partial H / \partial X_i, \quad i = 0, 1, \ldots n, \tag{4.102}$$

$$\dot{X}_i = -\partial H / \partial x_i, \quad i = 0, 1, \ldots n, \tag{4.103}$$

and condition (1) is satisfied, the time functions $X_0(t)$, $M(X(t), x(t))$ are constant, and hence condition (2) can be verified at any point in time.

This is a statement of the simplest form of Pontryagin's results. Let us look at the D.P. approach formally, without worrying about analytic considerations. We note first of all that the optimal value of the integral (4.99) depends only on the starting condition x_0, and we can thus invoke Bellman's Principle of Optimality, and if $F(x)$ is the value of

$\int_{t_0}^{t_1} f_0(x(t),u(t))dt$ beginning in state x at time t and using an optimal policy, we have

$$F(x) = \mathrm{opt}_u[f_0(x,u)\delta + F(x+f\delta)].$$ (4.104)

Note the difference between this and equations (4.72), (4.95), in that the time factor does not arise in (4.104). In the sense of Chapter 3 it is a stationary equation.

Expanding F to first order terms, and taking the limit as $\delta \to 0$ we, formally, derive the equation

$$0 = \mathrm{opt}_u[f_0(x,u) + \sum_{i=1}^{n} f_i(x,u)(\partial F/\partial x_i)(x)].$$ (4.105)

Thus formally we have derived part of Pontryagin's Maximum Principle, if $X_i(t) \equiv \partial F/\partial x_i(x(t))$, $i = 1, 2, \ldots n$; $X_0(t) \equiv 1$.

Pontryagin actually shows, formally, that the Hamiltonian equations (4.102), (4.103) can also be deduced, and hence, without enquiring too deeply into problems of differentiability, D.P. produces Pontryagin's results.

However Pontryagin's main criticism is that $\partial F/\partial x_i$ may not exist. In fact, with the following example, $\partial F/\partial x_i$ does not exist on the curves $x_1 = \frac{1}{2}x_2^2(x_2 \leqslant 0)$, $x_1 = -\frac{1}{2}x_2^2(x_2 \geqslant 0)$. Nevertheless $\partial F/\partial x_i$ exists everywhere else, and F is continuous everywhere, and so we ought to be able to solve the problem. The problem is:

find the control $u(t)$, $|u| \leqslant 1$ which minimises the time taken to get from (x_1,x_2) to the point $(0,0)$ where $\dot{x}_1 = x_2$, $\dot{x}_2 = u$.

We have

$$f_0 \equiv 1, \quad f_1 \equiv x_2, \quad f_2 \equiv u.$$

Equation (4.105) then becomes

$$0 = \min_u[1 + x_2(\partial F/\partial x_1) + u(\partial F/\partial x_2)].$$

Then $u = -\,\mathrm{sign}\,(\partial F/\partial x_2)$ and

$$1 + x_2(\partial F/\partial x_1) - (\partial F/\partial x_2) = 0 \text{ if } \partial F/\partial x_2 > 0$$ (4.106)

$$1 + x_2(\partial F/\partial x_1) + (\partial F/\partial x_2) = 0 \text{ if } \partial F/\partial x_2 < 0.$$

If we solve these in the normal way, forgetting about non-differentiability, and match different segments of the curves at points where

$\partial F / \partial x_2 = 0$, as obtained from (4.107) or (4.108), we derive the answer Pontryagin gets, viz: the (x_1, x_2) plane is divided into two regions (in one of which $u = 1$ and, in the other $u = -1$) as shown in Fig. 3.

If (x_1, x_2) is originally in the '$u = 1$' region, we keep $u = 1$ until we meet $x_1 = -\tfrac{1}{2} x_2^2$ and then switch to $u = -1$. Corresponding results hold if (x_1, x_2) is in the '$u = -1$' region initially.

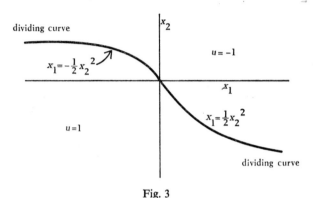

Fig. 3

Finally it is worth mentioning the two entirely different and conflicting attitudes of Bellman and Pontryagin. Pontryagin, p. 7, [38] says 'Thus Bellman's considerations yield a good heuristic method, rather than a mathematical solution of the problem', whereas Bellman, p. 180, [16] says that too much attention is paid (referring to Calculus of Variations) to mathematical exactness and little to computational routines. Both the calculus of variations and Pontryagin's Maximum Principle yield, in general, an exceedingly complex set of differential equations, and it is problematic whether the most sophisticated mathematical analysis will make these easier in future. On the other hand the discrete D.P. approach requires no sophistication and is quite general, the problem being one of reducing the size of the computational burden somehow.

4.4. Functional Approximation

By far and away the biggest stumbling block in the way of more general applications is the fact that we need, for many problems, a high dimensional vector to describe the state of the system. Consider, for example, the allocation problem in Section 4.1, which gave rise to the functional equation:

$$f_m(c_1, c_2, \ldots c_l) = \max_{0 \leqslant x_m \leqslant \min_k [c_k / \alpha_{km}]} [g_m(x_m) + f_{m-1}(c_1^* c_2^* \ldots c_l^*)]$$
$$(4.113)$$

where
$$c_k^* = c_k - \alpha_{km} x_m, \; k = 1, 2, \ldots l.$$

The Lagrange multiplier method has been suggested for this, to reduce dimensionality, but cannot be used to reduce dimensionality for general D.P. problems, and so we shall need a more general approach.

Suppose that we divided the ranges of $c_1, c_2, \ldots c_l$ by M partition points, sufficiently close that $c_1^*, c_2^*, \ldots c_l^*$ could be approximated by one of the points. The number of states we would have to consider would then be M^l at each stage. If $M = l = 10$ even our largest computer could not possibly do this, even with auxiliary tape storage.

Bellman [16, 19] shows how this can be done using the method of functional approximations which replaces the problem of storage of the functional values (at each stage) of the states by the problem of storing a set of coefficients of certain functions, at each stage.

Briefly, the function of $f_m(c_1, c_2, \ldots c_l)$ is replaced by a linear combination of certain functions,
$$z_1(c_1, c_2, \ldots c_l), \; z_2(c_1, c_2, \ldots c_l) \ldots z_T(c_1, \ldots c_l), \text{ viz.}$$
$$f_m(c_1, c_2, \ldots c_l) \sim \sum_{s=1}^{T} \alpha_{ms} z_s(c_1, c_2, \ldots c_l). \tag{4.114}$$

If an inner product operation for any two functions $g(c)$, $h(c)$ exists, such that $\{z_s\}$ form an orthonormal set, in the sense that
$$[z_s, z_r] = \delta_{rs} \tag{4.115}$$
where $\delta_{rs} = 1$ if $r = s$, $= 0$ if $r \neq s$, then we see that:
$$\alpha_{ms} = [f_m, z_s]. \tag{4.116}$$

Suppose, for example, that $z_s(c_1, c_2, \ldots c_l)$, after standardising the $\{c_k\}$ to range between $+1$ and -1, is a product of powers of normalised Legendre polynomials, viz.
$$z_s = \prod_{u=1}^{l} p_{n_{su}}(c_u) \tag{4.117}$$
where $p_{n_{su}}$ is the n_{su}th Legendre polynomial.

Then
$$\alpha_{ms} = \int_{-1}^{1} dc_1 \int_{-1}^{1} dc_2 \ldots \int_{-1}^{1} dc_l (f_m(c_1, c_2, \ldots c_l)) \prod_{u=1}^{l} p_{n_{su}}(c_u). \tag{4.118}$$

If, for example, we allow Legendre polynomial approximations up to a total degree R, we have $T = (R+l)!/R!l!$ coefficients in all, and hence our storage problem is reduced from one of storing M^l values to one of storing $(R+l)!/R!l!$ values, e.g. if $M = R = l = 10$, we reduce the problem from one of storing 10 000 000 000 values to one of storing 184 756 values, the latter one being achievable with sufficient auxiliary storage on the larger computers. For $R = 5$ a much more feasible result occurs, viz. 3003.

We do not reduce the storage problem without some loss necessarily, and there may be an increase in computational time, because we have to compute the $\{\alpha_{ms}\}$ which provides an extra two stages to the computations in general. Before we can compute $\{\alpha_{ms}\}$, we need to compute $f_m(c_1, c_2, \ldots c_l)$ at some selected points. This involves a calculation of $f_{m-1}(c_1^*, c_2^*, \ldots c_l^*)$ from the $(m-1)$ stage counterpart of (4.114) viz.

$$f_{m-1}(c_1^*, c_2^*, \ldots c_l^*) \sim \sum_{s=1}^{T} \alpha_{m-1\,s}, z_s(c_1^*, c_2^*, \ldots c_l^*). \qquad (4.119)$$

Bellman [16, 19] shows how (4.118) can be approximated by a special quadrature using Christoffel numbers (see Lowan [30] for some tabulations). If $p_S(x)$ is the Sth degree Legendre polynomial, then, for a particular degree $[R = (S-1)]$ of approximating polynomials, the Christoffel numbers correspond to roots of the equation

$$p_S(x) = 0. \qquad (4.120)$$

If we are concerned with a one-dimensional function, $f_m(x)$, then the Christoffel numbers are a set $a_1, a_2, \ldots a_S$, such that an approximation to the one-dimensional counterpart of (4.118) is

$$\alpha_{ms} \sim \sum_{k=1}^{S} a_k f_m(\mu_k) p_s(\mu_k), \qquad (4.121)$$

where $\mu_1 \mu_2, \ldots \mu_S$ are given by (4.120) and $a_1, a_2, \ldots a_S$ are the corresponding Christoffel numbers (which can be tabulated in advance once S is given).

The multidimensional counterpart is

$$\alpha_{ms} \sim \sum_{k_1=1}^{S} \sum_{k_2=1}^{S} \ldots \sum_{k_l=1}^{S} a_{k_1} a_{k_2} \ldots a_{k_l} f_m(\mu_{k_1}, \mu_{k_2}, \ldots \mu_{k_l}) \prod_{t=1}^{l} p_{nst}(\mu_{k_t}) =$$

$$\sum_{k_1=1}^{S} \sum_{k_2=1}^{S} \ldots \sum_{k_l=1}^{S} a_{k_1} a_{k_2} \ldots a_{k_l} f_m(\mu_{k_1}, \ldots \mu_{k_l}) z_s(\mu_{k_1}, \ldots \mu_{k_l}). \qquad (4.122)$$

Bellman [16, 19] states that (4.121) is exact if $f_m(c)p_s(c)$ is a polynomial in c of degree $2S-1$. It can be proved, inductively, that (4.122) is also exact if $f_m(c_1, c_2, \ldots c_l) \prod_{t=1}^{l} p_{nst}(c_t)$ is polynomial of degree $2S-1$ in each c_k individually. (See Appendix, p. 168.)

If z_s (see equation (4.117)) is such that $n_{su} \leqslant S-1$ and if $f_m(c_1, c_2, \ldots c_l)$ is polynomial of degree $(S-1)$ in the individual c_k, then this holds.

Hence we would, in our approximations, choose an approximating polynomial containing Legendre polynomials up to degree $(S-1)$.

The real purpose of introducing functional approximation is to overcome the storage difficulty. It is possible that, even when the storage problem is not beyond the bounds of present computers, this approach may save on computational time with some loss of accuracy, and, in any case, we are seldom sure enough of the validity of our model (e.g. objective criteria and parametric values) that we would insist on too close an approximation to the model's optimum point. Using this approach we see that if we use a Christoffel set of degree S, the only functional values we would need to compute and store at each stage would be $\{f_m(\mu_{k_1},\mu_{k_2}, \ldots \mu_{k_l})\}$, where μ_{k_r} is any one of the zeros of the Sth degree Legendre polynomial, i.e. S^l values. For $S = 6, l = 6$ we have 46 656 values, much less than the original 1 000 000 values, and quite feasible. If we wished to approximate by Legendre polynomials up to a total degree of 5, we would only have 462 parameters $\{\alpha_{ms}\}$ to compute at each stage. Thus apart from the fact that we have to compute $f_{m-1}(c_1^*,c_2^*, \ldots c_l^*)$ in accordance with (4.7) for each allowable x_m for each $(c_1,c_2, \ldots c_l)$ given by $(\mu_{k_1},\mu_{k_2}, \ldots \mu_{k_l})$ for any combination of $\mu_1, \mu_2, \ldots \mu_s$, there would be a considerable reduction even in computations. Further research work will no doubt shed light on the possibilities of reducing computational time.

To complete this, let us set down formally the procedure we would adopt to solve equation (4.113)

(i) Choose a set of approximating functions, z_s, $s = 1, 2, \ldots T$ where each z_s is the product of Legendre polynomials in each variable, each of degree $S-1$ (at most, of course, since a polynomial of degree 2 is also one of degree $(S-1)$).

(ii) Determine $\mu_1, \mu_2, \ldots \mu_s, a_1, a_2, \ldots a_s$ from appropriate tables.

(iii) Calculate $f_1(c_1,c_2, \ldots c_l)$ at each point $(\mu_{k_1},\mu_{k_2}, \ldots \mu_{k_l})$ where $\{\mu_{k_s}\}$ ranges over all $\{\mu_s\}$ giving S^l points to be evaluated in all.

(iv) Calculate $\{\alpha_{1s}\}$, $s = 1, 2, \ldots T$ from equation (4.122), i.e.

$$\alpha_{1s} = \sum_{k_1=1}^{S} \sum_{k_2=1}^{S} \ldots \sum_{k_l=1}^{S} a_{k_1}a_{k_2} \ldots a_{k_l} f_1(\mu_{k_1}\mu_{k_2} \ldots \mu_{k_l})z_s(\mu_{k_1} \ldots \mu_{k_l}).$$

(v) Calculate $f_2(c_1,c_2, \ldots c_l)$ at each point $(\mu_{k_1}, \ldots \mu_{k_l})$ by (from equations (4.113), (4.114))

$$f_2(c_1,c_2, \ldots c_l) = \max_{0 \leqslant x_2 \leqslant min_k[c_k/\alpha_{k_2}]}[g_2(x_2) + \sum_{s=1}^{T} \alpha_{1s}z_s(c_1^*, \ldots c_{l*})]$$

where

$$c_k^* = c_k - \alpha_{k_2}x_2.$$

7

(*vi*) Calculate $\{\alpha_{2s}\}$ as in (*iv*) and repeat cycle until $f_n(c_1, c_2, \ldots c_l)$ has been calculated.

Further discussions on the use of other forms of approximation may be found in Azen [6] and Beckwith.[8] It is perhaps fair to say that further real progress in the applicability of Dynamic Programming may well depend on the ideas brought to bear by Bellman as discussed in this section.

Chapter 5

STOCHASTIC PROCESSES

THE essential difference between the sort of system we shall discuss here and the deterministic ones discussed in Chapter 4 arises from the fact that the transformed state resulting from a decision at any stage is not predetermined, but can be described by a known probability function, dependent, possibly, on the action taken as well as the initial state.

It has been argued that the use of D.P. for deterministic systems gives rise to redundant computations, sometimes, because the optimal actions are computed for states which are never assumed, although we may not know these prior to the analysis. However in a stochastic system we do not know beforehand, even after the policy has been determined, which states will be assumed, and, in some problems, any state may have a non-zero probability of being assumed at any stage. For such situations we obviously need to know the appropriate act for every possible state. Two possible alternative approaches to determining policies for such systems are either to simulate various policies or to determine analytically or computationally the effects of various policies. The latter gives rise to what is known as 'Stochastic Programming' which converts a stochastic optimisation problem into an equivalent deterministic optimisation problem.

In general this is carried out with policies of specific classes (e.g. we might use an (S,s) type rule for stock control; such a rule states: if the stock level falls to s or below, order a quantity $S-x$, where x is the actual stock level), within which specific parameters are free to be chosen. The disadvantage of this approach is that we restrict our analysis to such policies as may seem reasonable, whereas the D.P. approach does not predetermine the form of the policy, it is completely free (within the restrictions placed on it by special considerations, which also restrict simulations and mathematical treatments in a like manner however). In Section 5.5 we consider a recently developed competitive approach (to D.P.) due to Manne [32] but which has not been, to date, tested relative to D.P. First impressions indicate that it is strictly comparable computationally and storagewise. Whether D.P. should be used depends both on the relevant computational costs and on the extra return achievable by its use, which is not in general known of course, but certainly, if the computational cost were very small compared with the overall level of operating cost (estimated), one might do better to use it rather than use the other alternatives. This must be left to the judgement of the decision-maker.

The standard work in the field of stochastic processes is Howard [27] and we shall begin with a discussion of it.

5.1. Finite Discrete Markov Processes

By a finite Markov process we mean one described by a finite number of states with transition probabilities from one state to another being dependent only on the initial state, and, in our case, the action taken. The 'discrete' terminology applies to the stage structure, i.e. we make our decisions at discrete time intervals.

The initial problem, as we shall specify it, is that we are in one of a finite number, m, of states, and need to choose an action, k, from a given set, dependent only on the state, and on the stage. The duration of the system is n periods. The return in the first period, if we take action k when the initial state is i and we move to state j, is r_{ij}^k and this transition is made with probability p_{ij}^k. We wish to minimise our expected cost over the next n periods of time.

If a discount factor, α, is used in the analysis, similar results hold except that the expected long run discounted return is bounded and a different stationary form to that in equation (5.3) is obtained, viz.

$$v(i) = \min_k[q_i^k + \alpha\Sigma_j p_{ij}^k v(j)]$$

since, in this case, $v_n(i) \rightarrow v(i)$ satisfying this equation. Reference can be made to Howard for this, since it is not beset with the difficulties over complete ergodicity and non-stationarity of policies which the case, now covered, meets.

In the Appendix, p. 169 we show that, if $v_n(i)$ is the expected cost over the next n periods of time using an optimal policy and beginning in state i, then we have:
if $n > 1$

$$v_n(i) = \min_k[q_i^k + \Sigma_j p_{ij}^k v_{n-1}(j)]$$
$$v_1(i) = \min_k[q_i^k], \qquad\qquad\qquad (5.1)$$

where

$$q_i^k = \Sigma_j p_{ij}^k r_{ij}^k.$$

We can solve this easily by working backwards, for any finite n. In many cases, n is very large and we would like to know how the solution behaves for large n. We can introduce discount factors if we feel they are relevant, but this usually applies only to systems with durations in the order of years and then we can question the use of probabilities. It is not relevant in many production problems.

Now let us suppose, for the moment, that $v_n(i) \to ng + v(i) + \varepsilon_n(i)$ as $n \to \infty$, where $\varepsilon_n(i) \to 0$ as $n \to \infty$. This happens when the transition matrix for the optimal policy, in particular, is regular i.e. the characteristic equation, $|P - \lambda I| = 0$, has only simple roots of modulus unity (see Bartlet [7]). Then we derive

$$ng + v(i) + \varepsilon_n(i) = \min_k [q_i^k + \Sigma_j p_{ij}^k (n-1)g + \Sigma_j p_{ij}^k v(j) + \Sigma_j p_{ij}^k \varepsilon_{n-1}(j)]. \quad (5.2)$$

Hence, for sufficiently large n, providing $g \neq 0$, we derive:

$$g + v(i) = \min_k [q_i^k + \Sigma_j p_{ij}^k v(j)]. \quad (5.3)$$

Howard [27] gives an algorithm for solving (5.3) viz.

(i) choose a starting policy $\{k_0(i)\}$.

(ii) if there are m states, putting $v_0(m) = 0$, solve the m equations, given below, for $v_0(1), v_0(2), \ldots v_0(m-1)$ and g_0, viz.

$$g_0 + v_0(1) = q_1^{k_0(1)} + \Sigma_j p_{1j}^{k_0(1)} v_0(j)$$

$$g_0 + v_0(2) = q_2^{k_0(2)} + \Sigma_j p_{2j}^{k_0(2)} v_0(j)$$

$$\cdot \qquad \cdot \qquad \cdot \qquad \cdot$$
$$\cdot \qquad \cdot \qquad \cdot \qquad \cdot$$
$$\cdot \qquad \cdot \qquad \cdot \qquad \cdot$$

$$g_0 + v_0(m) = q_m^{k_0(m)} + \Sigma_j p_{mj}^{k_0(m)} v_0(j),$$

(iii) using $\{f_0(i)\}$ calculated above, for each i find that value of $k_1(i)$ which minimises

$$q_i^{k_1(i)} + \Sigma_j p_{ij}^{k_1(i)} v_0(j).$$

(iv) using this new policy, $\{k_1(i)\}$, repeat cycle at (ii) until the process converges, as it will do in a finite number of steps, to the optimal policy.

This algorithm holds for equation (5.3) providing each matrix $\{p_{ij}^k\}$ is completely ergodic, in the sense that it has only one eigen-value equal to unity; for only then does a solution exist at stage (ii). It always holds when discount factors are used. However, in cases where this condition does not hold, Howard gives another algorithm, for a modified form of (5.3), which allows for the fact that the optimal policy may result in recurrent chains, and, instead of the limiting form as given above, we have, in general:

$$v_n(i) \to ng(i) + v(i) + \varepsilon_n(i). \quad (5.4)$$

A full account of this algorithm has been given in Howard,[23] and it will not be dealt with here. It is to be hoped that we do not encounter such difficulties in practice, for their resolution is extremely tedious. They do not occur if $p_k^{ij} > 0$ for all i, j, k.

Numerical Example:

Transition Probabilities

State	Action	Transformed State 1	2	Expected Costs
1	1	0·5	0·5	5
	2	0·7	0·3	3
2	1	0·8	0·2	2
	2	0·4	0·6	1

Solution Procedure

(*i*) Select initial policy $\{k_0(i)\}$ viz. $k_0(1) = k_0(2) = 1$.

(*ii*) Putting $v_0(2) = 0$, solve the equations (for g_0, $v_0(1)$):

$$g_0 + v_0(1) = 5 + 0·5v_0(1) + 0·5 \times 0$$
$$g_0 + 0 \quad = 2 + 0·8v_0(1) + 0·2 \times 0$$

to give:

$$g_0 = 3·84, \quad v_0(1) = 2·3$$

(*iii*) Find new action $k_1(1)$ from

$$\min \begin{bmatrix} 5 + 0·5 \times 2·3 + 0·5 \times 0 \\ 3 + 0·7 \times 2·3 + 0·3 \times 0 \end{bmatrix} = 4·61 \quad \text{i.e. } k_1(1) = 2$$

Find new action $k_1(2)$ from:

$$\min \begin{bmatrix} 2 + 0·8 \times 2·3 + 0·2 \times 0 \\ 1 + 0·4 \times 2·3 + 0·6 \times 0 \end{bmatrix} = 1·92 \quad \text{i.e. } k_1(2) = 2$$

(*iv*) Putting $v_1(2) = 0$, solve the equations (for $g_1, v_1(1)$):

$$g_1 + v_1(1) = 3 + 0·7v_1(1) + 0·3 \times 0$$
$$g_1 + 0 \quad = 1 + 0·4v_1(1) + 0·6 \times 0$$

to give:

$$g_1 = 2·14, \quad v_1(1) = 2·86.$$

(*v*) Find new action $k_2(1)$ from

$$\min \begin{bmatrix} 5 + 0·5 \times 2·86 + 0·5 \times 0 \\ 3 + 0·7 \times 2·86 + 0·3 \times 0 \end{bmatrix} = 5 \quad \text{i.e. } k_2(1) = 2$$

Find new action $k_2(2)$ from

$$\min \begin{bmatrix} 2 + 0·8 \times 2·86 + 0·2 \times 0 \\ 1 + 0·4 \times 2·86 + 0·6 \times 0 \end{bmatrix} = 2·43 \quad \text{i.e. } k_2(2) = 2$$

Since $\{k_2(i)\} = \{k_1(i)\}$ the procedure has converged and the optimal policy is to take the second alternative action for each state. The corresponding cost per unit period is 2·14.

* Let us now go back to our assumption concerning the limiting form of $v_n(i)$. There are two difficulties associated with this; viz.

(i) It is difficult to establish this directly from equation (5.1).

(ii) In any case, $\varepsilon_n(i)$ need not $\to 0$, it may oscillate.

Howard deals essentially with steady state policies right from the beginning, i.e. he analyses the limiting form of $v_n(i)$ for a specified steady state policy. It is by no means clear (as pointed out in a private communication by J. Bather, Manchester University, Department of Statistics) that, in general, steady state policies contain an optimal policy at all. Consider, in fact, the following example.

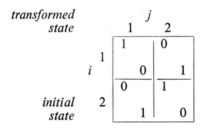

The top left hand elements in each square are the transition probabilities for $k = 1$, for each initial state, and the bottom right hand elements are the transition probabilities for $k = 2$, for each initial state.

The corresponding reward matrix is

	act	
	1	2
state 1	$-1/2+a$	$-1+a$
state 2	$-1/2+a$	$1+a$

$a > 0$

Then, if $v_n(k_1,k_2,i)$ is the expected overall return using policy (k_1,k_2), beginning in state i, we have:

$$v_n(1,1,1) = -\tfrac{1}{2}n.$$
$$v_n(2,2,1) = \left.\begin{array}{l} 0 \text{ if } n \text{ is even} \\ -1 \text{ if } n \text{ is odd} \end{array}\right\} + na$$
$$v_n(1,2,1) = -\tfrac{1}{2}n$$
$$v_n(2,1,1) = -\tfrac{1}{2}(n+1)$$

---

* The remainder of this section may be omitted except by the specialist reader.

Hence the maximum return, commencing in state 1, from a steady state policy, if n is odd, is $na-1$ and, if n is even, is na.

The long run gain is a. Now the policy $k_1 = 2$, $k_2 = 2$ for the first $(n-1)$ moves, if n is odd, followed by $k_1 = 1$, gives a larger overall return of $na-\frac{1}{2}$. The policy $k_1 = 1$ for the first move, $k_1 = k_2 = 2$ for the next $(n-1)$ moves gives an overall return of $na+\frac{1}{2}$ if n is even.

We therefore see that non-stationary policies may be optimal. However, if we are really after the long term gain per unit time, then the optimal set may always contain a stationary policy (and this we leave unproved) and, in the above example, the policy (2.2) is optimal in this sense, whether n is odd or even.

Concentrating on such steady policies the next point centres on the limiting form of $\varepsilon_n(i)$. This need not be zero, and, in fact, may be oscillatory.

This is borne out by the above example, and points to a mistake in Howard's analysis. In actual fact all we can say is that $|\varepsilon_n(i)|$ is bounded but may still be as large as $v(i)$.

If we begin, however, with Howard's final equation (5.3) we see that, for any stationary policy, the variable g is given by

$$g = \Sigma\Pi_i q_i$$

where Π_i is the steady state probability of being in state i using this policy, and q_i is the immediate expected cost when we are in state i and use this policy. This g is identical with the g occuring in the limiting form for $v_n(i)$. Therefore Howard's algorithm actually minimises the cost per unit time, and has nothing to do with ε_n and its behaviour.

One can therefore see that the connection between D.P. and Howard's results in very tenuous. On the other hand, it is highly likely that the algorithm provided would not have been forthcoming without the D.P. formulation.

5.2. An Alternative Computational Algorithm

The real advantage of the above approach is that it provides computational algorithms which can be used whatever the form of the data i.e. we need no special characteristics of the data involved. However, for systems with a large number of states, the work involved in step (*ii*) may be very involved, and one is tempted to ask whether something on the lines of Bellman's method of successive approximations might not be used. In certain cases this is possible, and the following algorithm may be used under certain conditions, viz. that, for any sequence of actions, there is a non-zero probability of moving from any state to some other state within a finite number of steps. This condition is satisfied if all transition probabilities are uniformly bounded below by a positive quantity. It is to be noted that these conditions are not be be applied simply to the transition matrices for any steady state policy; they must apply for any sequence of computations actually realised in the use of this algorithm. The algorithm is as follows.

Compute the sequences $\{V_n(i)\}$, $\{v_n(i)\}$, $\{g_n\}$

$$V_n(i) = \min_k[q_i^k + \Sigma_j p_{ij}^k v_{n-1}(j)] \qquad (5.5)$$

where

$$g_n = V_n(m), \ v_n(i) = V_n(i) - g_n$$

beginning with

$$v_0(i) \equiv 0.$$

The sequences $\{v_n(i)\}$, $\{g_n\}$, then converge uniformly to solution of Howard's final equation. We must note that even this does not imply that iterating equation (5.1) would give rise to a convergent policy.

A fuller account of this method, with proofs is given in White.[46]

Let us consider the example solved by Howard's method. Begin with $v_0(i) \equiv 0$, $i = 1, 2$.

$$n = 1 \quad V_1(1) = \min \begin{bmatrix} 5 \\ 3 \end{bmatrix} = 3$$

$$V_1(2) = \min \begin{bmatrix} 2 \\ 1 \end{bmatrix} = 1$$

$$\begin{aligned} g_1 &= V_1(2) &= 1 \\ v_1(1) &= V_1(1) - g_1 &= 2 \\ v_1(2) &= V_1(2) - g_1 &= 0 \end{aligned}$$

$$n = 2 \quad V_2(1) = \min \begin{bmatrix} 5 + 0.5 \times 2 + 0.5 \times 0 \\ 2 + 0.7 \times 2 + 0.3 \times 0 \end{bmatrix} = 4.4$$

$$V_2(2) = \min \begin{bmatrix} 2 + 0.8 \times 2 + 0.2 \times 0 \\ 1 + 0.4 \times 2 + 0.6 \times 0 \end{bmatrix} = 1.8$$

$$\begin{aligned} g_2 &= V_2(2) &= 1.8 \\ v_2(1) &= V_2(1) - g_2 &= 2.6 \\ v_2(2) &= V_2(2) - g_2 &= 0 \end{aligned}$$

$$n = 3 \quad V_3(1) = \min \begin{bmatrix} 5 + 0.5 \times 2.6 + 0.5 \times 0 \\ 3 + 0.7 \times 2.6 + 0.3 \times 0 \end{bmatrix} = 4.82$$

$$V_3(2) = \min \begin{bmatrix} 2 + 0.8 \times 2.6 + 0.2 \times 0 \\ 1 + 0.4 \times 2.6 + 0.6 \times 0 \end{bmatrix} = 2.04$$

$$\begin{aligned} g_3 &= V_3(2) &= 2.04 \\ v_3(1) &= V_3(1) - g_3 &= 2.78 \\ v_3(2) &= V_3(2) - g_3 &= 0 \end{aligned}$$

$$n = 4 \quad V_4(1) = \min \begin{bmatrix} 5+0\cdot5 \times 2\cdot78+0\cdot5 \times 0 \\ 3+0\cdot7 \times 2\cdot78+0\cdot3 \times 0 \end{bmatrix} = 4\cdot95$$

$$V_4(2) = \min \begin{bmatrix} 2+0\cdot8 \times 2\cdot78+0\cdot2 \times 0 \\ 1+0\cdot4 \times 2\cdot78+0\cdot6 \times 0 \end{bmatrix} = 2\cdot11$$

$$
\begin{aligned}
g_4 &= V_4(2) & &= 2\cdot11 \\
v_4(1) &= V_4(1)-g_4 & &= 2\cdot84 \\
v_4(2) &= V_4(2)-g_4 & &= 0
\end{aligned}
$$

$$n = 5 \quad V_5(1) = \min \begin{bmatrix} 5+0\cdot5 \times 2\cdot84+0\cdot5 \times 0 \\ 3+0\cdot7 \times 2\cdot84+0\cdot3 \times 0 \end{bmatrix} = 4\cdot99$$

$$V_5(2) = \min \begin{bmatrix} 2+0\cdot8 \times 2\cdot84+0\cdot2 \times 0 \\ 1+0\cdot4 \times 2\cdot84+0\cdot6 \times 0 \end{bmatrix} = 2\cdot14$$

$$
\begin{aligned}
g_5 &= V_5(2) & &= 2\cdot14 \\
v_5(1) &= V_5(1)-g_5 & &= 2\cdot85 \\
v_5(2) &= V_5(2)-g_5 & &= 0
\end{aligned}
$$

We readily see that convergence is setting in quite fast, and, if we repeat these steps, we converge to the answer obtained previously, viz.

$$g = 2\cdot14, \quad v(1) = 2\cdot86, \quad v(2) = 0.$$

5.3. Processes Involving Full or Partial Choice of Decision Interval

The standard problem treated above assumes that we make a decision once every period. There are problems where the decision concerns the choice of the next action epoch, apart from the choice of the next action. We shall discuss three possible types of problem, which are by no means all, of course. A full discussion of these problems is to be found in White,[45] and the following is a resumé of the results, which should be enough for practical applications.

5.3.1. A Fixed Action, Completely Controlled Decision Interval, Process

(a) *A Sequential Inspection Process.* Let us consider a process with m states, as before, in which a predetermined action (e.g. inspection, overhaul, replacement, etc.) is to take place from time to time, but in which the time at which the action is to take place is subject to choice.

Let p_{ij}^k be the probability that, if we are in state i now, we shall be in state j, k stages later, with no intervening decisions.

Let E_i^k be the expected cost (we shall talk in terms of 'cost minimisation', but 'return maximisation' can also be analysed in the same way) over the next k periods of time beginning in state i with no intervening actions.

Let $v_n(i)$ be the expected overall cost over the next n periods of time beginning in state i and using an optimal policy. Then we get

$$v_n(i) = \min_k[E_i^k + \Sigma_j p_{ij}^k v_{n-k}(j)].\tag{5.6}$$

It can be shown that, for policies, $\{k(i)\}$, in which all the $\{k(i)\}$ are bounded, a steady state policy is such that (assuming complete ergodicity):

$$v_n(i) \to ng + v(i) + \varepsilon_n(i)$$

where $|\varepsilon_n(i)|$ is bounded.

Substitution in the above equation and letting $\varepsilon_n(i) \to 0$ suggests the steady state set of equations:

$$v(i) = \min_k[E_i^k + \Sigma_j p_{ij}^k v(j) - kg].\tag{5.7}$$

We can easily show (see Appendix, p. 169) that

$$g = \min_k\{[E_i^k + \Sigma_j p_{ij}^k v(j) - v(i)]/k\}$$
$$= \min_k\{T[k,i,v(\cdot)]\} \text{ say.}\tag{5.8}$$

Restricting ourselves, therefore, to steady state policies, we see, as in Howard's work, that any g satisfying (5.8) for some $v(\cdot)$ is the minimum cost per unit time. As before, we simply use (5.6) to suggest the steady state equations, and then we verify that, indeed, a solution to these equations gives an optimal steady state solution, cost-wise, only.

We can even allow for infinite $\{k(i)\}$ in some cases; e.g. in the example quoted below, E_i^k has the form:

$$\alpha(i) + \beta(i)k + \gamma(i)\tau^k \text{ for some } 0 \leqslant \tau \leqslant 1,$$

and, for such cases, the above results still hold.

The following algorithm, which can be considered as an extension of Howard's, then applies, viz.

(i) Choose an arbitrary policy $\{k_0(i)\}$.

(ii) Solve the equations $g = T[k,i,v_0(\cdot)]$ for $g,v_0(\cdot)$, putting $v(m) = 0$.

(iii) Minimise $T[k,i,v_0(\cdot)]$ over k, for each i, giving a new policy $\{k_1(i)\}$.

(iv) Repeat cycle at (ii) until policies converge as they will do.

Results similar to those of Howard can be obtained, with the corresponding analysis, for non-completely ergodic systems.

Let us consider the traditional problem of sampling the output of a continuous production process, without feed back. To do this we beg a question, looked at in the next section, i.e. the problem of handling stochastic constraints, which, in this case, arises from a restriction on average outgoing quality level.

The problem as we shall state it is as follows. The cost per unit sample is one unit. The process in Markovian, in the sense that the probability that the next item is defective (acceptable) depends only on the condition of the present item (if known). This is thought to be an improvement on the old Dodge-Romig [21] approach, whose successive items were held to be independent, since one would expect that defective items occur through some temporary imbalance and hence likely to have local imbalance. The average number of defective items let through is to be preset at a value μ per item dispatched, and we wish to minimise the expected sampling cost.

Defining $v_n(i)$ to be the minimal cost of inspection over the next n items, when we have just inspected and found state i, our reduced equations become (without the quality restriction, putting $v(2) = 0$, with defective states and non-defective states being numbered 1, 2 respectively).

$$g = \min_k\{[1 + (p_{11}^k - 1)v(1)]/k\},$$
$$g = \min_k\{[1 + p_{21}^k v(1)]/k\}. \tag{5.9}$$

However, the unrestricted g is equal to:

$$\Sigma_i \xi_i E_i^{k(i)} / \Sigma_i [\xi_i k(i)],$$

where ξ_i is the steady state probability for state i for a specific policy.

Our quality restriction is equivalent to:

$$\Sigma_i \xi_i \left(\sum_{s=1}^{k(i)-1} p_{i1}^s + \mu p_{i1}^{k(i)}\right) / \Sigma_i \xi_i k(i) = \mu, \tag{5.10}$$

where p_{ij}^s is the probability that we move from state i to state j after s items.

$p_{i1}^{k(i)}$ is the probability that the $k(i)$th item will be defective, given state i now.

This is obtained as follows:

Expected number of defective items sent out between each inspection $= \mu \times$ expected number of items dispatched after one inspection but including the next.

Thus, since the inspection interval is $k(i)$ with probability ξ_i, we obtain

$$\Sigma_i \xi_i \sum_{s=1}^{k(i)-1} p_{i1}^s = \mu\{\Sigma_i \xi_i k(i) - \Sigma_i \xi_i p_{i1}^{k(i)}\},$$

the final term allowing for the fact that the $k(i)$th item may be defective and hence not dispatched. This gives equation (5.10).

Therefore, using the Lagrange parameter method, the classical discrete optimisation problem reduces to minimising the expected cost of sampling, with a new g equal to, for some η,

$$\Sigma_i \xi_i \left(E_i^{k(i)} + \eta \left(\sum_{s=1}^{k(i)-1} p_{i1}^s + \mu p_{i1}^{k(i)} \right) \right) \bigg/ \Sigma \xi_i k(i). \tag{5.11}$$

Hence we replace $E_i^{k(i)}$ by:

$$E_i^{k(i)} + \eta \left[\sum_{s=1}^{k(i)-1} p_{i1}^s + \mu p_{i1}^{k(i)} \right]. \tag{5.12}$$

Our equation (5.9) now becomes

$$g^* = \min_k \left\{ \left[1 + \eta \left(\sum_{s=1}^{k-1} p_{11}^s + \mu p_{11}^k \right) + (p_{11}^k - 1)v(1) \right] \bigg/ k \right\}$$

$$g^* = \min_k \left\{ \left[1 + \eta \left(\sum_{s=1}^{k-1} p_{21}^s + \mu p_{21}^k \right) + p_{21}^k v(1) \right] / k \right\}. \tag{5.13}$$

The procedure is to solve (5.13) and alter η until the required quality restriction is satisfied.

It is perhaps worth noting that, when successive states are entirely independent of the previous state, an optimal policy always requires the same sampling interval for both defective and non-defective items, and this again contrasts with the Dodge-Romig [21] results. For a proof see the Appendix, p. 169.

The following example illustrates the procedure. Let

$$p_{11}^1 = 0\cdot55, \quad p_{21}^1 = 0\cdot05, \quad \mu = 0\cdot04.$$

The equations become (with a slight adjustment):

$$g^* = 0\cdot1\eta + \min_k \left\{ [1 + \eta(0\cdot808 - 1\cdot728(0\cdot5)^k) + 0\cdot9((0\cdot5)^k - 1)v(1)]/k \right\}$$

$$g^* = 0\cdot1\eta + \min_k \left\{ [1 + \eta(1\cdot92(0\cdot5)^k - 0\cdot192) + 0\cdot1(1 - (0\cdot5)^k)v(1)]/k \right\}. \tag{5.14}$$

Table 10 gives the computational steps.

TABLE 10

η	Policy iterations		$v(1)$	Quality	Next Step Repeats
	$k(1)$	$k(2)$			
10	1	1	−16·48		
	1	5	3·2		
	1	8	1·18	0·036	x
9	1	8	1·25	0·0376	x
8	1	8	1·33	0·0376	x
7	1	9	1·4	0·039	x
6	1	10	1·472		
	1	15	1·474	0·044	x
6·5	1	10	1·4	0·040	x

The computations for $\eta = 6$ become very sensitive, and were carried out carefully for this reason. The optimal solution is $k(1) = 1$, $k(2) = 10$ with a corresponding value of g, obtained from putting $k(1) = 1$, $k(2) = 10$ in equations (5.9), equal to 0·12; i.e. approximately 1 unit in 8 is sampled on average.

(b) *Optimal Revision Policies.** Consider an electrolytic process producing a product continuously over time. Because of physical characteristics of the process, the electrical resistance will gradually increase with time. This will result in gradually increasing costs of operation, due to the increase in electrical energy dissipated as heat. Eventually these costs, when compared with the value of the product produced, will become uneconomical, and a decision will have to be taken as to when the process should be revised (overhauled, tec.). If the revision costs were zero, then we would tend to overhaul very frequently. However, in general, this is not so, and will result in longer run lengths.

Apart from the direct costs involved, we are also involved in a risk factor. Every time the process is overhauled, we cannot be certain that the electrical resistance characteristics will be identical for each cycle. They may be worse or they may be better. In general, we will have some data which will give us some idea as to the frequency of occurrence of each value of the electrical parameters concerned, and this can be used to guide our decision as to when to revise the process.

Suppose that, at the beginning of a cycle, we know the state of the system, i.e. the values of the parameters a,b (say), which will determine the profit to us if we run this cycle for m units of time. We call this $r(a,b,m)$.

We shall be interested in maximising the expected profit over the next n units of time. Once we know a and b, and also the revision policy we intend to use, (which tells us how long a cycle should be once a and b are known) then the expected overall return over the next n periods will depend on a,b and n only (remembering that, under a fixed policy, our decisions will be determined for us for each pair, a,b, at the beginning of a cycle).

We denote this return, using an optimal policy, by $f_n(a,b)$. The immediate return (over the cycle) is $r(a,b,m)$.

The return over the remaining $(n-m)$ units of time (i.e. after the first cycle) will depend on the new values of a and b after the process is revised. If a,b turn out to have values w,z, then the optimal return over the remaining $(n-m)$ units of time would be, using the Principle of Optimality:

$$f_{n-m}(w,z). \qquad (5.15)$$

* See White [47]

Since we will not be able to predict w,z, we can only take account of this using our accumulated data on the frequency of occurrence of values of w and z, i.e. we assume we have a probability distribution function $H(w,z)$.

The expected return then would be:

$$\int_w \int_z f_{n-m}(w,z)dH(w,z), \qquad (5.16)$$

or, in other words, the sum of the optimal returns for each possible values of w and z, multiplied by its probability of occurrence.

We then derive the relationship between $f_n(a,b)$ and the immediate and residual profits as follows, remembering that our decision m is still free,

$$f_n(a,b) = \max_{n \geqslant m \geqslant 0}[r(a,b,m) + \int_w \int_z f_{n-m}(w,z)dH(w,z)]. \quad (5.17)$$

We shall be interested in finding the optimal policy (which will be a function of a and b) when the lifetime is relatively long, i.e. n is very large.

Under certain very general conditions $f_n(a,b) = ng + f(a,b) + \varepsilon_n(a,b)$ where *$\varepsilon_n(a,b) \to 0$ as $n \to \infty$. The above equation then reduces to

$$f(a,b) = \max_{m \geqslant 0}[r(a,b,m) - mg + \int_w \int_z f(w,z)dH(w,z)].$$

Putting

$$\int_w \int_z f(w,z)dH(w,z) = \mu,$$

we obtain

$$f(a,b) = \max_{m \geqslant 0}[r(a,b,m) - mg + \mu]. \qquad (5.18)$$

If, as was the case with this problem,

$$r(a,b,m) = am - \tfrac{1}{2}bm^2 - c,$$

we obtain, by differentiating the right hand side, the optimal value of m.

Since we must have $m \geqslant 0$, we have

$$m = \max\,[0,(a-g)/b]. \qquad (5.19)$$

Substituting equation (5.19) and equation (5.18) we obtain

$$f(a,b) = \mu - c \text{ if } a \leqslant g$$
$$= \mu - c + (a-g)^2/2b \text{ if } a \geqslant g.$$

* $|\,\varepsilon_n(a,b)\,|$ need only be uniformly bounded for all a,b,n.

Going back to the definition of μ, we then find that g satisfies the equation

$$\mu = \int_{w=0}^{g} \int_{z=0}^{\infty} (\mu - c)dH(w,z) + \int_{w=g}^{\infty} \int_{z=0}^{\infty} \{(\mu - c) + (w - g)^2/2z\}dH(w,z)$$

i.e.

$$2c = \int_{w=g}^{\infty} \int_{z=0}^{\infty} \{(w-g)^2/z\}dH(w,z). \tag{5.20}$$

If $dH(w,z) = d\theta(z)d\Phi(w)$ and $\theta(z) = z-1$, $1 \leqslant z \leqslant 2$
$$\Phi(w) = w \qquad 0 \leqslant w \leqslant 1$$
$$c = \cdot05$$

we obtain the following equation for g, viz.

$$0\cdot1 = \int_{w=g}^{1} \int_{z=1}^{2} \{(w-g)^2/z\}dwdz$$

i.e.

$$0\cdot1 = \left(\int_{w=g}^{1} (w-g)^2 dw \right) \log_e(2) = (1-g)^3 \log_e(2)/3$$

i.e. $g = 0\cdot25$.

Hence the optimal rule is

$$m(a,b) = \max \left[0,(a-0\cdot25)/b \right].$$

More generally put

$$\int_{0}^{\infty} z^{-1}d\theta(z) = u.$$

Then (5.20) becomes

$$\int_{g}^{\infty} (w-g)^2 d\Phi(w) = 2cu^{-1}. \tag{5.21}$$

Special Cases

A. Rectangular Distribution for a

Let $d\Phi(w) = T^{-1}dw$, $0 \leqslant w \leqslant T$
$\qquad\qquad = 0$ otherwise.

Then we obtain, from (5.21)

$$(T-g)^3/3T = 2cu^{-1}$$

i.e. $\qquad\qquad\qquad g = T-(6cTu^{-1})^{\frac{1}{3}}.$

B. Exponential Distribution for a

Let $d\Phi(w) = \lambda \exp(-\lambda w)dw$, $w \geqslant 0$.

Then (5.21) gives

$$\lambda \int_g^\infty (w-g)^2 \exp(-\lambda w)dw = 2cu^{-1}$$

i.e.

$$\lambda \exp(-\lambda g) \int_0^\infty z^2 \exp(-\lambda z)dz = 2cu^{-1}.$$

Thus

$$g = \lambda^{-1} \log_e(2/\lambda^2 2cu^{-1}) = \lambda^{-1} \log_e(u/c\lambda^2).$$

C. Normal Distribution for a

Let

$$d\Phi(w) = (2\pi)^{-\frac{1}{2}}\sigma^{-1} \exp(-(w-\mu)^2/2\sigma^2)dw, \qquad -\infty \leqslant w \leqslant \infty$$

with $\phi(0)$ so small that negative values of a are not significant. Then (5.21) gives

$$(\sqrt{2\pi})^{-1}\sigma^{-1} \int_g^\infty (w-g)^2 \exp(-(w-\mu)^2/2\sigma^2)dw = 2cu^{-1}.$$

Put $s = (\mu-g)/\sigma$, $t = (w-g)/\sigma$. Then.

$$\int_0^\infty t^2 \exp(-(t-s)^2/2)dt = (8\pi)^{\frac{1}{2}}c/\sigma^2 u.$$

The left-hand side can easily be obtained, as a function of s, from standard tables, and hence, for each value of the right hand side, we can find a unique (if it exists) value of s, and thus of $g = \mu - \sigma s$.

5.3.2 *A Fixed Action, Partially Controlled Decision Interval, Process*

This is an extension of the previous model in that, although our action may require a maximal interval to the next action, the next action may be forced on us, prior to this, by some uncontrolled event.

Our problem is as follows. We again describe our system by one of a finite number of states, and we again have a choice of a specified set of acts. There is, associated with each act k, a probability p_{ijm}^k that the next action will be called for in precisely m units of time and the state then will be j, when the state is initially i and decision k is taken. There is also an immediate expected return associated with being in state i and taking decision k given by $q_i^k = \Sigma_j\Sigma_m p_{ijm}^k r_{ijm}^k$ where r_{ijm}^k is the actual (or expected) return associated with moving from state i to state j over m periods, having taken decision k.

8

Defining $v_n(i)$ to be the expected return over the next n periods of time, beginning in state i and using an optimal policy, we have:

$$v_n(i) = \max_k[q_i^k + \Sigma_j \Sigma_m p_{ijm}^k v_{n-m}(j)]. \qquad (5.22)$$

Provided m is always bounded (and we can make this as large as we wish, to include all practical considerations) then, as before, we can prove that, for any steady state policy, $v_n(i) \to ng + v(i) + \varepsilon_n(i)$ (again assuming complete ergodicity, to avoid further detail) where $|\varepsilon_n(i)|$ is bounded uniformly for all n, i.

Substituting in (5.22) suggests the following steady state equation (which is in fact valid, i.e. it gives a maximal gain per unit time):

$$v(i) = \max_k[q_i^k - (\Sigma_j \Sigma_m p_{ijm}^k m)g + \Sigma_j \Sigma_m p_{ijm}^k v(j)]. \qquad (5.23)$$

As in the previous section, we can derive a transformed set of equations, viz.

$$g = \max_k[\{q_i^k + \Sigma_j \Sigma_m p_{ijm}^k v(j) - v(i)\}/\{\Sigma_j \Sigma_m p_{ijm}^k m\}]. \qquad (5.24)$$

An algorithm similar to the one in the previous section is then readily derived, and needs little explanation.

One application of this is treated in White [45] where full details can be found. This concerns the problem of overhauling a furnace, subject to breakdowns. The decision to overhaul or not to overhaul is made at specific time intervals (a fixed multiple of the basic time period) from the time of completion of an overhaul or from the time the last inspection was made. The rate of production depends on the age since last overhaul, and on the production rate in the last time period, in a probabilistic manner. This can be zero when a 'blow up' occurs. A decision to overhaul, prior to a blow up, keeps the equipment idle for a specified time period and costs a certain amount of money. An overhaul for a blow up is much more expensive in time and money. If, on inspection, the decision is not to overhaul, a blow up prior to the next inspection forces an overhaul then. The problem is one of determining an optimal overhaul policy in terms of production rate and age (since last overhaul) of the equipment.

As a final point, it was possible to simplify the computations because of further properties of the functions involved.

5.3.3. A Variable Action, Partially Controlled Decision Interval, Process.

A Replacement Problem

We shall now consider a process controlled by two types of decision, one concerned with a variable action (e.g. choice of a piece of equipment) in a set A, and the other concerned with partial control of the next action epoch. A may depend, of course, on the existing state.

Specifically, the sequence is as follows. We have just taken an action in set A, and are, as a consequence, in state i. It is decided that the next action shall take place at time M from now, or prior to this, if forced upon us by uncontrolled events. When the next action epoch arises we choose an action k from the set A, which instantaneously changes the system from state j, in which the system happens to be when the action is called for, to state $I^k(j)$. The cycle is then repeated over a total life span of n periods.

There is a probability p_{ijm}^M that, if M is chosen when the state is i, then state is j when the next action is called for, and occurs m units of time later. The expected cost of taking action k, when this is called for m units of time after the last act, and the state has changed from state i after the last act to state j prior to this act, is q_{ijm}^k.

If we then define $v_n(i)$ to be the expected cost over the next n periods of time, beginning in state i and using an optimal policy, then $v_n(i)$ satisfies

$$v_n(i) = \min_{M \geqslant 0} \{ \Sigma_j \Sigma_m p_{ijm}^M \min_k [q_{ijm}^k + v_{n-m}(I^k(j))] \}. \tag{5.25}$$

For steady state policies, assuming M is bounded and complete ergodicity, we can show that $v_n(i) \to ng + v(i) + \varepsilon_n(i)$ as $n \to \infty$ where $|\varepsilon_n(i)|$ is bounded. Following the approach in the previous sections, we derive the following steady state equations:

$$v(i) = \min_{M \geqslant 0} \{ \Sigma_j \Sigma_m p_{ijm}^M (\min_k [q_{ijm}^k + v(I^k(j))] - mg) \}. \tag{5.26}$$

As in the previous sections we can change this to:

$$g = \min_{M \geqslant 0} [\{ \Sigma_j \Sigma_m p_{ijm}^M (\min_k [q_{ijm}^k + v(I^k(J))]) - v(i) \} / \{ \Sigma_j \Sigma_m m p_{ijm}^M \}]$$
$$= \min_{M(\cdot), k(\cdot)} [T(k(\cdot), M(\cdot), i, v(\cdot))] \text{ say.} \tag{5.27}$$

We can solve this, as in the previous section, by considering the binary policy $M(\cdot) \times k(\cdot)$ as a single policy. However, in certain circumstances, we can simplify the process. In particular, if $q_{ijm}^k = q_{ijm} + q_j^k$, then the following algorithm will be valid. Define

$$F(j) = \min_k [q_j^k + v(I^k(j))] = \min_k [\theta(k, j, v(\cdot))] \text{ say.} \tag{5.28}$$

Then:

(i) Choose an arbitrary policy $M_0(\cdot) \times k_0(\cdot)$,

(ii) Solve the equations $g = T(k_0(\cdot), M_0(\cdot), i, v_0(\cdot))$ for $v_0(\cdot)$, and g (putting one of the v's equal to zero).

(iii) Using $v_0(\cdot)$, find $F_0(\cdot)$, and hence $k_1(\cdot)$, from (5.28),

(iv) Using $k_1(\cdot)$, find $M_1(\cdot)$ by minimising $T(k_1(\cdot), M(\cdot), i, v_0(\cdot))$ for each i.

(v) Repeat cycle at (ii) using the new policy $M_1(\cdot) \times k_1(\cdot)$ and repeat until the sequences converge.

In White,[45] this was applied to the car replacement problem considered by Howard.[27] The state of the system at any time is the age, i of the car. The possible actions are the choices of the age of car to purchase next. The interval decisions are the choice of how long we keep the car before trading-in and purchasing another, with a replacement automatically necessitated if the present car breaks down completely in the meantime. The costs include purchase costs and operating costs plus negative trade-in costs.

In this case

$$q_j^k = a_j + b_k, \quad I^k(j) = I^k \text{ for all } j, k,$$

where b_k is the purchase cost of car aged k,

      a_j is the trade-in value of car aged j,

      q_{ijm} is the expected operating cost in keeping a car from age i to age j (in this case $m = j-i$).

We can then show that the system settles down to a fairly stable procedure, i.e. eventually we purchase a car at a fixed age, k, and keep it for a fixed period of time, M, before trading it in for a car of the same initial age, k, unless it breaks down in the meantime, when we begin with a car of the specified age, k, again. These results follow quite easily from the analysis and we can show that the optimal gain, g, and decisions k, M are given by

$$g = \min_M \min_k \left[\{ \Sigma_j \Sigma_m p_{I^k jm}^M (q_{I^k jm} + a_j + b_k) \} / \{ \Sigma_j \Sigma_m m p_{I^k jm}^M \} \right]. \quad (5.29)$$

The part that discrete finite Markov processes plays in D.P. cannot be over emphasised, because of the generality of the computational algorithms which require no restrictions on the forms of the data used.

5.4. Stochastic Constraints. Inventory Control Problems

It is sometimes possible to handle stochastic constraints in a D.P. model, using the method of Lagrange parameters.

Let us consider steady state solutions for Howard's completely ergodic case, for long duration systems. The equations are

$$g + v(i) = \min_k [q_i^k + \Sigma_j p_{ij}^k v(j)]. \quad (5.30)$$

For any policy, $k(\cdot)$, g is given by

$$g = \Sigma_s \xi_s q_s, \quad (5.31)$$

where ξ_s is the steady state probability of being in state s corresponding to the specified policy; and q_s is the instantaneous expected return when in state s and using this policy.

We know that solving (5.30) is equivalent to choosing a policy to maximise g in (5.31).

Let us now consider stochastic constraints of the form:

$$\Sigma_i a_{ti} \xi_i = \eta_t, \qquad t = 1, 2, \ldots l. \tag{5.32}$$

The problem can then be transposed to one of minimising $g - \Sigma_t \lambda_t \Sigma_i a_{ti} \xi_i$, and choosing $\{\lambda_t\}$ such that the constraints (5.32) are satisfied by the optimising $\{\xi_i\}$.

Now:

$$g - \Sigma_t \lambda_t \Sigma_i a_{ti} \xi_i = \Sigma_i \xi_i (q_i - \Sigma_t \lambda_t a_{ti}). \tag{5.33}$$

Hence we replace equations (5.30) by:

$$g^* + v^*(i) = \min_k [q_i^k - \Sigma_t \lambda_t a_{ti} + \Sigma_j p_{ij}^k v^*(j)]. \tag{5.34}$$

These equations are solved in the usual way and $\{\lambda_t\}$ varied until the constraints are satisfied.

Howard's method is particularly useful for inventory control problems, because, as stated before, we need to know nothing about analytic cost structures, etc. The decision k concerns how much stock to order when the present level is i.

We are usually very fortunate if we can calculate run-out costs and we usually put a constraint limiting the probability of run out, viz.

$$\xi_0 = a \tag{5.35}$$

where $i = 0$ corresponds to 'no stock'.

The equation (5.34) then becomes:

$$g^* + v^*(i) = \min_k [q_i^k - \lambda \delta_{io} + \Sigma_j p_{ij}^k v^*(j)], \tag{5.36}$$

with only one λ parameter to handle.

Of course, there are difficulties in choosing λ at each step, and presumably these will be solved by noting the behaviour of ξ_0 at each stage. As we get closer to $\xi_0 = a$, we can use the policy with which we last ended as a first approximation for the next stage.

As pointed out in the previous section it is not difficult to use the same approach to cater for the problem of controlling output quality in the sampling problem.

5.5 A Linear Programming Approach

A complete discussion of the following can be found in Manne.[32] Suppose that, instead of our policy telling us which decision k to take when we are in state i, we consider mixed policies, where p_i^k denotes the probability that if we are in state i we take action k.

Then, if ξ_i is the steady state probability of being in state i (which we assume to exist) and if ξ_{ik} is the steady state probability of being in state i and taking decision k we have:

$$\Sigma_k \xi_{ik} = \Sigma_j \Sigma_k \xi_{jk} p_{ji}^k, \qquad (5.37)$$

$$\xi_{ik} = p_i^k \xi_i. \qquad (5.38)$$

$$\Sigma_i \Sigma_k \xi_{ik} = 1. \qquad (5.39)$$

$$\xi_{ik} \geqslant 0. \qquad (5.40)$$

$$\Sigma_k \xi_{ik} = \xi_i. \qquad (5.41)$$

The objective function is then

$$g = \Sigma_i \Sigma_k \xi_{ik} q_i^k. \qquad (5.42)$$

It can be shown (see Manne [32]) that a minimal value of g, subject to the above constraints, can always be achieved by a pure policy, i.e. one in which, for a given i, $\xi_{ik} = 0$ except for one value of k. The problem then reduces to a linear programme of minimising (5.42) subject to (5.37), (5.39), (5.40). $\{p_i^k\}$ then comes from (5.38), (5.41).

In some cases this method may be preferable to Howard's algorithm, but, if we have, say 50 states and 50 alternative actions, we have 2500 variables and 51 constraints, excluding the non-negativity constraints— quite a task to solve. At this stage the choice must be left to the decision-maker himself.

5.6. Approximation Using Expectations

In certain stochastic situations the variability in outcome may be small enough to warrant the use of 'expected' outcomes, at least as a first approximation, to simplify the computations. We might proceed as follows, using, again, Howard's completely ergodic model, and assuming that the states form an ordered continuum (e.g. we might consider the inventory control problem, where the state is the stock level at anytime).

As before, consider the equations

$$g + v(i) = \min_k [q_i^k + \Sigma_j p_{ij}^k v(j)]. \qquad (5.43)$$

Consider, now, the equations obtained by assuming that the state i is deterministically transformed into a state $\mu^k(i)$ given by

$$\mu^k(i) = \Sigma_j j p_{ij}^k. \qquad (5.44)$$

It is, of course, necessary to choose the nearest tabulated value of i to $\mu^k(i)$. Thus if i runs from 0 to 10, in steps of 1, and $\mu^k(1) = 2\cdot8$, we would represent $\mu^k(1)$ by 3. In all actual calculations this has to be done.

The approximation obviously gets better if we have a large number of divisions for the i scale.

These equations are

$$G + V(i) = \min_k[q_i^k + V(\mu^k(i))]. \qquad (5.45)$$

Again we assume complete ergodicity.*

Let us consider any policy, and the steady state equations corresponding to (5.43) and (5.45) (dropping the index k for convenience). We have

$$g + v(i) = q_i + \Sigma_j p_{ij} v(j), \qquad (5.46)$$

and

$$G + V(i) = q_i + V(\mu(i)). \qquad (5.47)$$

Then we get

$$G - g + V(i) - v(i) = \Sigma_j p_{ij}(V(\mu(i)) - v(j))$$
$$= \Sigma_j p_{ij}(V(j) - v(j)) + \Sigma_j p_{ij}(V(\mu(i)) - V(j)). \qquad (5.48)$$

Then

$$G - g = \Sigma_i \xi_i \Sigma_j p_{ij}(V(\mu(i)) - V(j)), \qquad (5.49)$$

where ξ_i is the steady state probability for state i using the policy specified.

Now, to a second order approximation,

$$\Sigma_j p_{ij}(V(\mu(i)) - V(j)) \sim \Sigma_j p_{ij}(\mu(i) - j)^2 V''(\mu(i))/2! = \sigma^2(i)V''(\mu(i))/2. \qquad (5.50)$$

Here, of course, the notion of $V''(i)$ is purely formal, assuming i comes from a continuum, although computations are discrete. We could operate with the notion of 'second difference', but the above will illustrate our purpose, viz. one of showing how small variances influence the difference in the solutions to (5.46)–(5.47).

Thus

$$(G - g)/g = (G/g - 1) \sim \tfrac{1}{2}\Sigma_i \xi_i \sigma^2(i) V''(\mu(i))/(\Sigma_i \xi_i q_i). \qquad (5.51)$$

If the (for all policies reasonably acceptable) right-hand side of (5.51) is small, which it will be if $\{\sigma^2(i)\}$ is small, then an optimal policy for the deterministic problem will be near to an optimal policy for the stochastic problem. At the very worst this procedure may give a reasonable starting policy for solving (5.43), and the solution of (5.45) is usually quite trivial.

Numerical experimentation in this approach at the Centre for Business Research, Manchester, has shown sensational reductions in

---

* Modifications are possible in non-completely ergodic conditions.

computational time using this method to generate an initial policy, and the approximate policies, from the deterministic model, have been extremely near optimal (see Norman [33], [34]).

Let us consider the example discussed at the beginning of the Chapter. We calculate the means and variances thus:

		$\mu^k(i)$ Mean transformed state	$(\sigma^2)^k(i)$
i	k		Variances
1	1	1·5	0·25
1	2	1·3	0·21
2	1	1·2	0·16
2	2	1·6	0·24

This is a very crude problem in that there are only two discrete states. When the number of states becomes large the approximation becomes very efficient. We now need to choose representative states for the mean figures given. These are chosen as follows:

i	k	Transformed state
1	1	2
1	2	1
2	1	1
2	2	2

The equivalent deterministic equations then become

$$G + V(1) = \min \begin{bmatrix} 5 + V(2) \\ 2 + V(1) \end{bmatrix}$$

$$G + V(2) = \min \begin{bmatrix} 2 + V(1) \\ 1 + V(2) \end{bmatrix}$$

Following Howard's method of solution and beginning with $k_0(1) = 1$, $k_0(2) = 1$, we find that $G = 1$, $V(1) = 4$, $V(2) = 0$, $k_1(1) = 1$, $k_1(2) = 2$. This policy is then used as the starting policy for the probabilistic model.

Although little computational saving is offered for this simple example, for problems with a large number of states the savings can be considerable.

5.7. Analytic Derivation of Policies. Quadratic Cost Function

Holt *et al.*[26] discuss the derivation of linear decision rules in special cases where cost functions are quadratic in the decision and uncontrolled variables.

Without going into too much detail, the results, which are the basis behind the book, are as follows.

Decisions are made at regular intervals of time, the choice being a vector y. The state of the system at any time is described by a vector $*x$. Between decisions certain events occur in a stochastic manner, which can be described by a vector s.

The cost incurred in a specific period described by (x,y,s) is a quadratic function, $Q(x,y,s)$ which we express as follows:

$$Q(x,y,s) = q_0 + q_x'x + q_y'y + q_s's + x'Q_{xx}x + y'Q_{yy}y + s'Q_{ss}s +$$
$$x'Q_{xy}y + x'Q_{xs}s + y'Q_{ys}s, \qquad (5.52)$$

where q_0 is a scalar,

q_x, q_y, q_s are vectors, and

$Q_{xx}, Q_{xy}, \ldots$ etc., are all symmetric matrices.

The state of the system at the beginning of the next period is a linear combination of x, y, s, viz. $x \rightarrow Ax + By + Cs$ where A, B, C are matrices.

The problem is one of finding a decision rule which will optimise expected costs over a known number of periods.

The results are that the optimal decision rule for the first period can be obtained by treating all future events, s, for each period of time, as predetermined and equal to their expected values as given at the beginning of the process. This decision rule is a linear function of the state variable x and the forecasts of s. For each successive period we need to recompute the forecasts as extra information becomes available, and, providing the time space is long enough the same rule may be used. This solution holds independent of whether the successive s are correlated, or how information arrives to modify the situation.

Two points need to be made, viz.

1. The derivation of the solution assumes that no limitations are placed on the decision variable y. If such restrictions are placed, the solution is no longer valid, and the decision rule should then depend on the actual probability distributions, and indeed, on the manner in which they are modified as time goes on and more information arises. Even in cases of complete independence of the s, the results will not be true. In the actual cases considered we would need to restrict the decision variable y so that its components were non-negative, since we cannot have negative production and work force sizes. On page 61 of reference 26 equations (2–10) and (2–11) could give negative values for P_t and W_t. Of course, if it is known that there is little likelihood of this situation arising, then the results are perfectly acceptable. For inventory problems

* x includes information about future demands.

in general, since we wish to keep down stock levels, one would expect that this prospect was, under optimal conditions, not good.

2. A simple method of solution exists for this specific problem, but for more general cases of A, B, C for example, this method will not apply so easily, since the determination of special matrices will be complicated.

Let us now use the D.P. approach.

With the obvious definitions, assuming, for the present, that the s are uncorrelated, we obtain

$$f_n(x) = \min_y \left[E_s\{Q(x,y,s)\} + E_s\{ f_{n-1}(Ax+By+Cs)\} \right] \quad (5.53)$$

where $f_n(x)$ is the minimal expected cost over the next n time periods beginning in state x.

If we assume that y is perfectly free, we can then show inductively that

$$f_n(x) = u_n + v'_n x + x' W_n x, \quad (5.54)$$

where

$$u_{k+1} = u_k + q_0 + (q'_s + v'_k C)E_s(s) + E_s\{s'(Q_{ss} + C'W_k C)s\} - \tfrac{1}{4}(q_y + B'v_k +$$

$$(Q_{ys} + 2B'W_k C)E_s(s))'(Q_{yy} + B'W_k B)^{-1}(q_y + B'v_k +$$

$$(Q_{ys} + 2B'W_k C)E_s(s)). \quad (5.55)$$

$$v_{k+1} = q_x + (Q_{xs} + 2A'W_k C)E_s(s) + A'v_k - \tfrac{1}{2}(Q_{xy} + 2A'W_k B)(Q_{yy} +$$

$$B'W_k B)^{-1}(q_y + B'v_k + (Q_{ys} + 2B'W_k C)E_s(s)). \quad (5.56)$$

$$W_{k+1} = Q_{xx} + A'W_k A - \tfrac{1}{4}(Q_{xy} + 2A'W_k B)(Q_{yy} + B'W_k B)^{-1}(Q_{xy} + 2B'W_k A). \quad (5.57)$$

The basis of the proof is as follows. With $f_0(x) \equiv 0$, the unrestricted maximum of $E_s\{Q(x,y,s)\}$ is a quadratic function of x with coefficients depending on $E(s)$, and the covariance matrix of s. Thus $f_1(x)$ is quadratic in x. Then $f_2(x)$ is the unrestricted maximum of the sum of two quadratic terms, and is, therefore, itself, quadratic in x. Inductively we prove $f_n(x)$ is quadratic in x for $n = 1, 2, \ldots k$.

The optimal decision y, at the $(k+1)$th stage from the end is given by

$$y = -\tfrac{1}{2}(Q_{yy} + B'W_k B)^{-1}(q_y + Q_{yx} x + Q_{ys} E_s(s) + B'v_k + 2B'W_k(Ax +$$

$$CE_s(s))). \quad (5.58)$$

The deductions that y is linear in x and $E_s(s)$ (for the succeeding periods) is then straightforward from the above, since v_k is linear in $E_s(s)$ for the remaining periods (by induction).

For the last stage we have

$$v_1 = q_x + Q_{xs}E_s(s) - \tfrac{1}{2}Q_{xy}Q_{yy}^{-1}(q_y + Q_{ys}E_s(s)). \tag{5.59}$$

$$u_1 = q_0 + q_s'E_s(s) + E_s\{s'Q_{ss}s\} - \tfrac{1}{4}(q_y + Q_{ys}E_s(s))'Q_{yy}^{-1}(q_y + Q_{ys}E_s(s)). \tag{5.60}$$

$$W_1 = Q_{xx} - \tfrac{1}{2}Q_{xy}Q_{yy}^{-1}Q_{xy}. \tag{5.61}$$

It should be possible to investigate whether a steady state solution exists for large n by analysing the sequences $\{u_k\}$, $\{v_k\}$, $\{W_k\}$.

Now let us consider the case when the s may be correlated, or the more general case when all information I is included in the description of the system at each stage. We then have

$$f_n(x,I) = \min_y \left[E_{s/I}\{Q(x,y,s)\} + E_{s,\,I^*/I}\{f_{n-1}(Ax + By + Cs, I^*)\}\right]. \tag{5.62}$$

I^* is the new information position at the next stage.

It is then easy to show, with no restrictions on y, that

$$f_n(x,I) = u_n(I) + v_n'(I)x + x'W_n(I)x. \tag{5.63}$$

The recurrence relations are then similar to those given before, providing we replace all expectations on the right-hand side by $E_{s/I}$ and replace u_k, v_k and W_k by $E_{I^*/I}\{u_k(I^*)\}$ $E_{I^*/I}\{v_k(I^*)\}$ and $E_{I^*/I}\{W_k(I^*)\}$ respectively. However it is easily seen that $W_k(I)$ does not depend on I, and hence the recurrence relations for W_k remain the same. We can then use the recurrence relations for $v_k(I)$, to show that the solution given by Holt *et al.* concerning any dependence between the s etc., is still valid, providing no restrictions are placed on y.

To see that the solution need not hold if we restrict $y \geqslant 0$, we first of all see that, in this case, if any component of $Q_{yy}^{-1}(q_y + Q_{yx}x + Q_{ys}E_s\{s\})$ is positive, then some component of the unrestricted solution will be negative. Hence we see that $f_1(x)$ is not representable as a single quadratic form for all x, but rather as one of a set of quadratic forms depending on the area in which x lies. If we then go back to $f_2(x)$, we see that its relationship to $f_1(Ax + By + Cs)$ depends on where s lies, for now the range of s can be split up into several areas, in each of which $f_1(Ax + By + Cs)$ has a different quadratic form. Thus $f_2(x)$ will depend on the probability with which s falls in each particular area, and hence not only on $E_s(s)$. As we progress further back, then this effect is even more exaggerated for $f_k(x)$ will have a larger number of quadratic components than $f_{k-1}(x)$, and therefore require finer probability descriptions.

5.8. Control Processes with Probabilistic Duration

The sort of systems we have been dealing with so far are those in which the durations were known, finite or infinite, and, sometimes, known only after the solution had been obtained (cf. the optimal path problem). There are situations in which the duration of the systems is a stochastic variable dependent possibly on the policy chosen. We shall discuss two such problems in this area. It is to be noted that we determine directly so called 'stationary' or 'autonomous' equations into which the stage (or time) variable does not enter, and this is usually a characteristic of such processes. The essential feature of such problems is that the process terminates when a specified event occurs.

5.8.1. *An Optimal Economic Lot Size Problem*

A. *The Discrete Version and a Directed Computational Algorithm*

A decision-maker is faced with satisfying an order for N items. His production process is defective, and he does not know, for certain, how many good items will be produced from an input batch of any size. Excess production has no value.

Insufficient good items require extra set-ups at a cost. What production policy should he use?

We shall assume that past experience provides him with evidence that if he puts n items into production he will produce m good items with probability $p(n,m)$. Also the unit production cost is c and the set-up cost is s.

Let $f(N)$ be the expected cost of satisfying the order using an optimal policy. Then, for $N \geqslant 1$

$$f(N) = \min_{n \geqslant N} \left[s + nc + \sum_{m=0}^{N-1} p(n,m) f(N-m) \right]. \qquad (5.64)$$

The first term represents the immediate cost. $f(N-m)$ represents the optimal residual expected cost, using the Principle of Optimality, if only m good items are produced, thus leaving us with $(N-m)$ items to provide. This can be transformed (see Appendix, p. 170) into:

$$f(N) = \min_{n \geqslant N} \left[\left\{ s + nc + \sum_{m=1}^{N-1} p(n,m) f(N-m) \right\} \middle/ \{1 - p(n,0)\} \right]. \qquad (5.65)$$

From this equation we can easily compute $f(0) (= 0)$, $f(1)$, $f(2)$, and so on.

We need not restrict ourselves to $n \geqslant N$ of course, but this seems a reasonable aid to computational reductions.

It is to be noted that this is another case of a directed state set, with the corresponding computational process.

Example

Suppose we limit ourselves to an input batch of 5 items at most. Let $s = c = 1$. Let the input-output probability table be as follows:

		0	1	2	3	4	5
				m			
	1	·70	·30	·00	·00	·00	·00
	2	·40	·30	·30	·00	·00	·00
n	3	·30	·30	·20	·20	·00	·00
	4	·20	·20	·20	·20	·20	·00
	5	·10	·20	·20	·20	·20	·10

$$p(n,m)$$

Then

$$f(1) = \min \begin{bmatrix} n = 1: (1+1)/(1-\cdot7) = 6\cdot7 \\ n = 2: (1+2)/(1-\cdot4) = 5\cdot0 \\ n = 3: (1+3)/(1-\cdot3) = 5\cdot7 \\ n = 4: (1+4)/(1-\cdot2) = 6\cdot3 \\ n = 5: (1+5)/(1-\cdot1) = 6\cdot6 \end{bmatrix} \leftarrow = 5\cdot0.$$

For one item the optimal solution is to plan to produce two every time a deficit occurs.

$$f(2) = \min \begin{bmatrix} n = 1: (1+1+\cdot3\times5)/(1-\cdot7) = 11\cdot7 \\ n = 2: (1+2+\cdot3\times5)/(1-\cdot4) = 7\cdot5 \\ n = 3: (1+3+\cdot3\times5)/(1-\cdot3) = 7\cdot9 \\ n = 4: (1+4+\cdot2\times5)/(1-\cdot2) = 7\cdot5 \\ n = 5: (1+5+\cdot2\times5)/(1-\cdot1) = 7\cdot8 \end{bmatrix} \begin{matrix} \leftarrow \\ \\ \leftarrow \end{matrix} = 7\cdot5.$$

If 2 items are required the optimal input is either 2 or 4, reverting to an input of 2 if a deficit of 1 item occurs at any time.

B. A Continuous Version. The Method of Successive Approximations

If N is very large, then the above procedure may be tedious, and it may be better to consider a continuous version. If $G(z)$ is a distribution function for the proportion of defective product in any batch (this can be relaxed if required, but the analysis is the same), then the corresponding equation to (5.64) is:
if $x > 0$

$$f(x) = \min_{y \geqslant x} \left[s + cy + \int_{1-x/y}^{1} f(x - (1-z)y) \, dG(z) \right]. \quad (5.66)$$

$x - (1-z)y$ is the residual quantity to be produced if the input quantity is y and a proportion, z, of this, is defective.

Putting

$$1 - x/y = t,$$
$$R(x) = (f(x)/s) - 1 \quad (x > 0),$$
$$R(0) = -1, \text{ and}$$
$$c/s = \alpha, \tag{5.67}$$

this becomes, for $x > 0$,

$$R(x) = \min_{0 \leqslant t \leqslant 1} \left[\alpha x/(1-t) + (1 - G(t)) + \int_t^1 R((z-t)x/(1-t))dG(z) \right].$$
$$\tag{5.68}$$

It can be proved that Bellman's method of successive approximations can be used in very general conditions for this (see White [45, 52]). A distinction between this and Bellman's assumptions for the applicability of the method of successive approximations (see Bellman [9]), is that Bellman assumes that either the transformations are of the 'shrinking point' type in which the modulus of a transformed state is less than a certain multiple (less than unity) of the modulus of the initial state, (in the language of Chapter 3, for some k, and all x, $\| T(d) \cdot x \| \leqslant k \| x \|$, $0 \leqslant k < 1$) or of the 'shrinking function' type, (less than unity), in which either future path values carry less weight than present path values (e.g. a discount factor) or the probability of termination at the next stop is uniformly less than a constant (less than unity) for all possible situations. The equation (5.68) is neither of these cases but is, rather, a mixture of them. A complete discussion of this problem can be found in White.[45, 52]

The advantage of the continuous method is that we can divide the x range into a smallish number of ranges, and compute $f_n(x)$ at each of the partition points, using the method of successive approximations, and to interpolate at other points. This cannot be done with the directed method, for we need the value of $f(N-1)$ before we begin to compute $f(N)$.

As an example let $\alpha = \cdot 1$, $G(z) \equiv z$, $x \leqslant 1000$. Then, if $x \neq 0$,

$$R_1(x) = \min_{0 \leqslant t \leqslant 1} \left[\cdot 1x/(1-t) + (1-t) \right]$$
$$= 2(\cdot 1x)^{\frac{1}{2}} \text{ if } x \leqslant 10(t_1(x) = 1 - (\cdot 1x)^{\frac{1}{2}})$$
$$= \cdot 1x + 1 \text{ if } x \geqslant 10(t_1(x) = 0).$$

$$R_2(x) = \min_{0 \leqslant t \leqslant 1} \left[\cdot 1x/(1-t) + (1-t) + \int_t^1 R_1((z-t)x/(1-t))dG(z) \right].$$

This is solved in discrete terms by approximating $G(z)$ with discrete probabilities of $\cdot 1$ at each of the points $z = \cdot 1, \cdot 2, \ldots \cdot 9, 1 \cdot 0$. The optimal value of t among the set $0, \cdot1, \cdot2, \ldots \cdot9$ is chosen. If we wished to get a better approximation then a finer division of the t-range is needed.

Now if $(z-t) \geq \cdot1$, $x \geq 100$, then $(z-t)x/(1-t) \geq 10$. Hence

$$R_1\{(z-t)x/(1-t)\} = \cdot1(z-t)x/(1-t)+1,$$

whence

$$R_2(x) = \min \begin{bmatrix} t=0: \; \cdot1x+1+\cdot1\sum_{z=\cdot1}^{1\cdot0} (\cdot1zx+1) \\[2ex] t>0: \; \min_{t>0}\left[\cdot1x/(1-t)+(1-t)+\left\{-\cdot1+ \right.\right. \\[2ex] \left.\left. \cdot1\left(\sum_{z=t+\cdot1}^{1\cdot0} (\cdot1((z-t)x/(1-t))+1)\right)\right\}\right] \end{bmatrix}$$

We then calculate $R_2(90)$ (using the tabulated values of $R_1(x)$) as tabulated below.

| | | | | | $(z-t)$ | | | | | | | $9/(1-t)+$ | |
t	0	·1	·2	·3	·4	·5	·6	·7	·8	·9	1·0	$(1-t)$	Σ
·0	x	1·90	2·80	3·70	4·60	5·50	6·40	7·30	8·20	9·10	10·0	10·00	*15·95*
·1	−1	2·00	3·00	4·00	5·00	6·00	7·00	8·00	9·00	10·0		10·90	16·20
·2	−1	2·13	3·25	4·38	5·50	6·63	7·75	8·88	10·0			12·05	16·80
·3	−1	2·27	3·54	4·81	6·08	7·35	8·62	10·0				13·40	17·67
·4	−1	2·50	4·00	5·50	7·00	8·50	10·0					15·60	19·15
·5	−1	2·80	4·60	6·40	8·20	10·0						18·50	21·60
·6	−1	3·25	5·50	7·75	10·0							23·10	25·65
·7	−1	4·00	7·00	10·0								30·30	32·30
·8	−1	5·50	10·0									45·20	46·65
·9	−1	10·0										90·10	91·00

$$R_1((z-t)90/(1-t))$$

$$\Sigma = 9/(1-t)+(1-t)+\cdot1\sum_{z \geq t} R_1(90(z-t)/(1-t)).$$

Thus

$$R_2(90) = 15\cdot95$$
$$t_2(90) = 0$$

We calculate similarly $R_2(80)$, $R_2(70)$, $\ldots R_2(10)$, $R_2(9)$, $R_2(8)$, $\ldots$ $R_2(1)$. The results are shown at the top of p. 118.

x	$R_2(x)$	$t_2(x)$
$\geqslant 100$	$\cdot155x+1\cdot90$	0
90	15·95	0
80	14·40	0
70	12·86	0
60	11·30	0
50	9·74	0/·1
40	8·14	·1
30	6·51	·1
20	4·86	·2
10	3·05	·3
9	2·84	·4
8	2·62	·4
7	2·41	·4
6	2·18	·5
5	1·93	·5
4	1·68	·5
3	1·39	·6
2	1·07	·6
1	·74	·6
0	-1	—

Using these results we can now calculate $R_2(x)$ for $x = 1000, 900, \ldots$ 100, 90, 80, $\ldots$ 10, interpolating from the table for $R_2(x)$ when necessary. We cannot calculate $R_3(9)$, $R_3(8)$, $\ldots$ unless we calculate $R_2(\cdot9)$, $R_2(\cdot8)$, $\ldots R_2(\cdot1)$. We may be able to do this by curve fitting to $R_2(x)$ for all x if we wish. However, the essential point is that we can compute the optimum solution without having to compute $R_n(x)$ for all x and this is important if x is very large.

5.8.2 An Optimal Component Replacement Process

A. The Discrete Version and a Directed Computational Algorithm

Some systems exist whose lifetime is virtually independent of some or all components of the system; e.g. a car or a television set are subject to general ageing, independent of many components. In other systems, components of some kind may be required to carry out a set programme and the life of the system may depend more on environmental factors than on the tools, components, etc., needed to carry out the programme.

As time passes replacements for some components will be needed as they fail. Also the expectation of the future life of the system may decrease as time goes on. Hence, when a component is to be replaced, if we have a choice of component (e.g. new or reconditioned), we need to strike a balance between the cost of the component replacement and the life which can be expected from it, bearing in mind the reducing life span of the system as a whole. Thus it is obviously a problem in the probabilistic duration area.

The problem we shall consider is one of minimising the expected overall cost to the end of the system's life.

In many cases we begin again with a new system (e.g. a new car, etc.) and this is easily formulated in much the same manner if the case merits it. The student may wish to treat this as an exercise, bearing in mind, now, that we not only replace the components of the major system, but also replace the major system several times over a known period, n, say. We can let $n \to \infty$. Of course this no longer becomes a problem in which the duration is uncertain.

Let c_i be the cost of the ith alternative replacement,

$p_i(k)$ be the probability that the ith type of replacement will last k units of time ($k \geqslant 1$), and

$q(t,k)$ be the probability that when the system is of age t it will last at least a further k units of time.

Define $v(t)$ to be the expected cost from the time of replacing a component, when the system is of age t, to the end of the system's life, using an optimal policy.

Then

$$v(t) = \min_i \left[c_i + \sum_{k \geqslant 1} p_i(k) q(t,k) v(t+k) \right]. \tag{5.69}$$

c_i is the immediate cost. The age of the system when this replacement component fails is $(t+k)$ (where k has probability $p_i(k)q(t,k)$) and the residual expected cost, using the Principle of Optimality, is $v(t+k)$ and thus (5.69) is derived.

Since the states are directed we can solve this, providing we can assume that an upper limit, T, exists to the system's life. The same difficulties arise as in the previous section when T is large, and a continuous formulation may be better.

Consider the following example, with $T = 20$.

$$p_i(k)$$

i	c_i	$k:$	1	2	3	4	5
1	1		·1	·2	·3	·2	·2
2	1·05		0	·2	·3	·3	·2
3	1·10		0	0	·2	·4	·4

$$q(t,k)$$

k:	1	2	3	4	5
0	1	1	1	1	·9
1	1	1	1	·9	·9
2	1	1	·9	·9	·9
3	1	·9	·9	·9	·9
4	·9	·9	·9	·8	·8
5	·9	·9	·8	·8	·8
6	·9	·8	·8	·8	·8
7	·8	·8	·8	·7	·7
8	·8	·8	·7	·7	·7
9	·8	·7	·7	·7	·7
10	·7	·7	·7	·6	·6
11	·7	·7	·6	·6	·6
12	·6	·6	·6	·6	·6
13	·6	·6	·6	·5	·5
14	·5	·5	·5	·5	·5
15	·5	·5	·5	·4	·4
16	·4	·4	·4	·4	·3
17	·3	·3	·3	·3	·3
18	·2	·2	·2	·2	·2
19	·1	·1	·1	·1	·1
20	0	0	0	0	0

(t labels the rows.)

Define i_t (optimal) to be the optimal component to use when we require a replacement at age t.

We then obtain

$$v(20) = 0$$

$$v(19) = \min \begin{bmatrix} i = 1: 1 + \cdot1 \times \cdot1 \times 0 & = 1 \\ i = 2: 1\cdot05 + 0 \times \cdot1 \times 0 = 1\cdot05 \\ i = 3: 1\cdot10 + 0 \times \cdot1 \times 0 = 1\cdot10 \end{bmatrix} \leftarrow = 1$$

$$i_{19} = 1$$

$$v(18) = \min \begin{bmatrix} i = 1: 1 + \cdot1 \times \cdot2 \times 1 + \cdot2 \times \cdot2 \times 0 & = 1\cdot02 \\ i = 2: 1\cdot05 + 0 \times \cdot2 \times 1 + \cdot2 \times \cdot2 \times 0 & = 1\cdot05 \\ i = 3: 1\cdot10 + 0 \times \cdot2 \times 1 + 0 \times \cdot2 \times 0 & = 1\cdot10 \end{bmatrix} \leftarrow = 1\cdot02$$

$$i_{18} = 1$$

$$v(17) = \min \begin{bmatrix} i = 1: \\ 1 + \cdot1 \times \cdot3 \times 1\cdot02 + \cdot2 \times \cdot3 \times 1 + \cdot3 \times \cdot3 \times 0 & = 1\cdot09 \\ i = 2: \\ 1\cdot05 + 0 \times \cdot3 \times 1\cdot02 + \cdot2 \times \cdot3 \times 1 + \cdot3 \times \cdot3 \times 0 = 1\cdot11 \\ i = 3: \\ 1\cdot10 + 0 \times \cdot3 \times 1\cdot02 + 0 \times \cdot3 \times 1 + \cdot2 \times \cdot3 \times 0 & = 1\cdot10 \end{bmatrix} \leftarrow = 1\cdot09$$

$$i_{17} = 1$$

$$v(16) = \min \begin{bmatrix} i = 1: 1 + \cdot1 \times \cdot4 \times 1\cdot09 + \cdot2 \times \cdot4 \times 1\cdot02 + \\ \qquad\qquad \cdot3 \times \cdot4 \times 1 + \cdot2 \times \cdot4 \times 0 = 1\cdot25 \\ i = 2: 1\cdot05 + 0 \times \cdot4 \times 1\cdot09 + \cdot2 \times \cdot4 \times 1\cdot02 + \\ \qquad\qquad \cdot3 \times \cdot4 \times 1 + \cdot3 \times \cdot4 \times 0 = 1\cdot20 \\ i = 3: 1\cdot10 + 0 \times \cdot4 \times 1\cdot09 + 0 \times \cdot4 \times 1\cdot02 + \\ \qquad\qquad \cdot2 \times \cdot4 \times 1 + \cdot4 \times \cdot4 \times 0 = 1\cdot18 \end{bmatrix} = 1\cdot18$$

$$\leftarrow$$

$$i_{16} = 3$$

The student can now verify the following, approximate solutions, for all t.

t	$v(t)$	i_t
0	3·97	3
1	3·70	3
2	3·47	3
3	3·22	3
4	3·01	3
5	2·85	3
6	2·72	3
7	2·46	3
8	2·34	3
9	2·26	1
10	2·03	3
11	1·90	3
12	1·80	1
13	1·68	1/3
14	1·55	1
15	1·36	3
16	1·18	3
17	1·09	1
18	1·02	1
19	1·00	1
20	0	—

B. A Continuous Version and the Method of Successive Approximations

If we let $G_i(u)$ be the distribution function for the life of the ith type of component, and $G(z)$ be the distribution function for the life of the system, our equation becomes:

$$v(t) = \min_i \left[c_i + \int_0^\infty v(t+u)\{(1 - G(t+u))/(1 - G(t))\}dG_i(u) \right]. \quad (5.70)$$

Putting $V(t) = (1 - G(t))v(t)$, we obtain

$$V(t) = \min_i \left[(1 - G(t))c_i + \int_0^\infty V(t+u)dG_i(u) \right]. \quad (5.71)$$

Under certain general conditions (see White [45, 52]) Bellman's method of successive approximations is valid, and the same remarks concerning advantages of this apply in the previous section.

5.9. Dynamic Programming and Investment Analysis

If there is one area in which D.P. holds great potential, in principle at least, it is the area of investment analysis, for this is one area where present investment decisions influence future decisions, sometimes, quite considerably.

The following three examples arose from a research project at the Centre for Business Research, Manchester University. The first one was not taken to its final conclusion because of the size of the task involved, but nevertheless an important point arises from it. The last one was completed as far as it was deemed necessary.

The second one illustates a misconception in objectives held by some investors.

5.9.1. *Dynamic Programming, Investment Values, and the Present Worth Concept*

A fair amount of literature exists on attempts to determine values of investment opportunities for the purpose of investment selection. These are usually very subjective and open to criticism of one kind or another. The only really satisfactory way of resolving such problems is to realise that the value of an opportunity arises from its contribution to future performance in some manner. Restricting ourselves to monetary factors only, we see that an investment value depends on the income stream it generates in the future and also on how this is used to generate further income, and so on. The value, therefore, depends partly on some assumption about future investment policy, and partly on some description of future investment opportunities (both on the nature and on arrival pattern of these).

One approach to investment valuations is to use the present worth concept. If an investment opportunity can be represented by a time series of net returns, $r(\cdot) = (r_1, r_2, \ldots r_s \ldots)$, then the present worth of this is $w(r(\cdot)) = \sum_1^n \alpha^s r_s$, where $0 \leqslant \alpha \leqslant 1$.

In itself this has no interpretation directly, but we note that $w(r(\cdot)) = \alpha^n \sum_1^n \alpha^{s-n} r_s$. Therefore, if $i = \alpha^{-1} - 1$, the present worth of an opportunity is proportional to the total net income we have at the end of the investment's life if we invest each income at a constant rate of interest equal to i.

Such an approach is subject to the following objections:

(i) The actual income received from future investments is not a constant interest rate, and will depend on both the opportunities and investment policy relevant to that time.

(*ii*) The common practice is to assume *i* equal to some present overall rate of interest, and this conflicts with the purpose of valuation (viz. optimal choice), unless of course, we assume we are operating optimally now.

(*iii*) The procedure of finding the rate of interest, *i*, which makes the present worth equal to zero, and using this interest as an indicant of value is similarly questionable.

(*iv*) The present worth measure does not tell us when to accept or reject an investment, only which is supposed to be the better (we include a null investment if we are faced with only one choice).

We can make a further objection and that is that the value of an investment opportunity will, in general, depend on other existing opportunities, for it may be that, in terms of income patterns, a combination of several may be preferable to one.

A full account of the problem can be found in White,[48] and the purpose of the above notes is to cast some doubt on the validity in principle, of the present worth concept. This has been used even in D.P. formulations (see Fisher [25]) in which the problem has been to choose optimal opportunities over time, but, in which, each opportunity has been given a present worth value, quite unjustifiably so on *a priori* grounds at least.

It is not to be construed that present worth valuations are of no use, for they are undoubtedly correlated with true value of an opportunity, but not necessarily perfectly, and, if one existed, a perfect indicant may not be of this form. There are certain situations in which investment values, independent of present conditions and opportunities, do exist, and within this class, there are others where the present worth valuation is correct. We cannot only establish this, we can actually compute the correct interest rate. This depends on our long term objectives and on our preference operators in uncertain situations. We shall make some assumptions, which will no doubt be as open to question as the *a priori* postulation of present worth values, but at least we shall have a basis on which to build our investment analysis, which is modifiable, in principle, to suit other postulates.

Our assumptions are:

(*i*) The system is closed, i.e. no income is obtained other than from investment of income, and no dividends are paid, etc.; no overdrafts will be allowed, but reserve cash in bank earns a nominal current interest rate.

(*ii*) The arrival of opportunities is probabilistic, and the income streams for each opportunity are probabilistic.

(*iii*) The objective will be to maximise the expected sum of liquid reserves plus total cash invested to date after n periods of time.

This latter assumption may be very questionable, and the ascertainment of objective criteria will, in general, require considerable thought. The purpose of this criterion is to represent, in some sense, the overall cash being generated and stored (in equipment) in the system over some time period. The problem could be formulated in terms of 'total market value' providing the pattern of changes in market value are known. The fact that the above criterion may not be appropriate in no way invalidates the procedural principles put forward.

With these main assumptions we now make several definitions.

(*i*) X is the total cash in reserve at the moment.

(*ii*) T is the total amount of money invested to date (excluding cash reserves in bank).

(*iii*) R is the set of investments held at the moment (described in some appropriate language).

(*iv*) Z is the set of investment opportunities existing at the moment.

(*v*) I is any information existing at the time of decision-making, which influences

(*a*) the probabilities of returns for investments;

(*b*) the arrival of returns for investments;

(*c*) the arrival of future investments.

We also, include, in I, the immediate past events, such as income from each of the investments in the previous period, bank current account rate, plus changing patterns in investment opportunities. We may also include X, T, R, Z if relevant to the probabilities. The only thing we exclude is the actual decision at that time.

* If we let $\Phi(I^*/I)$ be the distribution function of the new information state at the beginning of the next period when the present one is I, and if $f_n(X,T,R,Z,I)$ is the expected sum of cash reserve plus cash investment to date at the end of n periods, beginning in condition X, T, R, Z, I now, and using an optimal policy, we derive: if the decision is to invest $y_1, y_2, \ldots y_k \ldots$ in opportunities $z_1(\cdot), z_2(\cdot), \ldots z_k(\cdot), \ldots (z_k(\cdot)) \in Z$ if $n > 0$

$$f_n(X,T,R,Z,I) = \max_{\{y_k\} \geqslant 0, \Sigma y_k \leqslant X} \left[\int_{I^*} f_{n-1}(X^*,T^*,R^*,Z^*,I^*) \right.$$
$$\left. d\Phi(X^*,T^*,\ldots I^*/X,T,\ldots I) \right] \tag{5.72}$$

$$f_0(X,T,R,Z,I) = X + T.$$

---

* This part may be missed out by the less mathematical students who can turn to the simplest form on page 126 which is self-contained.

where $z_i(\cdot)$ is an element of Z,

y_i is the quantity invested in $z_i(\cdot)$,
$X^* = (X-\Sigma y_i)(1+u)+r+\Sigma y_i z_i$,
$T^* = T+\Sigma y_i$,
$Y = \cup_i y_i z_i(\cdot)$,
$R^* = R\cup Y$,
r is the return, in the intervening period, from R,
z_i is the return, in the intervening period, from $z_i(\cdot)$,
u is the current account interest rate.

All returns are proportional to scale of investment within the sets Z, R.

We can then easily show inductively that:

$$f_n(X,T,R,Z,I) = T+u_n(R,I)+\beta_n(I)X+X \max_{z(\cdot)\in Z}[v_n(z(\cdot),I)] \quad (5.73)$$

where u_n, β_n, v_n satisfy:

$$u_{n+1}(R,I) = \int_{I^*} \{\beta_n(I^*)r+u_n(\Delta R,I^*)+rV_n(Z^*,I^*)\}d\Phi(I^*/I). \quad (5.74)$$

$$\beta_{n+1}(I) = \int_{I^*} \{\beta_n(I^*)+V_n(Z^*,I^*)\}d\Phi(I^*/I). \quad (5.75)$$

$$v_{n+1}(z(\cdot),I) = \max\left[0,\int_{I^*} \{1+u_n(\Delta z(\cdot),I^*)+(z-1-u)(\beta_n(I^*)+\right.$$

$$\left. V_n(Z^*,I^*))\}d\Phi(I^*/I)\right]. \quad (5.76)$$

$$V_n(Z,I) = \max_{z(\cdot)\in Z}[v_n(z(\cdot),I)]. \quad (5.77)$$

$\Delta g(\cdot) = \Delta[g(1),g(2),\ldots g(k)\ldots] = [g(2),g(3)\ldots]$ for all $g(\cdot)$, i.e., Δ simply shifts the time forward one period. It must be remembered that $I^*(I)$ contain X^*, T^*, R^*, $Z^*(X,T,R,Z)$. Some duplication is involved but this is convenient for expository purposes.

The consequence of this analysis is that we do have an investment value $v_n(z(\cdot),I)$, and that an optimal decision is to invest all money in that one with the highest value greater than zero, or not to invest at all if all values are less than zero.

If we simplify the analysis and assume that no probability changing information is to be used, and if we assume that there is a distribution function, $\Phi(S)$, for the set of opportunities, S, available at any time (independent of everything), then we can, again, determine a very much simplified investment value, for long duration systems (i.e. n large) viz.

$$v(z(\cdot)) = \max\left[0,\sum_{t=1}^{\infty} \lambda^{-(t-1)}z(t)-(1+\mu)\right], \quad (5.78)$$

where λ satisfies the equation,

$$\lambda = \int_S \left\{ \max_{s(\cdot) \in S} \left[\max \left[(1+\mu), \sum_{t=1}^{\infty} \lambda^{-(t-1)} s(t) \right] \right] \right\} d\Phi(S), \quad (5.79)$$

μ is the mean current account bank rate.

When only one opportunity at a time occurs, and if this always gives a constant income stream (i.e. $z(\cdot) = [z,z,z,\ldots]$) then we can define the system adequately by

$X =$ the cash held in the bank,
$T =$ the cash invested to date,
$R =$ the present (constant) return from investments now held, and
$z =$ the maximum return per unit offered by all opportunities now present.

Our functional equation then becomes
$n \geqslant 1$

$$f_n(X,T,R,z) = \max_{0 \leqslant y \leqslant X} \left[\int_u \int_s f_{n-1}((X-y)(1+u) + \right.$$

$$\left. R + yz, T+y, R+yz, s) d\Phi(s) d\theta(u) \right] \quad (5.80)$$

$$f_0(X,T,R,z) = X+T.$$

The terms on the right-hand side of (5.80) are self evident.

X changes to $(X-y)(1+u)+R+yz$,
T changes to $T+y$,
R changes to $R+yz$, and
z changes to s.

We then find that, if $\mu = E(u)$

$$f_1(X,T,R,z) = \max_{0 \leqslant y \leqslant X} \left[\int_u \int_s \{(X-y)(1+u)+R+yz+T+y\} \right.$$

$$\left. d\Phi(s) d\theta(u) \right],$$

$$= \max_{0 \leqslant y \leqslant X} [X(1+\mu)+T+R+y(z-\mu)],$$

$$= T+R+(1+\mu)X+Xv_1(z),$$

where $v_1(z) = \max [z-\mu,0]$.
The solution, for one period is $y = X$ if $v_1(z) \geqslant 0$

$$y = 0 \text{ if } v_1(z) \leqslant 0.$$

If we assume, inductively, that

$$f_k(X,T,R,z) = T+u_kR+\beta_kX+Xv_k(z),$$

we can prove that this is true for $(k+1)$ and, hence, inductively, establish it for all k.

A recurrence relation between $(u_k, \beta_k, v_k(\cdot))$ and u_{k+1}, β_{k+1}, $v_{k+1}(\cdot)$ can be derived (special cases of 5·74–5·77) and the limiting form, as $k \to \infty$, found.

The limiting value, $v(z)$, is given by the following and the solution is to take $y = X$ if $v(z) \geqslant 0$, $y = 0$ if $v(z) \leqslant 0$.

$$v(z) = \max [0, (\lambda/(\lambda-1))z - (1+\mu)]$$
$$= (\lambda/(\lambda-1)) \max [0, z - \eta]$$

where λ, η satisfy, respectively

$$\lambda = \int_s \max \left[(1+\mu), s \sum_{t=1}^{\infty} \lambda^{-(t-1)} \right] d\Phi(s)$$

$$\eta(\eta - \mu) = (1 + \mu - \eta) \int_{s \geqslant \eta} (s - \eta) d\Phi(s) \qquad (5.81)$$

and $\Phi(s)$ is the distribution function for $s(s(\cdot) \equiv [s, s, \ldots s)]$.

The main point, therefore, is that it may be possible, with the appropriate approach, to determine investment values from more fundamental considerations than have hitherto been used. The 'present worth' approach is not necessarily valid in general, but is valid in certain cases.

5.9.2. The Use of Expected Yield in Stock Market Investments

During an investigation of the possibility of applying D.P. to portfolio analysis the general use of 'expected yield' as a criterion for investment selection was evident, although actual attempts to measure it were unknown at the time.

Further reflection seemed to indicate, in fact, that 'expected yield' was not in fact the correct one, and that expected return, or something on these lines, was more appropriate. The following exercise confirmed that there is indeed a significant difference in some cases. Further exercises in portfolio analysis can be found in White & Norman.[49]

Let us suppose that we have a certain amount of money, and, from time to time, investment opportunities, giving a rate of return of r per unit investment, arise, with a probability distribution function $F(r)$, independently and identically distributed in each time period.

The yield over N periods is defined as being equal to $(\sqrt[N]{(x/x_0)} - 1)$ if we begin with x_0 and end up with x. The return at the end of N periods is of course, $x - x_0$.

If $v_m(x)$ is the expected yield over the next m periods of time beginning with x, and using an optimal policy, then, if $m \geqslant 1$, $x > 0$,

$$v_m(x) = \max_{0 \leqslant y \leqslant x} \left[\int_r v_{m-1}(x + ry) dF(r) \right]. \qquad (5.82)$$

$$v_0(x) = \sqrt[N]{(x/x_0)} - 1. \tag{5.83}$$

$$v_m(0) \equiv 0. \tag{5.84}$$

Then

$$v_1(x) = \sqrt[N]{(x/x_0)} \max_{0 \leqslant p \leqslant 1} \int_r \left[\sqrt[N]{(1+pr)} dF(r) \right] - 1$$

$$= k_1 \sqrt[N]{(x/x_0)} - 1. \tag{5.85}$$

Inductively we have

$$v_m(x) = k_1^{mN} \sqrt[N]{(x/x_0)} - 1. \tag{5.86}$$

The optimal solution is to always invest a fixed proportion of money given by that value of p which maximises

$$\int_r \sqrt[N]{(1+pr)} dF(r).$$

The optimal policy, for expected return, on the other hand, is given by 'invest all money if $E(r) = \mu \geqslant 0$, otherwise invest nothing'.

The two policies are identical only if $r \geqslant 0$ for all r. Otherwise, with risky situations, the policy giving optimal expected yield may give a much smaller expected return than the optimal one.

It may, fortuitously, be true that the utility function for money is proportional to $\sqrt[N]{x}$, but, since N is variable in general, this is not really tenable. However, the important point to be gained from this is that, once again, D.P. can be used to analyse some of the conceptual difficulties arising in investment problems (in this case, in helping to analyse the implications of various objective criteria).

5.9.3. *The Optimal Use of Reserve Cash*

There are situations in which cash is held in reserve to meet commitments expected to arise from time to time in the future. Rather than keep the cash idle it may be lent out on short term loans, say, recallable after a period of time, with the risk that, while this cash is so invested, any call off in the meantime may enforce an overdraft, at a rate of interest greater than that obtainable on short term loans. The problem is then one of determining, on the basis of total liquid reserves at the end of each period of time, how much to put into short term loans.

The assumptions we shall make are:

(*i*) The investment decisions are made once per unit time, and this period coincides with the loan period.

(*ii*) Deposits in any period occur at the end of the period and have a distribution function $\theta(u)$, independent of the time period.

(*iii*) Claims and expenses are settled at the end of the period, and have a combined distribution function $X(z)$ independent of time period.

(*iv*) The major call off (by the company's stockbrokers) occurs at the beginning of the period (after the short term loan decision has been made) and has a distribution function $\Phi(w)$, independent of the period.

(*v*) The current account, short term, and overdraft interest rates are c,t,d respectively with $c<t<d$.

(*vi*) All short term loans are assumed to be automatically freed at the end of a period, leaving a total available cash reserve whose sum is this plus the amount still in the bank.

Defining $v_n(x)$ to be the expected total effective cash balance after n periods of time using an optimal policy, then we have, putting $n-z=\xi$, and letting the distribution function for ξ be $G(\xi)$, if $n\geqslant 2$

$$v_n(x) = \max_{\min[0,x]\leqslant r\leqslant x}\left[\int_w\int_\xi v_{n-1}((1+t)x+\xi-w-rt+\right.$$

$$\min\left[c(r-w),d(r-w)\right])dG(\xi)d\Phi(w)\Big]$$

$$v_1(x) = \max_{\min[0,x]\leqslant r\leqslant x}\left[\int_w\int_\xi \{(1+t)x+\xi-w-rt+\right.$$

$$\min\left[c(r-w),d(r-w)\right]\}dG(\xi)d\Phi(w)\Big]. \qquad (5.87)$$

One obvious method of solving this is to compute $v_1(x)$, and then $v_2(x)$ and so on. However, it is possible to extract considerable information from the above equations and prove, inductively, that, if $r_n(x)$ is the optimal policy at the nth stage (from the end): if $r_n(x)<x$ then

$$\Phi^{-1}((d-t)/(d-c))\leqslant r_n(x)\leqslant\Phi^{-1}(((1+d)/(1+t))^{n-1}((d-t)/(d-c))). \qquad (5.88)$$

Φ^{-1} is the inverse function of Φ.

In the example concerned, d,t,c were very small, and hence, to a very good order of approximation, for a very long time period, the optimal policy approximates:

$$r_n(x) = \min\left[\eta,x\right], \quad \eta = \Phi^{-1}((d-t)/(d-c)). \qquad (5.89)$$

For cases where d,t,c are not so small we can still simplify the process, for we can show that if we define $g_n(x) = v_n(x)/(1+d)^n$ then $\{g_n(x)\}\rightarrow$

$g(x)$, as $n\rightarrow\infty$, uniformly for any bounded x, satisfying (under fairly general conditions)

$$g(x) = (1+d)^{-1} \max_{\min[0,x]\leqslant r\leqslant x}\left[\int_w \int_\xi g(x(1+t)+\xi-w+\right.$$

$$\left. \min\left[c(r-w),d(r-w)\right])dG(\xi)d\Phi(w)\right]. \qquad (5.90)$$

Further than this, we can establish that there exists an $_*x$ and and x^* such that

$$g(x) = a+x \text{ if } x\leqslant_*x$$
$$= 0 \quad \text{ if } x\geqslant x^*.$$

If we then make the problem discrete, with the state $i = 1$ corresponding to the lowest value x greater than $_*x$, and $i = m$ corresponding to the highest values of x less than x^*, then we can reduce the equation to

$$g(i) = \max_r[q_i^r+(1+d)^{-1}\Sigma_{1\leqslant j\leqslant m}p_{ij}^r g(j)] \qquad (5.91)$$

where

$$q_i^r = (1+d)^{-1}\Sigma_{j<1}(a+j)p_{ij}^r.$$

This can be solved using Howard's method, the interesting point being that the original states were not bounded.

A full account of this can be found in White and Norman.[53]

5.10. Dynamic Programming in Selling and Purchasing

As a final round up to the potential application of D.P. in stochastic control problems, let us consider two very simple problems, which, however, typify a much more general complex class of situations than are presented below.

5.10.1. *The Optimal Disposal of an Asset*

Suppose that a person has an asset (e.g. a piece of land) for which he is offered a certain amount of money from period to period. Let us assume that these offers have a distribution function $F(s)$, independent of the time period and previous offers. Suitable modifications can be made if correlations or trends exist.

Let us assume that, if he accepts the offer, he can invest the money at a fixed rate of interest r, or he can wait until the next period and consider any new offers which may arise, no offer being renewed.

Define $f_n(y)$ to be the expected return he will get when he receives an offer of value y and he uses an optimal policy over the remaining n periods.

Then if $n>1$ and $p = (1+r)$,

$$f_n(y) = \max\left[p^n y, \int_0^\infty f_{n-1}(s)dF(s).\right] \qquad (5.92)$$

Since he must accept any offer if he still has his asset at the beginning of the last period, we have

$$f_1(y) = py. \qquad (5.93)$$

Now maximising $f_n(y)$ is equivalent to maximising

$$g_n(y) \equiv p^{-n}f_n(y),$$
$$g_n(y) \text{ satisfies}$$
$$g_n(y) = \max\left[y, p^{-1}\int_0^\infty g_{n-1}(s)dF(s)\right]. \qquad (5.94)$$

If n is finite, we proceed as follows.

$$g_1(y) = y$$
$$g_2(y) = \max\left[y, p^{-1}\int_0^\infty sdF(s)\right]$$
$$= y \text{ if } y \geqslant p^{-1}\int_0^\infty sdF(s) \ (= \mu_1 \text{ say}), \qquad (5.95)$$
$$= \mu_1 \text{ if } y \leqslant \mu_1.$$

Now define

$$p^{-1}\int_0^\infty g_n(s)dF(s) = \mu_n. \qquad (5.96)$$

Then

$$g_n(y) = \max\left[y, \mu_{n-1}\right]$$
$$= y \text{ if } y \geqslant \mu_{n-1}$$
$$= \mu_{n-1} \text{ if } y \leqslant \mu_{n-1}. \qquad (5.97)$$

Then

$$\mu_n = p^{-1}\int_0^\infty g_n(s)dF(s) = p^{-1}\int_0^{\mu_{n-1}} \mu_{n-1}dF(s) + p^{-1}\int_{\mu_{n-1}}^\infty sdF(s),$$
$$(5.98)$$

i.e.

$$\mu_n = p^{-1}\mu_{n-1}F(\mu_{n-1}) + p^{-1}\int_{\mu_{n-1}}^\infty sdF(s). \qquad (5.99)$$

Define $G(z) = \int_z^\infty sdF(s)$. Then

$$\mu_n = p^{-1}\mu_{n-1}F(\mu_{n-1}) + p^{-1}G(\mu_{n-1}). \qquad (5.100)$$

With n periods remaining, the optimal policy is to accept (reject) if $y \geqslant \mu_n (\leqslant \mu_n)$ and μ_n is determined by equation (5.100). It is easily established that if $G(0) \leqslant M < \infty$, $\{\mu_n\} \to \mu$ as $n \to \infty$ and that if $F(s)$ has a density function, μ satisfies (see Appendix, p. 170):

$$\mu(p - F(\mu)) = G(\mu). \qquad (5.101)$$

As an example consider the following.

Let $dF(s) = ae^{-as}$.

Then

$$F(\mu) = 1 - e^{-a\mu}; \quad G(\mu) = e^{-a\mu}(\mu + a^{-1}).$$

Hence

$$\mu(p - 1 + e^{-a\mu}) = e^{-a\mu}(\mu + a^{-1})$$

i.e.

$$a\mu(p - 1) = e^{-a\mu} \qquad (5.102)$$

and with $a\mu = t$, $(p-1)t = e^{-t}$, the solution is obtained as shown in Fig. 4.

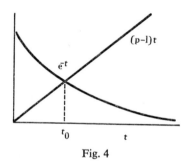

Fig. 4

The optimal policy:

accept offer y if $y \geqslant a^{-1} t_0$;

wait at least another period if $y \leqslant a^{-1} t_0$.

5.10.2. Optimal Purchasing with Deadline

Situations arise in which a certain quantity of raw material is required at a specific time. If the price of this material (e.g. copper, tin, etc.) fluctuates, then there arises the problem of deciding, given the purchase price at any time, whether to purchase at that price or wait a further period, during which the prices may go up or down. This bears some similarity to the investment problem of section 5.9.

Let us assume that a density function, $g(z)$, for the purchase price per unit, z, exists and is invariant from one period to another (modifications can be made if this is not so or if correlations between successive prices exist, as they may undoubtedly do so).

Let us suppose we are faced with a price, p, with n periods left and wish to minimise the expected cost of purchasing by the deadline time. If we have a different value function, then the optimal policy may result in purchasing a piece at a time, but with expected linear costs it is easy to prove that we either purchase all or none. Bearing this in mind we might as well assume that our requirement is only one unit.

Let $f_n(p)$ be the expected cost of purchasing by the deadline time, using an optimal policy, with n periods to go, and faced with a market price of p per unit, then we have:
$n > 1$

$$f_n(p) = \min \left[\int_s^p f_{n-1}(s)g(s)ds \right],$$

$$f_1(p) = p. \tag{5.103}$$

We see easily that if

$$\int_s^{} f_k(s)g(s)ds = c_k,$$

$$f_k(p) = \min \left[\begin{matrix} p \\ c_{k-1} \end{matrix} \right], \tag{5.104}$$

$$c_k = \int_{s \leqslant c_{k-1}} sg(s)ds + c_{k-1} \int_{s \geqslant c_{k-1}} g(s)ds. \tag{5.105}$$

Quite obviously, as $n \to \infty$, then it becomes more profitable to wait for the smallest possible value of p, which will arise eventually with a larger probability as n increases. In general the case of large n is not pertinent to this type of problem.

The optimal policy is, with k periods left,

$$\begin{matrix} \text{purchase} & \text{if } p \leqslant c_k, \\ \text{wait} & \text{if } p \geqslant c_k. \end{matrix}$$

Perhaps enough has been said in this chapter to establish that not only is D.P. important in stochastic control processes, but that also, there are many artifices which we may employ to simplify the computational solution, the manner in which we go about it depending on the problem being faced. The part that D.P. plays in resolving conceptual problems, as typified by value problems in investment, cannot be overstressed and, indeed, D.P. can be expected to play a central role in value theory in general.

Chapter 6

ADAPTIVE PROCESSES

CHAPTER 5 dealt with processes in which we were able to describe the change of state from stage to stage in a stochastic manner, the parameters and form of which were assumed known, possibly in terms of the decisions as well as the uncontrolled environment. There are, however, a large class of problems for which the stochastic descriptions are still adequate, but whose form and/or parameters are unknown, and it is with a sub-class of these that we shall be dealing here, viz. those in which the parameters themselves are subject to stochastic laws and can be modified as information is acquired from stage to stage. This sort of problem comes under the heading of 'adaptive programming', and is a mixed learning and optimising type problem.

It is perhaps worth noting that the term 'adaptive' can be applied to a problem in any environment whose nature becomes known, somehow, by the acquisition of knowledge over time. Although we shall be dealing mainly with environments of the type mentioned above, we would like to include search problems in the adaptive class, and will discuss one later. Within this broad context, non-probabilistic environments, as discussed by Bellman,[12] associated with sequential machines, also qualify.

6.1. Describing the Problem Situation

The typical situation we shall discuss can be described as follows. We wish to control some system, for which some measure of performance exists, dependent on the decisions taken and the conditions assumed throughout the relevant life of the system. The condition of the system at any time can be described by two sets of variables, viz. s and x_n. The latter set represent n observations made on certain variables, not subject to the control of the decision-maker, except in as much as the variables to be observed can be chosen. s represents all other variables necessary to describe the condition of the system for the purposes of model construction, e.g. we might have, for an inventory type system, $s = [s]$, $x_n = [x_n]$, where s is the present inventory level and x_n was the previous demand quantity.

The variable x_n is assumed to obey some stochastic law; i.e. it is assumed that x_n has a cumulative probability distribution. If this distribution were known, then we would be back in the class of problems discussed in Chapter 5. On the other hand, if nothing were known about the distribution then we would be in the class of multi-stage game type problem discussed in Bellman.[9] The class of problems which we shall treat here requires that the stochastic law for x_n, can, itself, be described stochastically. In short, we shall assume that the form of the distribution for x_n is known, but, within this form, is an unknown parameter α (this can be a vector in general, but no loss of generality occurs if we assume that it is a single variable) subject to a probability distribution function $G_0(\alpha)$, initially. The distribution function for x_n is then $F_n(x_n/\alpha)$.

There are difficulties inherent in the use of *a priori* probability functions, $G_0(\alpha)$, quite obviously, and one has to be careful in deciding when such an approach is valid. This book is concerned with D.P. and not with the fundamental problems in probability theory, and hence these problems must be accepted within the context of the book. Raiffa and Schlaiffer [39] discuss these problems quite well. Perhaps the main point in the favour of such representations is that they do allow us to formalise the learning process, which goes on as information is acquired over time, in a somewhat reasonable manner.

One example, in which the use of such representations might be useful, is the batch sampling situation. In such a set up, the observations, which are made, are simply whether an item is defective or non-defective. The probability of an item being defective or not defective depends, for random sampling, on the quality, p, of the batch, which represents the proportion of defective items in the batch. With enough information from the sampling of previous batches, one would presumably have some idea of the distribution of quality p over the batches, and this is, therefore, an *a priori* distribution for p. Of course, this distribution is based only on samples, and we never really know the quality of a batch, except under special circumstances (e.g. 100% sample) and hence we are, in a sense, begging many questions even here. Nevertheless it is expected that some idea of the quality distribution of batches must be acquired, although how accurate this may be a very open question.

Suffice it to say that the justification of the use of *a priori* probabilities is extremely difficult, and must be left to the judgement of the decision-maker himself to some extent.

Once we have accepted the use of *a priori* distributions, we are now in a position to determine the *a posteriori* distributions for both the parameters and the next observation, x_{n+1}, viz.

$$dF_n(x_{n+1}/x_n) = \int_\alpha dG_0(\alpha)dF_{n+1}(x_n,x_{n+1}/\alpha) \Big/ \int_\alpha dG_0(\alpha)dF_n(x_n/\alpha) \qquad (6.1)$$

10

$$dG_n(\alpha/\pmb{x}_n) = dG_0(\alpha)dF_n(\pmb{x}_n/\alpha)\Big/\int_\alpha dG_0(\alpha)dF_n(\pmb{x}_n/\alpha). \qquad (6.2)$$

We now have the ingredients for formulating our problem. The only other requirement is that of specifying our preference between policies, and we shall choose to prefer the policies which give rise to the maximum expected value of the paths generated by the policies under the given environment description. Given, of course, the validity of our main postulates in Chapter 3, we can then relate the value of being in state (s_n,x_n) at the nth stage, to the value of being in state (s_{n+1},x_{n+1}) at the $(n+1)$th stage, as in Chapter 5, since we now know the probability distribution of (s_{n+1},x_{n+1}) given (s_n,x_n). In principle the approach is identical with that of Chapter 5.

It is worthwhile making two observations here, viz.

(*i*) It is not necessary that the observations shall be independently distributed, although in such cases, if sufficient statistics exist in the classical sense, we can use them to simplify the problem, something we cannot do for dependent observations.

(*ii*) It was pointed out previously that we do not limit our adaptive class to probabilistically describable environments. Even for probabilistically describable environments there are some problems which do not come within the format given above without modifications; e.g. some search problems. If however, we consider α not to be necessarily a parameter determining probability distributions but a general proposition, such as 'the system, or environment, is in condition α', then the same format applies.

6.2. Comparison of Dynamic Programming and the Statistical Decision Function Approach

It is worth making some comment on the use of statistical decision functions for problems of the above type. For an extensive discussion of the statistical decision function approach see Wald [44] and Raiffa and Schlaiffer.[39]

Basically, Wald considers the following problem. A decision function δ is a rule for deciding, at each stage of the process, whether to terminate (and hence choose one of the terminal acts) or to take further observations, and, if so, which one to take (we can allow for the choice of observations in the D.P. formulation quite easily, although the examples will usually involve one further sample of the variable x). One difference between Wald and Raiffa is that the latter's decision functions all define the type of experiment, but this is easily absorbed under one δ.

If α is the true state of nature, then there exists a risk function $r(\alpha,\delta)$ representing the expected loss (or gain), including sampling costs and terminal losses or gains, for each decision function δ. Then, if $G_0(\alpha)$ is the *a priori* distribution function for α, the overall risk for a specific δ is given by:

$$r(\delta) = \int_\alpha r(\alpha,\delta)dG_0(\alpha). \tag{6.3}$$

Wald defines an admissible decision function, δ^*, as one for which '$r(\alpha,\delta^*)\geqslant r(\alpha,\delta)$' does not hold for all α and any δ, and is essentially concerned with the determination of complete classes of admissible decision functions in the sense that if δ is any decision function not in the class then there is a δ^* in the class such that $r(\alpha,\delta^*)\leqslant r(\alpha,\delta)$ for all α. Raiffa is concerned only with problems in which an *a priori* distribution, $G_0(\alpha)$, is known to exist, and a decision function δ which minimises $r(\delta)$ is said to be a Bayes solution relative to $G_0(\alpha)$. There is, however, a connection, for, under certain conditions (see Wald), the complete class of admissible decision functions are all Bayes solutions, relative to some corresponding *a priori* distribution function, $G_0(\alpha)$, each such distribution depending on the specific decision function, δ.

For general forms of risk function, $r(\alpha,\delta)$, we cannot use the D.P. approach to obtain Bayes solutions, for the costs associated with any path traversed may be such as to rule out the Optimality Principle (see Chapter 3). In this case we can use only the decision function approach, which consists, in general, of selecting classes of decision functions, specified completely, apart from certain parameters, and then finding the optimum parameters. This of course means that, in general, only sub-optimum solutions are found, except, perhaps, for isolated cases.

For most cases, however, including those catered for by Wald, the risk function is separable into the sum of costs and terminal risks, and the Principle of Optimality holds. For Wald's method, if $c(x,s)$ is the observational cost of * x and s (where s specifies the manner in which x was observed) and if $r(\alpha,a)$ is the terminal risk of taking action a when the true state is α, we would compute $H(x,s/\delta,\alpha)$ (which is the distribution function for the observations x,s prior to termination, given δ and α). Then:

$$r(\delta) = \int_{\alpha,}\int_x (c(x,s)+r(\alpha,\delta(x)))dH(x,s/\delta,\alpha)dG_0(\alpha). \tag{6.4}$$

* $x = [x_1,x_2,\ldots x_n]$.

However, we note that, in this case, once we have observed x and the corresponding s, then we obviously choose our next decisions to optimise our future performance. If the new *a posteriori* distribution for α, after observing x and corresponding s, is dependent only on x and s, and if this is equal to $G(\alpha/x,s)$ we have, defining $v(x,s)$ to be the expected risk, beginning in condition x,s and using an optimal policy:

$$v(x,s) = \min \left[\begin{array}{c} \min_a \left[\int\limits_\alpha r(\alpha,a)dG(\alpha/x,s) \right] \\ \min_{s*} \left[\int\limits_\alpha \int\limits_{x*} \{c(x^*,s^*) - c(x,s) + v(x^*,s^*)\}dG(\alpha/x,s) \right. \\ \left. dF(x^*/x,s^*,\alpha) \right]. \end{array} \right] \quad (6.5)$$

s might have been equivalent to 'observations $x_1, x_2, \ldots x_n$ have been taken'; s^* might then be equivalent to : s plus 'observe $x_{s+1}, \ldots x_{s*}$'.

$F(x^*/x,s^*,\alpha)$ is the distribution function for x^* given x,s^*, and s^* is the combination of s and the new sampling decision. In the cases we shall discuss, s simply gives the number of observations to date, i.e. if $x = [x_1, x_2, \ldots x_n]$ then $s = n$.

The advantage of the D.P. approach is that no assumptions are made about the form of the decision function δ. Of course the real problem is whether the extra computations usually needed are justified by the decrease in risk which the D.P. approach will given. Even if we are only interested in the admissible decision functions, and no apparent *a priori* distribution exists, we can, because of Wald's result on the equivalence of the complete set of admissible solutions and the set Bayes solutions, still use the D.P. approach to generate the Bayes solutions for each $G_0(\alpha)$. It is of interest to note that the choice of an admissible decision function is equivalent to assuming an *a priori* distribution does exist and finding the Bayes solution relative to this distribution.

In both cases (the statistical decision function case and the D.P. case) the existence of known risk functions $r(\alpha,\delta)$ is assumed. There are situations in which such functions are replaced by stochastic constraints such as 'the probability that act a^* will be taken, when the true value of α is α^*, must be no greater than $p(\alpha^*,a^*)$'. The decision function approach may then still be used, for we can compute, for each δ, the probabilities concerned and then constrain ourselves to such a subclass of δ satisfying the constraints. We cannot handle this problem using D.P., but, in this form, the problem is not quite complete, for the constraints imply that some risk function does exist (for how are they, derived in the first place?) and all that is required is a little more attention to determining the effects of taking certain actions in certain conditions.

6.3. Sufficient Statistics

A discussion of sufficient statistics in the classical sense can be found in any treatise on mathematical statistics, and will not be discussed in detail here. For our purposes, a vector z_n, is said to be a sufficient statistic in the classical sense if:

$$dF_n(x_1, x_2, \ldots x_n/\alpha) = d\Phi(z_n/\alpha)dX_n(x_1, x_2, \ldots x_n) \qquad (6.6)$$

where X_n does not depend on α.

Sufficient statistics play an important role in the D.P. approach, in that they help to reduce the dimensionality of the problem sometimes. In circumstances where the observations are independently distributed, not even necessarily identically distributed, we can show (see Appendix, p. 171) that, if a sufficient statistic exists, then this can be used to represent the complete set of observations in the functional equation derived using the D.P. approach, and this may reduce the dimensionality problem considerably. For example, in the batch-sampling problem, think of the dimension of the state variable describing the complete time series of observations, and think how much simpler the problem becomes when we realise that, if n is the number of acceptable items and m is the number of defective items, to date, then (m,n) is a sufficient statistic for the system. We might be faced with the problem of deciding on how much capacity to add in the given year, given past data for demand for a product for so many years, and we may believe that demand is increasing linearly with time apart from some Normal error with unknown mean and variance. We can apply the D.P. approach to this problem, but, without the existence of sufficient statistics $\Sigma_1^n x_t$, $\Sigma_1^n x_t^2$, $\Sigma_1^n t x_t$ and n, any idea of computation can be forgotten once and for all. Here we can reduce an n-dimensional problem to a 4-dimensional problem (3 if we exclude n as a state variable).

Therefore, within this field of D.P., we can expect that the theory of sufficient statistics will be of paramount importance. A very good discussion of the use of sufficient statistics in statistical decision theory may be found in Raiffa and Schlaffer.[39] However it ought to be pointed out that sufficient statistics in the classical sense are not sufficient for D.P. purposes in general, because, although they are sufficient to describe the probability distribution of the unknown parameter α, they are not sufficient, in general, for describing the conditional distribution of the $(n+1)$th observation, given the previous n observations. In fact we get:

$$dF_n(x_{n+1}/x_1 x_2 \ldots x_n) = \frac{\int_\alpha d\Phi_{n+1}(z_{n+1}, \alpha)dX_{n+1}(x_1, x_2, \ldots x_{n+1})dG_0(\alpha)}{\int_\alpha d\Phi_n(z_n, \alpha)dX_n(x_1, x_2, \ldots x_n)dG_0(\alpha)}.$$

Only when the right hand side of the above expression depends only on z_n and x_{n+1} can we use z_n as a sufficient state variable in the functional equation we obtain, and this is in general not so. It is so when we have independence of observations, and then (see Appendix, pp. 171, 172)

$$dF_n(x_{n+1}/x_1 x_2 \ldots x_n) = \int_\alpha d\Phi_n(z_n,\alpha) dF(x_{n+1}/\alpha) dG_0(\alpha) \Big/ \int_\alpha d\Phi_n(z_n,\alpha)$$
$$dG_0(\alpha). \quad (6.7)$$

$$dG_n(\alpha/x_1, x_2, \ldots x_n) = dG_0(\alpha) d\Phi_n(z_n/\alpha) \Big/ \int_\alpha d\Phi_n(z_n,\alpha) dG_0(\alpha). \quad (6.8)$$

We assume from here onwards, that the distributions are identical as well as independent, although we only need independence for our proof of sufficiency.

6.4. Examples

6.4.1. *Estimating a Parameter*

Let $k(\beta - \alpha)^2$ be the cost of taking β to be the true parameter when α is the actual value.

Let
$$dG_0(\alpha) = (\sqrt{2\pi})^{-1} e^{-\alpha^2/2} d\alpha$$
$$dF(x/\alpha) = (\sqrt{2\pi})^{-1} e^{-(x-\alpha)^2/2} dx.$$

Let
$$s = (\sum_1^n x_i)/n.$$

Then:

$$dF_n(x_{n+1}/s,n) = \frac{(\sqrt{2\pi})^{-1} e^{-x_{n+1}^2/2} \left\{ \int_\alpha e^{-(n+1)\alpha^2/2 + \alpha x_{n+1} - \alpha^2/2} d\alpha \right\} dx_{n+1}}{\int_\alpha e^{-n\alpha^2/2 + nas - \alpha^2/2} d\alpha}$$

$$= (\sqrt{2\pi})^{-1}((n+1)/(n+2))^{\frac{1}{2}} e^{-((n+1)/2(n+2))(x_{n+1} - ns/(n+1))^2}$$
$$dx_{n+1}$$

$$dG_n(\alpha/s,n) = \{ e^{-(n+1)\alpha^2/2 + nas} \Big/ \int e^{-(n+1)\alpha^2/2 + nas} d\alpha \} d\alpha$$

$$= ((n+1)/2\pi)^{\frac{1}{2}} e^{-((n+1)/2)(\alpha - ns/(n+1))^2} d\alpha.$$

Thus x_{n+1} is normally distributed with mean $ns/(n+1)$ and variance $(n+2)/(n+1)$. α is normally distributed with mean $ns/(n+1)$ and variance $1/(n+1)$. Thus s,n are sufficient statistics for the D.P. formulation, and our functional equation becomes, if c is the unit sample cost,

$$f(s,n) = \min \left[\begin{array}{l} \min_\beta \int\int_\alpha k(\beta-\alpha)^2((n+1)/2\pi)^{\frac{1}{2}} e^{-((n+1)/2)(\alpha - ns/(n+1))^2} d\alpha \\ c + \int_x ((n+1)/2\pi(n+2))^{\frac{1}{2}} e^{-((n+1)/(n+2))(x - ns/(n+1))^2/2} \\ \qquad\qquad f((ns+x)/(n+1), n+1) dx \end{array} \right]$$

Now

$$\min_\beta \left[\int_\alpha k(\beta-\alpha)^2((n+1)/2\pi)^{\frac{1}{2}} e^{-(n+1)(\alpha-ns/(n+1))^2/2} d\alpha \right]$$
$$= \min_\beta \left[k\{(\beta-ns/(n+1))^2 + 1/(n+1)\} \right]$$
$$= k/(n+1).$$
$$\hat\beta = ns/(n+1).$$

We see straight away that, if $k/(n+1) \leqslant c$, then an optimal solution is to take no further observation, and to choose $\beta = ns/(n+1)$, and $f(s,n) = k/(n+1)$, independent of s. Then let N be such that $k/(N+1) \leqslant c < k/N$. Then if $n \geqslant N$, $f(s,n) = k/(n+1)$. Also $f(s,N-1) =$

$$\min \begin{bmatrix} k/N \\ c+k/(N+1) \end{bmatrix} = f(N-1), \text{ say.}$$

Repeating this line of reasoning, we see that for all s, $f(s,n)$ is independent of s, and we can write it as $f(n)$, where

$$f(n) = k/(n+1), \quad n \geqslant N$$

$$f(n) = \min \begin{bmatrix} k/(n+1) \\ c+f(n+1) \end{bmatrix}, \quad n < N.$$

It is easily seen (see Appendix, p. 172) that the optimal solution is of the form:

'take a prefixed sample of size m, determine s, and take $\hat\beta$ equal to $ms/(m+1)$.'

Let us consider the following example to see how m can be calculated.

EXAMPLE $k = 10$, $c = 1$

Then $10/(9+1) \leqslant 1 < 10/9$. Hence $N = 9$

n	A. $c+f(n+1)$	B. $k/(n+1)$	min $[A,B]$	Action
9	>1	1	1	T
8	2	1·11	1·11	T
7	2·11	1·25	1·25	T
6	2·25	1·43	1·43	T
5	2·43	1·67	1·67	T
4	2·67	2·00	2·00	T
3	3·00	2·5	2·50	T
2	3·5	3·33	3·33	T
1	4·33	5·00	4·33	S
0	6·00	∞	6·00	S

T = Terminate and choose $\hat\beta = ns/(n+1)$
S = Take a further sample at least.

6.4.2 *Large Batch Sampling*

Let us consider the problem of sampling a very large batch of items, which may be classified as defective or non-defective. Let us also assume that sampling is carried out on a 'one at a time' basis (although this restriction can easily be removed if economies of scale exist), at a cost c per item.

The purpose of sampling is to prevent bad patches from going out, and any such scheme has the attendant risk of also misclassifying good batches as bad (which are then scrapped or inspected completely and defects made up). Therefore, for each quality, p (representing the true proportion of defective items in the batch), there will exist cost functions $a(p)$, $r(p)$, respectively representing the expected cost of accepting and rejecting batches of quality p. I shall not enquire into the derivation of these costs, but shall merely assume, not only that they can be determined, but are uniformly bounded for all p. This gives rise to one difficulty since we shall assume that the batch is infinite, and, therefore, if we rejected a batch and carried out a complete inspection, the costs should, for consistency, be infinite, although in practice they are finite. However, we are at liberty to approximate our cost functions as we wish and putting a bound on all relevant costs is just one such approximation.

The traditional approach to this problem is to fix the probabilities that, say, a batch of quality p_0 will be rejected and the probability that a batch of quality p_1 will be accepted, and then to choose a minimal expected sample size policy. However, a brief reflection will reveal that this tends to hide the real fact that the reason certain probabilities are desired to be small is that certain consequences are anticipated from such errors and hence functions $a(p)$, $r(p)$, do exist. Not only this of course they exist for all values of p.

As the sampling proceeds we shall accumulate a series of observations, each one representing either a defective item or a nondefective item. It is easily seen that if $G_0(p)$ is an initial *a priori* distribution for p (which will be obtained somehow from past information on other batches, and this, in itself, poses difficulties, since such information is only sample information; for our purposes we must accept the existence of $G_0(p)$) then, if we obtain a series of observations $x_1, x_2, \ldots x_N$, we have

$$dG_N(p/x_1, x_2, \ldots x_N) = dG_0(p)p^m(1-p)^n \bigg/ \int_p p^m(1-p)^n dG_0(p) = dG_{m.n}(p)$$

$$(6.9)$$

$$dF_N(0/x_1,x_2,\ldots x_N) = \int_p dG_0(p)p^{m+1}(1-p)^n \bigg/ \int_p dG_0(p)p^m(1-p)^n =$$

$$p(m,n) \qquad (6.10)$$

$$dF_N(1/x_1,x_2,\ldots x_N) = \int_p dG_0(p)p^m(1-p)^{n+1} \bigg/ \int_p dG_0(p)p^m(1-p)^n =$$

$$1-p(m,n) \qquad (6.11)$$

where $[x_1,x_2,\ldots x_N]$ contains m defective outcomes and n non-defective outcomes, and 0, 1 represent defective and non-defective outcomes respectively.

This means that the statistic (m,n) is a sufficient statistic, not only in the classical sense, but also for the adaptive programming model. We are now in a position to derive our formal model, and if we define $v(m,n)$ to be expected cost, to termination, of the sampling cost plus risks, when we have so far observed m defective items, and n non-defective items, and we are using an optimal sampling policy, we have

$$v(m,n) = \min \begin{bmatrix} \text{accept:} & \int_p a(p)dG_{m,n}(p) \\[2ex] \text{reject:} & \int_p r(p)dG_{m,n}(p) \\[2ex] \text{take a further sample:} \\ c+p(m,n)v(m+1,n)+(1-p(m,n))v(m,n+1) \end{bmatrix}. \quad (6.12)$$

If, for convenience, we put

$$u(m,n) = \min \begin{bmatrix} \int_p a(p)dG_{m,n}(p) \\[2ex] \int_p r(p)dG_{m,n}(p) \end{bmatrix}, \qquad (6.13)$$

we get

$$v(m,n) = \min \left[u(m,n); c+p(m,n)v(m+1,n)+(1-p(m,n))v(m,n+1) \right].$$

$$(6.14)$$

There are two methods of solution for this equation as follows.

(i) *Bellman's method of successive approximation*

Define $v_1(m,n) = u(m,n)$.
Then, for $k \geqslant 2$, define $v_k(m,n)$ as follows:

$$v_k(m,n) = \min \left[u(m,n); c+p(m,n)v_{k-1}(m+1,n)+(1-p(m,n))v_{k-1} \right.$$

$$\left. (m,n+1) \right]. \qquad (6.15)$$

We can show that, under certain conditions, the sequence $\{v_k(m,n)\}$ converges to a function $v(m,n)$ which is a unique solution of the functional equation above. One proof is given in the Appendix, p. 173, and another can be found in Wald [44] using a different approach (actually Wald begins with the recurrence relations rather than the functional equation, and is not concerned with uniqueness).

The conditions we shall require are that:

(a) $u(m,n) \geqslant 0$ for all m, n

(b) for $(m+n)$ sufficiently large, given $\varepsilon > 0$,
$$u(m,n) \leqslant \varepsilon.$$

If we are prepared to overlook uniqueness considerations, convergence to a solution of (6.14) is assured if

$$u(m,n) \geqslant u \text{ for all } m, n \text{ and some } u > -\infty.$$

(ii) A computational algorithm for directed sets

We note that the state (m,n) is partially directed by the relation $(m',n') \geqslant (m,n)$ if $m' \geqslant m$, $n' \geqslant n$, and that all realised states are fully directed. We can use this property to simplify the computations as follows.

Under the conditions (a), (b) on $u(m,n)$, given above, for $(m+n)$ sufficiently large

$$v(m,n) = u(m,n).$$

Let this be true for $m+n \geqslant T$, say.

We can then compute $v(m,n)$ for $m+n = T-1$ and so on, inductively, until we have the complete solution.

It is worth noting that Bellman's method has its advantages, in that, sometimes, it may be possible to get analytic solutions using his approach, or the convergence may be quite fast. At the same time we have had to use the property that $u(m,n) \to 0$ as $(m+n)$ becomes large to establish the directed method, and it is conceivable that this may not hold. Bellman's method still applies however, subject only to $u(m,n)$ being bounded from below, except that uniqueness is much more difficult to establish under more general conditions.

Wald [44] gives a numerical example using the directed method, which I quote. The conditions are:

$$\begin{aligned}
a(p) &= 0, & p &< 3/4 \\
&= 1, & p &\geqslant 3/4 \\
b(p) &= 0, & p &> 1/4 \\
&= 1, & p &\leqslant 1/4 \\
G_0(p) &= p \\
c &= \cdot004.
\end{aligned}$$

Then the equations become

$$v(m,n) = \min\left[u(m,n); \cdot 004 + p(m,n)v(m+1,n) + (1-p(m,n))v(m,n+1)\right].$$
(6.16)

$$p(m,n) = \int_0^1 p^{m+1}(1-p)^n dp \Big/ \int_0^1 p^m(1-p)^n dp = (m+1)/(m+n+2).$$
(6.17)

$$u(m,n) = \min\left[\int_{\frac{1}{4}}^1 p^m(1-p)^n dp \Big/ \int_0^1 p^m(1-p)^n dp;\right.$$

$$\left.\int_0^{\frac{1}{4}} p^m(1-p)^n dp \Big/ \int_0^1 p^m(1-p)^n dp\right]$$

$$= \min\left[\phi(m,n); \phi(n,m)\right],$$
(6.18)

where

$$\phi(n,m) = n!m!/(n+m+1)! - (3^{m+1}n!m!/4^{m+n+1})\sum_{s=1}^{n+1} 3^s/$$

$$(m+s)!(n-s+1)!$$

$$= (n!m!/(n+m+1)!)\left(1-(3^{m+1}/4^{m+n+1})\sum_{s=1}^{n+1}\binom{m+n+1}{m+s}3^s\right).$$
(6.19)

It is obvious that, if $(m+n)$ is sufficiently large, then $\phi(m,n) < \cdot 004$, and in fact this occurs for $m+n \geqslant 10$. Table 11 gives the complete

TABLE 11

$v(m,n)$

Number of 1's

n

Number
of 0's

	0	1	2	3	4	5	6	7	8	9	10	11
0	·0252	·0212	·0126	·0039	·0010	·0002	·0001	·0000	·0000	·0000	·0000	—
1	·0212	·0265	·0225	·0141	·0046	·0013	·0004	·0001	·0000	·0000	·0000	—
2	·0126	·0225	·0250	·0210	·0129	·0042	·0013	·0005	·0001	·0000	·0000	—
3	·0039	·0141	·0210	·0225	·0185	·0100	·0035	·0012	·0004	·0001	·0000	—
4	·0010	·0046	·0129	·0185	·0210	·0161	·0076	·0028	·0010	·0003	·0001	—
m5	·0002	·0013	·0042	·0100	·0161	·0176	·0136	·0056	·0022	·0008	·0003	—
6	·0001	·0004	·0013	·0035	·0076	·0136	·0143	·0103	·0042	·0016	·0006	—
7	·0000	·0001	·0005	·0012	·0028	·0056	·0103	·0115	·0075	·0031	·0012	—
8	·0000	·0000	·0001	·0004	·0010	·0022	·0042	·0075	·0094	·0054	·0023	—
9	·0000	·0000	·0000	·0001	·0003	·0008	·0016	·0031	·0054	·0079	·0039	—
10	·0000	·0000	·0000	·0000	·0001	·0003	·0006	·0012	·0023	·0039	·0074	—
11	—	—	—	—	—	—	—	—	—	—	—	

evaluation, and the optimal policy is: to take a further sample only if (m,n) is inside the boundary line; to accept the batch if (m,n) is outside the boundary line if $m<n$; and otherwise to reject the batch (presumably for complete inspection, etc.).

As a final point Bellman [12] indicates how the β type distribution, with two degrees of freedom, (of which the above is a special case) may be of some use in simplifying the computations, for if

$$dG_0(p) = p^{a-1}(1-p)^{b-1}dp/\beta(a,b),$$

then

$$p(m,n) = (m+a)/(m+n+a+b). \tag{6.20}$$

6.4.3 *An Adaptive Version of the Economic Lot Size Problem*

In Chapter 5 we discussed the problem of deciding how large an initial input batch size should be to minimise the expected cost of satisfying the order, where the costs are set-up costs and production costs, and the process produces defective items in a known probabilistic manner.

One criticism against the previous approach might be that if the product is special in some sense, so that any excess production or scrapped production has either no value, as we assumed, or purely scrap values, then it is not likely that we shall have adequate past statistics from which to derive probability distributions, and these are likely to be very subjective if we use them at all. However, we cannot deny that some such probabilistic measures are in mind when deciding on batch size. One such explanation arises from the fact that, usually, products are not completely specialised; they do bear similarities in many ways to other products for which statistics, taken over the whole variety of such products, are available. It may therefore be reasonable to postulate that the process will produce defective items with an unknown probability for which we have an *a priori* distribution function $G_0(p)$. We are now ready to formulate the problem as an adaptive programming problem, the real distinction between this and the approach used in Chapter 5 being that we modify our ideas about the probability distribution of p as we examine our products, which, as before, are inspected when the batch is completed. Before proceeding, it is worth pointing out that the production process need not of course, be binomial, and indeed, any parametrisable distribution can be handled.

Defining (since (m,n) form a sufficient statistic for p) $f(N,m,n)$ as the expected cost of satisfying an order for N items when we have already produced m defective items and n acceptable items and we use an optimal policy, we derive the following functional equation:

$$f(N,m,n) = \min_{M \geqslant N} \left[s + Mc + \right.$$

$$\left. \sum_{0 < l \leqslant N} q(M,N-l,m,n)f(l,M+m-N+l,n+N-l) \right], \quad (6.21)$$

where s,c are the set-up and unit production costs respectively, and $q(M,N-l,m,n)$ is the probability that, if M items are put into production and m defectives and n acceptable items have so far been produced, then $(N-l)$ acceptable items will be produced. Its value is given by

$$q(M,N-l,m,n) = \binom{M}{N-l} \int_0^1 p^{M+m+l-N}(1-p)^{N-l+n}dG_0(p) \Big/$$

$$\int_0^1 p^m(1-p)^n dG_0(p). \quad (6.22)$$

There are two possible methods of solution for the above equation, the first one being Bellman's method of successive approximations, and the second one being akin to the solution given in Chapter 5 for directed sets (or, at least, partially directed as our states are here).

(i) Bellman's method of successive approximations

Define $f_1(N,m,n)$ as follows:

$$f_1(N,m,n) = s + Nc \text{ if } N > 0$$
$$= 0 \text{ otherwise.} \quad (6.23)$$

Then define $f_k(N,m,n)$, $k \geqslant 2$, as follows.
If $N \neq 0$

$$f_k(N,m,n) = \min_{M \geqslant N} \left[s + Mc + \right.$$

$$\left. \sum_{0 < l \leqslant N} q(M,N-l,m,n)f_{k-1}(l,m+M-N+l,n+N-l) \right]$$

$$(6.24)$$

$$f_k(0,m,n) \equiv 0.$$

Under certain conditions, we can show that the sequence $[f_k(N,m,n)]$ converges monotonely to a function $f(N,m,n)$ which is a unique solution of the functional equation derived initially. These conditions are: for fixed n,

$$\int_0^1 p^m (1-p)^{n-N} dG_0(p) \Big/ \int_0^1 p^m(1-p)^n dG_0(p)$$

should be uniformly bounded for all $m \geqslant m^*$ $(< \infty)$, m^* depends on n,N. If $dG_0(p) = 0$ for $p \geqslant p_0$, $p_0 < 1$, then this always true, for an upper bound is then $(1 - p_0)^{n-N}$ in this case.

The proof that this algorithm is valid is given in the Appendix, pp. 174–176.

(ii) A computational algorithm for directed sets

We note that, if the initial state is (N,m,n), then the new state, after the decision, is (N',m',n') where $N' \leqslant N$, $m' \geqslant m$, $n' \geqslant n$, and, in this sense the transformation is a directed one, i.e. the states are, in general, partially ordered, and realised states are completely ordered. This property can be used to help in the computations.

Let us assume that N,n are given, and that, for $m \geqslant m^*(N,n)$ we know $f(N,m,n)$.

Let us also assume $f(l,m',n')$ is known for $1 \leqslant l < N$, and all m',n' (actually we only need $m' \geqslant m$, $n' \geqslant n$, but, if $f(N,m,n)$ is to be computed for all m,n, then we eventually need all m',n').

Then $f(N,m^*-1,n)$ can be computed directly from the original functional equation.

To find $f(N,m,n)$ for $m \geqslant m^*$ we note that the functional equation can be transformed to give, if $q(M,0,m,n) \neq 1$:

$$f(N,m,n) = \min_{M \geqslant N} \left[\left\{ s + Mc + q(M,0,m,n)(f(N,m+M,n) - f(N,m,n)) \right. \right.$$

$$\left. \left. + \sum_{0 < l < N} q(M,N-l,m,n)f(l,m+M+l-N,n+N-l) \right\} \right/$$

$$\left. (1 - q(M,0,m,n)) \right]. \qquad (6.25)$$

If $q(M,0,m,n) = 1$, then we may use the original equation directly of course.

Now, under certain conditions, we can, by taking m sufficiently large, make $|f(N,m+M,n) - f(N,m,n)|$ as small as we wish. Therefore, for m sufficiently large, an approximate solution is given by

$$f(N,m,n) \sim \min_{M \geqslant N} \left[\left\{ s + Mc + \right. \right.$$

$$\left. \sum_{0 < l < N} q(M,N-l,m,n)f(l,m+M+l-N,n+N-l) \right\} \right/ (1 - q(M,0,m,n)) \right].$$

$$(6.26)$$

The value of m^*, for any desired level of approximation, can be obtained by using the results given in the Appendix, p. 178. Alternatively, we may just make m^* very large nominally and check that $|f(N,m,n) - f(N,m',n)|$ is sufficiently small for $m,m' \geqslant m^*$.

The final prerequisite is that we can compute $f(1,m,n)$, and this can be obtained in an analogous manner, since $f(0,m',n') \equiv 0$ for all m',n'. For m sufficiently large, given n, we have

$$f(1,m,n) \sim \min_{M \geqslant 1}[(s+Mc)/(1-q(1,0,m,n))]. \qquad (6.27)$$

The only condition, in addition to the uniform boundedness conditions stated in the previous algorithm, is that

$$\int_0^1 p^{m+M-N+l}(1-p)^{n+N-l}dG_0(p) \bigg/ \int_0^1 p^m(1-p)^n dG_0(p)$$

tends to a limit (in this case $\leqslant 1$) as m tends to ∞, for any M,N,n,l.

This condition is certainly likely to hold for most well behaved distribution functions $G_0(p)$.

6.4.4. A Pricing Problem

Let us assume that we have a relatively new product whose price we wish to set. We know that the price will influence the number sold in a given time period, but we are not quite sure how. Experience has taught us that the number sold per unit time of similar products is of the form $a-bp+\varepsilon$ where ε is normally distributed with zero mean and variance σ^2. The parameters a, b, σ vary among the group of similar products according to some distribution function $G_0(a,b,\sigma)$. Our problem is one of deciding, at the end of each time period, what price to set for the new product to maximise, say, the expected overall profit over n periods of time.

Defining $v_k(z_1,z_2,\ldots z_{n-k}; p_1,p_2 \ldots p_{n-k})$ as expected the profit over the next k periods of time when we have previously priced the item at $p_1, p_2, \ldots p_{n-k}$ and have sold $z_1,z_2, \ldots z_{n-k}$ items respectively, and when we use an optimal policy, we see that assuming prob $\{a-bp+\varepsilon \leqslant 0\}$ is small, $k \geqslant 1$

$$v_k(z_1,z_2,\ldots z_{n-k};p_1,p_2,\ldots p_{n-k}) =$$

$$\max_p \left[\int\!\!\int_{a,b,\sigma,\varepsilon} \{(p-c)(a-bp+\varepsilon)+v_{k-1}(z_1,z_2,\ldots z_{n-k},a-bp+\varepsilon;\right.$$

$$\left. p_1,p_2,\ldots p_{n-k},p)\}dF(\varepsilon/\sigma)dG_{n-k}(a,b,\sigma/z_1,z_2,\ldots z_{n-k};p_1,p_2,\ldots p_{n-k})\right].$$

$$v_0(z_1,z_2,\ldots z_n;p_1,p_2,\ldots p_n) \equiv 0 \qquad (6.28)$$

where c is the unit production cost.

It is easily seen that

$$dG_{n-k}(a,b,\sigma/z_1,z_2,\ldots z_{n-k};p_1,p_2,\ldots p_{n-k}) = (\sqrt{(2\pi)}\sigma)^{-(n-k)}$$

$$e^{-(A+b^2B-2abC-2aD+2bE+a^2)/2\sigma^2}dG_0(a,b,\sigma) \bigg/ \int_{a,b,\sigma}(\sqrt{(2\pi)}\sigma)^{-(n-k)}$$

$$e^{-(A+b^2B-2abC-2aD+2bE+a^2)/2\sigma^2}dG_0(a,b,\sigma). \qquad (6.29)$$

Since $dF(\varepsilon/\sigma) = (\sqrt{(2\pi)}\sigma)^{-1}e^{-\varepsilon^2/2\sigma^2}d\varepsilon$, we see easily that A,B,C,D,E are sufficient statistics, together with $(n-k)$, for the problem, where

$$A = \sum_1^{n-k} z_i^2,$$

$$B = \sum_1^{n-k} p_i^2,$$

$$C = \sum_1^{n-k} p_i,$$

$$D = \sum_1^{n-k} z_i, \text{ and}$$

$$E = \sum_1^{n-k} p_i z_i. \tag{6.30}$$

The new functional equation becomes
$k \geqslant 1$

$$v_k(A,B,C,D,E) = \min_p \Bigg[\iint_{a,b,\sigma,\varepsilon} \{(p-c)(a-bp+\varepsilon) +$$

$$v_{k-1}(A+(a-bp+\varepsilon)^2, B+p^2, C+p, D+a-bp+\varepsilon, E+p(a-bp+\varepsilon))\}$$

$$dF(\varepsilon/\sigma)dG_{n-k}(a,b,\sigma/A,B,C,D,E) \Bigg] \tag{6.31}$$

$v_0(A,B,C,D,E) = 0.$

No doubt, many more realistic modifications can be made, but one cannot doubt that the pricing process is, in every sense, an adaptive process, initially on similar products, plus, perhaps, other information of various kinds.

It is interesting to note the difference between the classical approach and the D.P. approach. Initially the only information is in $G_0(a,b,\sigma)$, and the initial pricing is based somehow on this (e.g. it may be taken in accordance with $v_1(A,B,C,D,E)$ with $n = 1$).

After a time, the statistician will step in and provide the best statistical estimates of a, b and σ. These estimates have nothing to do with the decision-maker, and hence we have two independent types of optimisation mixed together, whereas the D.P. approach does not differentiate between optimal information and optimal use, they are both embedded in one process. It is to be noted that choosing p not only influences our profit but also our information content.

6.4.5. *A Capacity Expansion Problem*

Let us consider something in the same vein as problem 6.4.4, but, in which, the price, and hence profit, is fixed, and, in which, the demand is growing over time in some manner. We may, perhaps, assume that the growth is linear with time, with a normally distributed error, i.e. the demand is equal to $(a+bt+\varepsilon)$. As before considerations of other products, and perhaps information we already have, on this product, provides us with some likelihood function, $G_0(a,b,\sigma)$ for the parameters.

Our problem is this. We have accumulated information, $x_1,x_2,\ldots x_{n-k}$, on the demand (not sales) for the product over the last $(n-k)$ periods, and we want to know how much extra capacity, if any, to invest in. The risks are that sales may be lost if capacity is too low, but equipment may be idle if capacity is too high.

Let c be the unit cost of extra capacity and let r be the net income from a unit sale. Then if $v_k(x_1,x_2,\ldots x_{n-k},z)$ is the expected profit over the next k periods of time, when our past demands have been $x_1,x_2,\ldots x_{n-k}$, and our present capacity is z, then, if u is the increase in capacity we choose,

$$v_k(x_1,x_2,\ldots x_{n-k},z) = \max_{u \geqslant 0} \left[\int_{a,b,\sigma,s} \{r \min [z+u,s] - \right.$$

$$cu + v_{k-1}(x_1,x_2,\ldots x_{n-k},s,u+z)\} dF(s/a,b,\sigma,n-k+1)$$

$$\left. dG_{n-k}(a,b,\sigma/x_1,x_2,\ldots x_{n-k}) \right]. \qquad (6.32)$$

We can, if we wish, make some assumption about cash values of equipment in the last period, and even introduce discount factors for the lost interest on money tied up in equipment, but the general form is similar. The resolution of these problems is a task in itself.

To proceed, we can show, as with example 6.4, that sufficient statistics exist, viz. $z,n-k$, together with

$$S = \Sigma x_t^2$$

$$X = \Sigma x_t$$

$$A = \Sigma tx_t. \qquad (6.33)$$

We then have

$k \geqslant 1$

$$v_k(S,X,A,z) = \max_{u \geqslant 0} \left[-cu + \int_{a,b,\sigma,s} \{r \min [z+u,s] + \right.$$

$$v_{k-1}(S+s^2,X+s,A+(n-k+1)s,z+u)\} dF(s/a,b,\sigma,n-k+1)$$

$$\left. dG_{n-k}(a,b,\sigma/S,X,A) \right], \qquad (6.34)$$

11

where

$$dG_{n-k}(a,b,\sigma/S,X,A) = N_{n-k}(a,b,\sigma)\Big/\int_{a,b,\sigma} N_{n-k}(a,b,\sigma)dG_0(a,b,\sigma).$$

$$N_{n-k}(a,b,\sigma) = \sigma^{-(n-k)}e^{-(S-2aX-2bA)/2\sigma^2}e^{-((n-k)a+(n-k)(n-k+1)ab+(n-k)}$$
$$^{(n-k+1)(2n-2k+1)b^2)/2\sigma^2}$$

$$dF(s/a,b,\sigma,n-k+1) = (\sqrt{(2\pi)}\sigma)^{-1}e^{-(s-a-b(n-k+1))^2/2\sigma^2}ds. \tag{6.35}$$

Of course the Normal distribution is only an approximation, since we would not have $s<0$ in practice.

6.4.6. A Search Problem

So far we have been discussing problems where the environment is described stochastically with unknown parameters, which are themselves described stochastically. There is a special subclass of these problems in which the environment is known to be in one and only one state, and for which there exists a probability distribution for the states, which is modified on the basis of observations, to be chosen, until some final terminating decision is made.

Such a situation arises in search processes where we are trying to locate an item or to identify the precise values of some variable, and about which we have some *a priori* probability distribution.

Let us assume that we have made n observations, perhaps of a complex nature, and that we now have an *a posteriori* distribution function, $G_n(s)$, for the state s of the system.

Let us also assume that the process terminates when a certain event E occurs, and that we wish to minimise the expected time to terminating the process.

Let $F_n(e/G_n,a,s)$ be the distribution function for event e, when G_n is given, action a is taken, and the true state of the system is s. Let $t(a,s)$ be the time consumed in carrying out a when the true state is s.

Then, if $v(G_n)$ is the expected time to completion, when G_n is given, and we use an optimal policy, we have

$$v(G_n) = \min_a \left[\int_s t(a,s)dG_n(s)+\int_{e\,\notin\,E} v(G_{n+1}/G_n,a,e)dF_n(e/G_n,a)\right], \tag{6.36}$$

where

$$dF_n(e/G_n,a) = \int_s dF_n(e/G_n,a,s)dG_n(s),$$

and $G_{n+1}(s)$ is the new *a posteriori* distribution function for s, given G_n,a,e and is given by

$$dG_{n+1}(s/G_n,a,e) = dG_n(s)dF_n(e/G_n,a,s)\Big/\int_s dF_n(e/G_n,a,s)dG_n(s). \tag{6.37}$$

As a simple example, let s take discrete values $1, 2, \ldots N$, and let $dG_n(s) = p_s$. Let E be the event: 'the item has been located'. Let a be the choice of location to search next. Thus, if we decide to search location s, and the state is actually r, then E will occur only if $r = s$. Let $t(a,s) = t(a)$.

The functional equation then becomes

$$v(p_1, p_2, \ldots p_N) = \min_a [t(a) + (1 - p_a)v(p_1^*, p_2^*, \ldots p_{a-1}^*, 0, p_{a+1}^*, \ldots p_N^*)],$$

(6.38)

where

$$p_r^* = p_r/(1 - p_a).$$

(6.39)

The solution is quite easy for this problem (see Bellman [9]), for we see that, if $v_{rs}(p_1, \ldots p_N)$ is the expected time searching first location r, and then location s, and then continuing optimally, then

$$v_{rs}(p_1, p_2, \ldots p_N) - v_{sr}(p_1, p_2, \ldots p_N) = t(r) + (1 - p_r)t(s) - t(s) -$$

$$(1 - p_s)t(r).$$

Therefore, we would search location r prior to location s, assuming s succeeds r or vice versa, only if $t(r)/p_r \leqslant t(s)/p_s$. Since this inequality is preserved at all stages (i.e.

$$(t(r)/p_r \leqslant t(s)/p_s) \rightleftharpoons (t(r)/p_r' \leqslant t(s)/p_s'),$$

where p_r', p_s' are modifications of p_r, p_s respectively, on the basis of intervening observations) we see that we can decide on the order of observations right at the beginning, viz. choose the smallest value of $t(r)/p_r$, then the next smallest, and so on, until the process terminates.

The original functional equation can of course be applied to a wider variety of problems than the one discussed, and further examples can be found in Bellman,[9] including, for example, the possibility that observations yield only partial information about the condition of a specific location.

It was pointed out before, that adaptive programming is not confined to probabilistically describable systems. It is applicable to any situation in which a process of acquiring information of any kind about the environment, or condition of the system, is relevant to the problem on hand, although, without the use of probabilities, we need to use minimax criteria. Bellman [12] deals with a class of such problems under the heading 'Sequential Machines'.

APPENDICES

PROOF OF SOME RESULTS

Appendix to Chapter 1

A1.1. The Classical Optimisation Problem

A discrete optimisation problem takes the following form:
find $x_1, x_2, \ldots x_n$ which maximise (minimise) $\theta(x_1, x_2, \ldots x_n)$ subject to constraints

$$\phi_i(x_1, x_2, \ldots x_n) = 0, \quad i = 1, 2, \ldots m.$$

Constraints of the inequality form, '$\phi_i(x_1, x_2, \ldots x_n) \leqslant 0$' can be changed into those of the equality type, by introducing unconstrained variables, $\{y_i\}$, $i = 1, 2, \ldots m$, so that the inequality constraints become

$$\phi_i(x_1, x_2, \ldots x_n) + y_i^2 = 0, \quad i = 1, 2, \ldots m.$$

The problem is 'discrete' in that the space, over which optimisation takes place, is an integer vector product over some space X^1 (see Chapter 3 for the definition of a 'discrete' D.P. process). The continuous analogue of a discrete optimisation problem (see p. 75) is the classical Calculus of Variations problem in which the thing we are optimising is a function, i.e. a point in a vector space which is a continuous vector product of a basic space.

Except in as much as integer type solutions are required, the same applies to all Non-Linear Programming. The application of the Differential Calculus converts an optimisation problem to one of finding any feasible solution to a set of inequalities (including equalities).

Thus, assuming differentiability, by introducing the Lagrange parameters, the solution of the above optimisation problem is a solution of the equations

$$\frac{\partial \theta}{\partial x_i} + \Sigma_j \lambda_j \frac{\partial \phi_j}{\partial x_i} = 0, \quad i = 1, 2, \ldots n,$$

$$\phi_j(x_1, x_2, \ldots x_n) = 0, \quad j = 1, 2, \ldots m,$$

for which the Hessian $\left[\dfrac{\partial^2 \theta}{\partial x_i \partial x_j} + \Sigma_s \lambda_s \dfrac{\partial^2 \phi_s}{\partial x_i \partial x_j} \right]$ is negative definite. The inequality conditions for the solution come from this property.

It need hardly be stated that determining these inequalities and solving them are two entirely different problems, and the latter one can be far from easy. Added to this, of course, we face problems of differentiating between local optima and absolute optima. If we now include integer solutions only, the difficulties are even more pronounced and various refinements are necessary to get a solution.

The general L.P. problem is one of maximising $\theta(x_1, x_2, \ldots x_n) \equiv \Sigma_1^n \alpha_j x_j$, subject to constraint $\Sigma_j \alpha_{ij} x_j = \beta_i$, $i = 1, 2, \ldots m$, $x_j \geqslant 0$, $j = 1, 2, \ldots n$. In terms of equality constraints only, this reduces to

$$\Sigma_j \alpha_{ij} x_j = \beta_i, \qquad i = 1, 2, \ldots m,$$

$$x_j - y_j^2 = 0, \qquad j = 1, 2, \ldots n.$$

The solution conditions are then

$$\alpha_j + \Sigma_i \lambda_i \alpha_{ij} + \mu_j = 0, \qquad j = 1, 2, \ldots n,$$

$$\mu_j y_j = 0, \qquad j = 1, 2, \ldots n,$$

$$x_j = y_j^2, \qquad j = 1, 2, \ldots n,$$

$$\Sigma_j \alpha_{ij} x_j = \beta_i, \qquad i = 1, 2, \ldots m,$$

and the matrix

$$\begin{bmatrix} 0_{nn} & 0_{nn} \\ 0_{nn} & -\mathrm{diag}(\mu_j) \end{bmatrix}$$

is negative definite, 0_{nn} being a zero matrix of order $n \times n$.

The latter restriction requires that

$$\mu_j \geqslant 0, \qquad j = 1, 2, \ldots n.$$

It is easily seen that these combined equations are the combined primal-dual equations for a standard L.P. procedure. The simplex algorithm is, effectively, a mechanism for solving these equations. The optimality of the final solution is expressible in this form whatever the algorithm used to solve the problems.

A1.2. Point and Functional Equations

Suppose x is a point in n-dimensional Euclidean space, E_n; A is a non-singular $n \times n$ matrix, and b is another point in E_n. Then the equation

$$Ax = b$$

gives a unique point solution $x = A^{-1}b$.

Suppose, now, that a function f is defined on E_n and suppose f satisfies the following equation

$$f^2(x) = f(x)$$

for all $x \in E_n$.

f may then have one of two basic solutions, viz.

$$f(x) = 1 \quad \text{for all } x \in E_n$$

$$f(x) = 0 \quad \text{for all } x \in E_n,$$

or it may have a more general solution, viz.

$$f(x) = 0 \quad \text{for all } x \in R_n \subseteq E_n,$$
$$f(x) = 1 \quad \text{for } x \in E_n - R_n = \tilde{R}_n.$$

The solution f is a 'function' over E_n and not a 'point' in E_n.

Other functional equations might be $f(x+y) = f(x) + f(y), f_m(x+y) = f_{m-1}(x) + f_{m-1}(y)$, where, in the second case, we have equations relating different functions.

Let us now consider the first linear point equation. Let I be the space indexing the components of E_n, i.e. $I \equiv [1, 2, \ldots n]$. The point equation over E_n can now be replaced by a functional equation over I, viz.

$$\Sigma_j a_{ij} f(j) = b_i, \quad i = 1, 2, \ldots n.$$

Effectively what D.P. does (and this will be seen in later chapters) is to replace a point equation in E_n by a functional equation over some $E_m \times I$. To be useful we need to have $m \ll n$ in general. Thus, referring to equation (4.2) the equations expressing optimality, through the Calculus approach, over E_n, are

$$g_i'(x_i) = \lambda \alpha_i, \quad i = 1, 2, \ldots n,$$
$$\Sigma_i \alpha_i x_i = c.$$

These are replaced by the functional equation, over $E_1 \times I$,

$$f_m(z) = \max_{0 \leqslant x_m - z / \alpha_m} [g_m(x_m) + f_{m-1}(z - \alpha_m x_m)].$$

The transposition from the simultaneous equation form to the functional equation form is brought about by creating a sequence of related problems by the appropriate choice of new variables. This transition is not to be identified with the above transition showing how a point equation can be transformed into a functional equation over I, this being simply for illustration purposes. The D.P. formulation comes from the recognition that we can consider $[x_1, x_2, \ldots x_n]$ as a point in E_n or as a path in $E_1 \times I$. The functional equation is then over $E_1 \times I$.

Appendix to Chapter 2

THE OPTIMAL PATH PROBLEM

A2.1. Method of Successive Approximations

(*i*) The sequence $\{f_n(i)\}$, given by equations (2.5) and (2.6), converge monotonely to a function $\{f(i)\}$ satisfying equation (2.2).

Proof

From equation (2.6)

$$f_n(i) = \min_s [c_{is} + f_{n-1}(s)] \leqslant f_n(i) \qquad \text{(taking } s = i\text{).}$$

Thus $\{f_n(i)\}$ forms a monotonic decreasing sequence. Since $c_{ij} \geqslant 0$, we see that $f_n(i) \geqslant 0$ for all n,i. Hence the sequence $\{f_n(i)\}$ is bounded below. Hence the sequence converges to a function $\{f(i)\}$. Since we have only a finite number of states, this convergence is uniform. Since the convergence is uniform, given $\varepsilon > 0$, $\exists$ a n_0 such that, for $n \geqslant n_0$ and all i, $|f_n(i) - f(i)| \leqslant \varepsilon$. Equation (2.6) then gives:

$$\min_s [c_{is} + f(s) - 2\varepsilon] \leqslant f(i) \leqslant \min_s [c_{is} + f(s) + 2\varepsilon].$$

Since we can make ε as small as we wish, the required result follows.

(*ii*) The sequence $\{f_n(i)\}$ converges in at most $(N-1)$ steps, i.e.

$$\{f_{N+t-1}(i)\} = \{f_{N-1}(i)\} \text{ for } t \geqslant 0.$$

Proof

Suppose that, for some i, $f_N(i) \neq f_{N-1}(i)$. Let the optimal sequence obtained from $f_N(i)$ be: $i_0(= i)$, i_1, i_2, ... i_N ($= N$). Since there are $(N+1)$ points in this sequence, at least two must be identical, say i_p and i_{p+r}. Then

$$f_N(i) = \{c_{i_0 i_1} + c_{i_1 i_2} + \ldots c_{i_{p-1} i_p} + f_{N-r-p}(i_p)\} + \{c_{i_p i_{p+1}} + \ldots c_{i_{p+r-1} i_{p+r}}\}.$$

The latter bracket is a loop, and the first bracket is at least equal to the optimal cost of getting from i_0 to N in at most $(N-r)$ steps.

Thus $f_N(i) \geqslant f_{N-r}(i)$ for some $r \geqslant 1$.

But $f_N(i) \leqslant f_{N-r}(i)$ for all $r \geqslant 1$.

Hence $f_N(i) = f_{N-r}(i)$ for some $r \geqslant 1$

Since $f_{N-1}(i) \leqslant f_{N-r}(i)$ for all $r \geqslant 1$, we see that

$$f_N(i) = f_{N-r}(i) \geqslant f_{N-1}(i) \geqslant f_N(i)$$

and this contradicts the above. Since $\{f_N(i)\} \equiv \{f_{N-1}(i)\}$, then $\{f_{N+t-1}(i)\} \equiv \{f_{N-1}(i)\}$ for all $t \geqslant 0$.

A2.2. Method of Approximation in Policy Space

The sequence $\{f_n(i)\}$ converges to a solution of equation (2.2) and each policy derived successively has no loops, hence ensuring the solution of the simultaneous equations.

Proof

Let A be a policy with no loops and let B be the next policy derived from A using the method given. Then if $f_A(i), f_B(i)$ are the path value from i to N using policies A,B respectively, and $s_A(i), s_B(i)$ denote the policy decisions when at point i, we see that:

$$f_A(i) = c_{is_A(i)} + f_A(s_A(i))$$
$$f_B(i) = c_{is_B(i)} + f_B(s_B(i)).$$

Then:

$$f_A(i) - f_B(i) = \{c_{is_A(i)} + f_A(s_A(i)) - (c_{is_B(i)} + f_A(s_B(i)))\} +$$
$$\{f_A(s_B(i)) - f_B(s_B(i))\}.$$

Let $\Delta f(i) = f_A(i) - f_B(i)$ and denote the first bracket by γ_i. Then

$$\Delta f(i) = \gamma_i + \Delta f(s_B(i)).$$

By virtue of the algorithm given, $\gamma_i \geqslant 0$.

Now suppose policy B involved a loop, which we may, by renumbering, take to be $1 \to 2 \to 3 \ldots k \to 1$.

Then

$$\Delta f(1) = \gamma_1 + \Delta f(2)$$
$$\Delta f(2) = \gamma_2 + \Delta f(3)$$
$$\cdot \qquad \cdot \qquad \cdot$$
$$\cdot \qquad \cdot \qquad \cdot$$
$$\cdot \qquad \cdot \qquad \cdot$$
$$\Delta f(k) = \gamma_k + \Delta f(1).$$

Adding up both sides, we get:

$$0 = \Sigma_s \gamma_s.$$

Since $\gamma_s \to 0$, for all s, we see that $\gamma_s = 0$ for $s = 1, 2, \ldots k$. Hence the contraction of policy B to this loop would be identical with the contraction of policy A to this loop, and since A has no loops, B can have no loops.* We then use the inductive argument, since, initially, $\{s_0(i)\}$ is taken to have no loops.

It is easy to see now that, since $\gamma_i \geqslant 0$, for all i, then so is $\Delta f(i) \geqslant 0$ for all i. Hence the sequence $\{f_n(i)\}$ is monotone decreasing; since $f_n(i) \geqslant 0$ always, the same reasoning as in the method of successive approximations, gives the desired results.

* If $s_A(i)$ minimises $c_j + f_A(j)$, then we set $s_B(i) = s_A(i)$.

A2.3. Uniqueness of Solution

Equation (2.2) has a unique solution $\{f(i)\}$ among the class of all functions with $f(N) = 0$.

Proof

Let $\{f(i)\}$, $\{F(i)\}$ be two solutions to equation (2.2) with $f(N) = F(N) = 0$. Let $\{s(i)\}$ be the policy associated with $\{f(i)\}$.

Then, from equation (2.2),

$$f(i) = \min_s [c_{is} + f(s)],$$
$$F(i) = \min_s [c_{is} + F(s)].$$

Then

$$f(i) - F(i) \geqslant f(s(i)) - F(s(i)) \geqslant f(s(s(i))) - F(s(s(i))) \geqslant \ldots$$

Repeating this process, since ultimately we arrive at point N, we see that

$$f(i) - F(i) \geqslant 0, \text{ all } i.$$

Reversing the process, by letting $S(i)$ be the policy associated with $F(i)$, we can prove $F(i) - f(i) \geqslant 0$, all i.

Hence $f(i) - F(i) = 0$, all i, as required.

Appendix to Chapter 3

A3.1. Expected Path Values

In Section 3.2, the following path value, in terms of state variables $x_r, x_{r+1}, \ldots x_s$, was given, viz.

$$_sV_r(x_r,d_r,x_{r+1}, \ldots x_s) = \min_{t=0,1,2, \ldots s-r-1}[c_{r+t}(x_{r+t},d_{r+t},x_{r+t+1})].$$

In the case where the system is stochastic it was stated in Chapter 3 that certainly no obvious relationship existed between expected minimum for a path and the expected minimum for a contracted path in terms of the state variables $x_r, \ldots x_s$. Thus if we define

$$_sv_r(x_r,\pi_r(\cdot)) = E_{x_{r+1},x_{r+2}, \ldots , x_s/x_r,\pi_r(\cdot)}\{_sV_r(x_r,\pi_r(x_r),x_{r+1}, \ldots x_s)\},$$

then we certainly do not obtain

$$_sv_r(x_r,\pi_r(\cdot)) = E_{x_{r+1}/x_r,\pi_r(\cdot)}\{\min[c_r(x_r,\pi_r(x_r),x_{r+1});_sv_{r+1}(x_{r+1},\pi_{r+1}(\cdot))]\}.$$

However let us introduce an extra variable set $z_r, z_{r+1}, \ldots z_s$ where

$$z_t = \min[z_{t-1},c_{t-1}(x_{t-1},\pi_{t-1}(x_{t-1}),x_t)].$$

Define

$$_sv_r^*(x_r,z_r,\pi_r^*(\cdot))$$

to be equal to

$$E_{x_{r+1},x_{r+2}, \ldots , x_s/x_r,\pi_r^*(\cdot)}\{_sV_r^*(u_r,\pi_r^*(u_r), \ldots u_s)\},$$

where $u_r \equiv [x_r,z_r]$, $\pi_r^*(\cdot)$ is the policy induced by $\pi_r(\cdot)$ and $_xV_r^*$ is the path value induced by $_sV_r$ in the space of $\{u_r\}$, i.e.

$$_sV_r^*(u_r,\pi_r^*(u_r), \ldots u_s) = \min[z_r;_sV_r(x_r,\pi_r(x_r), \ldots x_s)].$$

The induced state values now satisfy the equation

$$_sv_r^*(x_r,z_r,\pi_r^*(\cdot)) = E_{x_{r+1},x_{r+2}, \ldots , x_s/x_r,\pi_r(\cdot)}\{\min[z_r;c_r(x_r,\pi_r(x_r),x_{r+1});$$

$$c_{r+1}(x_{r+1},\pi_{r+1}(x_{r+1}),x_{r+2}); \ldots c_{s-1}(x_{s-1},\pi_{s-1}(x_{s-1}),x_s)]\}$$

$$= E_{x_{r+1} \mid x_r,\pi_r(\cdot)}\{E_{x_{r+2}, \ldots x_s/x_{r+1},\pi_{r+1}(\cdot)}\{\min[\min[z_r;$$

$$c_r(x_r,\pi_r(x_r),x_{r+1})];c_{r+1}(x_{r+1},\pi_{r+1}(x_{r+1}),x_{r+2});$$

$$\ldots c_{s-1}(x_{s-1},\pi_{s-1}(x_{s-1}),x_s)]\}\}$$

$$= E_{x_{r+1} \mid x_r,\pi_r(\cdot)}\{E_{x_{r+2}, \ldots x_s/x_{r+1},\pi_{r+1}(\cdot)} \min[z_{r+1},$$

$$c_{r+1}(\ldots),c_{r+2}(\ldots) \ldots]\}$$

$$= E_{x_{r+1} \mid x_r \cdot \pi_r(\cdot)}\{_sv_{r+1}^*(x_{r+1}, \min[z_r,c_r(x_r,\pi_r(x_r),x_{r+1})],$$

$$\pi_{r+1}^*(\cdot))\}\}.$$

Thus since $_sv_r(x_r,\pi_r(\cdot)) = {_sv_r^*}(x_r,x_r,\pi_r^*(\cdot))$ we have converted the original path values into ones which satisfy the second postulate, and from which the original path values can be derived. This is, of course, just one example of increasing the dimensionality of a problem to ensure that D.P. may be used.

A3.2. Principal of Optimality

It was mentioned in Chapter 3 that, even if postulate 2 holds for the state values of a system, the optimality principle may not do so. This is quite easy to demonstrate, for consider an equation of type 2 as follows,

$$_nv_r(x_r,\pi_r(\cdot)) = \alpha_r(x_r,\pi_r(x_r)) + \beta_r(x_r,\pi_r(x_r)) \cdot {_nv_{r+1}}(x_{r+1},\pi_{r+1}(\cdot)) +$$
$$\gamma_r(x_r,\pi_r(x_r))_nv_{r+1}^2(x_{r+1},\pi_{r+1}(\cdot)),$$

where

$$x_{r+1} = T_r(\pi_r(x_r)) \cdot x_r.$$

It is then fairly obvious that $_nv_r(x_r,\pi_r(\cdot))$ does not assume an optimal value simply if $d_r(=\pi_r(x_r))$ is chosen on the assumption that $_nv_{r+1}(x_{r+1},\pi_{r+1}(\cdot))$ is optimal.

Appendix to Chapter 4

A4.1. Validity of Lagrange Multiplier Method

Let our problem be one of maximising $\phi(x)$ subject to $\theta(x) = 0$. (We can do the same with several constraints, but one constraint is sufficient to illustrate the proof.)

Let the modified Lagrangian be

$$H(x,\lambda) = \phi(x) - \lambda\theta(x).$$

Let $x(\lambda)$ be the maximising function for $H(x,\lambda)$.

Then $H(x(\lambda),\lambda) \geqslant H(x,\lambda)$ for all x.

Suppose that we can vary λ until we get $x(\lambda^*)$ such that $\theta(x(\lambda^*)) = 0$.

Then we see easily that, for all x such that $\theta(x) = 0$,

$$\phi(x(\lambda^*)) = H(x(\lambda^*),\lambda^*) \geqslant H(x,\lambda^*) = \phi(x).$$

It is not necessary that the variable $x(\lambda)$ should trace a path meeting the region given by $\theta(x) = 0$, and, if this is the case, the method fails.

For example, let

$$\phi(x) = e^{-(x_1 - a)^2 - (x_2 - b)^2}, \ \theta(x) = x_2 - x_1,$$

Then the true optimum is given by

$$x_1 = x_2 = (a+b)/2$$

and is equal to $e^{-(a-b)^2/2}$.

Now

$$H(x,\lambda) = e^{-(x_1 - a)^2 - (x_2 - b)^2} - \lambda(x_2 - x_1).$$

For any $\lambda \neq 0$ the maximising values of x_2, x_1 have one infinite value between them at least (both will be infinite if we allow negative values of course, but the sufficiency condition holds if we restrict x to any region, i.e. if $x(\lambda)$ maximises $H(x,\lambda)$ subject to $x \in R$, and if $\theta(x(\lambda)) = 0$, then $x(\lambda)$ maximises $\phi(x)$ subject to $x \in R$, $\theta(x) = 0$) and hence we can never arrive at the point $x_1 = x_2 = (a+b)/2$ for any $\lambda \neq 0$. For $\lambda = 0$ we get the point $x_1 = a$, $x_2 = b$. Hence the method fails in this case.

A necessary condition that $x(\lambda)$ shall eventually meet $\theta(x) = 0$ is that there exist a λ such that, if x^* is the true optimum, $\phi(x^*) \geqslant \phi(x) - \lambda\theta(x)$ for all $x \in R$, and this condition fails in the above example. Such a λ will exist if

$$\min_{x:\theta(x) \geqslant 0} \left[(\phi(x^*) - \phi(x))/\theta(x)\right] \geqslant \max_{x:\theta(x) \leqslant 0} \left[(\phi(x^*) - \phi(x))/\theta(x)\right].$$

It is easy to construct examples in which $\phi(x)$ has local optimal unrestricted, except for $x \in R$, either side of the manifold $\theta(x) = 0$, which violate the previous conditions.

A4.2. Proof of Inequality (4.8)

Referring to the relevant section for the background information, we see that, if $X(x,\lambda) = J(x) - \Sigma_s \lambda_s H_s(x)$, then

$$X(x(\lambda),\lambda) \geqslant X(x(\lambda'),\lambda)$$

$$X(x(\lambda'),\lambda') \geqslant X(x(\lambda),\lambda').$$

Then

$$X(x(\lambda),\lambda) - X(x(\lambda),\lambda') \geqslant X(x(\lambda'),\lambda) - X(x(\lambda') - \lambda')$$

i.e.

$$\Sigma_s(\lambda'_s - \lambda_s)H_s(x(\lambda)) \geqslant \Sigma_s(\lambda'_s - \lambda_s)H_s(x(\lambda'))$$

i.e.

$$\Sigma_s(\lambda'_s - \lambda_s)(H_s(x(\lambda)) - H_s(x(\lambda'))) \geqslant 0.$$

A4.3. Proof of Convergence of $\{v_n(0)\}$ in Equation (4.15)

Let $v_n(0) = u_n$ for convenience.

Then if $m^*(n-1)$ is the optimal $(n-1)$ period decision, we have

$$u_{n-1} = \sum_{k=0}^{m^*-1} \alpha^k c(k) + \alpha^{m^*}(p - s(m^*)) + \alpha^{m^*} u_{n-1-m^*},$$

$$u_n \leqslant \sum_{k=0}^{m^*-1} \alpha^k c(k) + \alpha^{m^*}(p - s(m^*)) + \alpha^{m^*} u_{n-m^*}.$$

Since $u_n \geqslant u_{n-1}$ quite obviously (the proof is trivial) we then have

$$0 \leqslant u_n - u_{n-1} \leqslant \alpha^{m^*}\{u_{n-m^*} - u_{n-1-m^*}\}.$$

Let

$$\Delta_n = \max_{l \leqslant n}[u_l - u_{l-1}].$$

Then, since $u_k = 0$ $(k \leqslant 0)$,

$$\Delta_n = \max_{0 \leqslant l \leqslant n}[u_l - u_{l-1}],$$

$$\leqslant \max_{0 \leqslant l \leqslant n}[\alpha^{m^*(l-1)}\{u_{l-m^*(l-1)} - u_{l-1-m^*(l-1)}\}],$$

$$\leqslant \alpha \max_{0 \leqslant l \leqslant n}[u_{l-m^*(l-1)} - u_{l-1-m^*(l-1)}],$$

(providing we assume $m^*(l) \geqslant 1$ for all l, which it will be in most cases, and, in any case, if we restrict to integer values, this must be so)

$$\leqslant \alpha \max_{0 \leqslant l' \leqslant n-1}[u_{l'} - u_{l'-1}],$$

$$= \alpha \Delta_{n-1}.$$

Thus, repeating this argument, we have $\Delta_n \leqslant \alpha^{n-1}\Delta_1$. Now

$$\Delta_1 = u_1 \quad (\text{since } u_0 = 0)$$

$$= c(0) + \alpha(p - s(1)),$$

(we assume that the last piece of equipment is sold and a new one bought in formulating (4.14), but we do not need to do so. We can, in fact, assume that, if the optimising m equals n, then the equipment is sold, but this just complicates the analysis, since then $v_n(t)$ would satisfy the equation

$$v_n(t) = \min\left[\sum_0^{n-1} \alpha^k c(k) - \alpha^n s(t+n);\right.$$

$$\left.\min_{0 \leqslant m \leqslant n-1}\left[\sum_0^{m-1} \alpha^k c(k+t) + \alpha^m(p - s(t+m)) + \alpha^m v_{n-m}(0)\right]\right].$$

We can analyse this equation in the same way and still establish convergence.)

We therefore see that $\Delta_n \leqslant \alpha^{n-1} M$ for some $M < \infty$ and all n. This establishes that $\{u_n\}$ converges and the limit must then satisfy (4.16).

A4.4. Proof of Convergence of $\{v_n(t,T)\}$ in Equation (4.19)

We have, using a similar approach to the above,

$$0 \leqslant v_n(t,T) - v_{n-1}(t,T) \leqslant \alpha^{m^*}(v_{n-m^*}(0,T+m^*) - v_{n-1-m^*}(0,T+m^*)),$$

where m^* is the optimal decision for the $(n-1)$ stage problem.

Hence the result follows if $\{v_n(0,T)\}$ is uniformly convergent for all T. Let $v_n(0,T) = u_n(T)$ for convenience. Then

$$0 \leqslant u_n(T) - u_{n-1}(T) \leqslant \alpha^{m^*}(u_{n-m^*}(T+m^*) - u_{n-1-m^*}(T+m^*)),$$

where m^* is the optimal $(n-1)$ stage decision, and we must have $m^* \geqslant 1$ since we have new equipment each time and our decision is how long to keep it. If we allow m to be non-integral then we impose the condition $m \geqslant 1$.

Let
$$\Delta_n(T) = \max_{\substack{\sigma \geqslant T \\ l \leqslant n}}[u_l(\sigma) - u_{l-1}(\sigma)].$$

Then
$$\Delta_n(T) \leqslant \alpha \Delta_{n-1}(T+1) \ldots \leqslant \alpha^{n-1}\Delta_1(T+n-1).$$

In this case $0 \leqslant \Delta_1(T) \leqslant c(0,T) + \alpha(p(T) - s(1,T))$.
Hence, providing

$$\sum_0^{n-1} \alpha^r\{c(0,T+r) + \alpha(p(T+r) - s(1,T+r))\}$$

is uniformly convergent for all T, the results follow.

A4.5. Derivation of Equations (4.60), (4.61)

Let
$$t(y,x) = \rho(y/x).$$
Then
$T_2(x)$ is given by
$$T_1(y) = \rho(y/x),$$
i.e.
$$\rho(p/y) = \rho(y/x).$$

12

Thus $y = (px)^{\frac{1}{2}}$ and $T_2(x) = T_1((px)^{\frac{1}{2}}) = \rho((p/x)^{\frac{1}{2}})$.

Now let $T_r(x) = \rho((p/x)^{1/r})$, $\mu_r(x) = (px^{r-1})^{1/r}$.

Then $T_{r+1}(x)$ is given by

$$T_r(y) = \rho(y/x).$$

Thus
$$\rho((p/y)^{1/r}) = \rho(y/x).$$
$$y = (px^r)^{1/r+1} \quad \text{and} \quad T_{r+1}(x) = \rho((p/x)^{1/r+1}).$$

Hence the results follow inductively.

A4.6. Proof of the Exactness of Equation (4.122)

Let $g(x) = g(x_1, x_2, \ldots x_l)$ be polynomial of degree $2S-1$ in x_k individually, $k = 1, 2, \ldots l$.

Then

$$g(x) = \sum_{n_1=0}^{2S-1} \sum_{n_2=0}^{2S-1} \cdots \sum_{n_l=0}^{2S-1} \alpha_{n_1 n_2 \ldots n_l} x_1^{n_1} x_2^{n_2} \cdots x_l^{n_l}.$$

Then

$$\int_{-1}^{1} dx_1 \int_{-1}^{1} dx_2 \cdots \int_{-1}^{1} dx_l (g(x)) = \sum_{n_1=0}^{2S-1} \sum_{n_2=0}^{2S-1} \cdots \sum_{n_l=0}^{2S-1} \alpha_{n_1 n_2 \ldots n_l}$$

$$\int_{-1}^{1} x_1^{n_1} dx_1 \int_{-1}^{1} x_2^{n_2} dx_2 \cdots \int_{-1}^{1} x_l^{n_l} dx_l.$$

Now

$$\int_{-1}^{1} x_k^{n_k} dx_k = \sum_{j=1}^{S} a_j \mu_j^{n_k}, \qquad k = 1, 2, \ldots l$$

(this relation is exact if $n_k \leqslant 2S-1$).

Therefore

$$\int_{-1}^{1} dx_1 \int_{-1}^{1} dx_2 \cdots \int_{-1}^{1} dx_l (g(x))$$

$$= \sum_{n_1=0}^{2S-1} \sum_{n_2=0}^{2S-1} \cdots \sum_{n_l=0}^{2S-1} \alpha_{n_1 n_2, , , n_l} \prod_{k=1}^{l} \sum_{j=1}^{S} a_j \mu_j^{n_k}$$

$$= \sum_{j_1=1}^{S} \sum_{j_2=1}^{S} \cdots \sum_{j_l=1}^{S} a_{j_1} a_{j_2} \cdots a_{j_l} \sum_{n_1=0}^{2S-1} \sum_{n_2=0}^{2S-1} \cdots \sum_{n_l=0}^{2S-1} \alpha_{n_1 n_2, , , n_l} \mu_1^{n_1} \mu_{j_2}^{n_2} \cdots \mu_{j_l}^{n_l}$$

$$= \sum_{j_1=1}^{S} \sum_{j_2=1}^{S} \cdots \sum_{j_l=1}^{S} a_{j_1} a_{j_2} \cdots a_{j_l} g(\mu_{j_1}, \mu_{j_2}, \ldots \mu_{j_l}).$$

This is the required result.

Appendix to Chapter 5

STOCHASTIC PROCESSES

A5.1. Validity of Howard's Functional Equation

Defining $v_n(i,\pi_n)$ to be the expected return over the next n periods of time beginning in state i and using policy π_n, we see that, because of the additivity assumption,

$$v_n(i,\pi_n) = q_i^{\pi_n(i)} + \Sigma_j p_{ij}^{\pi_n(i)} v_{n-1}(j,\pi_{n-1}),$$

where π_{n-1} is the forward contraction of π_n to the remaining $(n-1)$ periods (see Chapter 3).

Then if $v_m(s) = \max_{\pi_m} [v_m(s,\pi_m)]$ we see that, since $p_{ij}^{\pi_n(i)} \geqslant 0$,

$$
\begin{aligned}
v_n(i) &= \max_{\pi_n}[v_n(i,\pi_n)] \\
&= \max_{\pi_n(i)\pi_{n-1}}[q_i^{\pi_n(i)} + \Sigma_j p_{ij}^{\pi_n(i)} v_{n-1}(j,\pi_{n-1})] \\
&= \max_{\pi_n(i)}[q_i^{\pi_n(i)} + \Sigma_j p_{ij}^{\pi_n(i)} \max_{\pi_{n-1}}[v_{n-1}(j,\pi_{n-1})]] \\
&= \max_{\pi_n(i)}[q_i^{\pi_n(i)} + \Sigma_j p_{ij}^{\pi_n(i)} v_{n-1}(j)] \\
&= \max_k[q_i^k + \Sigma_j p_{ij}^k v_{n-1}(j)].
\end{aligned}
$$

Of course the same results apply if we include a discount factor α.

A5.2. Proof of Equation (5.8)

We have

$$v(i) \leqslant E_i^k + \Sigma_j p_{ij}^k v(j) - kg \text{ for all } k.$$

Hence

$$g \leqslant \{E_i^k + \Sigma_j p_{ij}^k v(j) - v(i)\}/k \text{ for all } k.$$

For the optimal policy, equation (5.8) gives equality for some $k^*(i)$. Hence

$$g = \min_k[\{E_i^k + \Sigma_j p_{ij}^k v(j) - v(i)\}/k].$$

A5.3. Proof that Optimal Sampling Policy Implies Equal Intervals when Items are Independent

Our condition requires that $\{p_{1i}^k\} = \{p_{2i}^k\}$. From equations (5.13) our results will follow if we can show that $v(1) = 0$, for the other elements are identical in both equations.

However, we easily derive, by subtracting both equations, $0 \geqslant -v(1)/k(1)$, and $0 \leqslant -v(1)/k(2)$. Hence $v(1) = 0$.

A5.4 Proof of Transformed Equation (5.65)

We have, for all n,

$$f(N) \leqslant s + nc + \sum_{m=1}^{N-1} p(n,m)f(N-m) + p(n,0)f(N)$$

i.e. for all n,

$$f(N) \leqslant \left\{ s + nc + \sum_{m=1}^{N-1} p(n,m)f(N-m) \right\} \Big/ \{1 - p(n,0)\}.$$

Hence, since the above inequality becomes an equality for the optimal $n = n^*$,

$$f(N) = \min_n \left[\left\{ s + nc + \sum_{m=1}^{N-1} p(n,m)f(N-m) \right\} \Big/ \{1 - p(n,0)\} \right].$$

A5.5. Proof of Equation (5.101)

From equation (5.95) we see easily that $g_2(y) \geqslant g_1(y)$. From equation (5.97), $g_n(y) - g_{n-1}(y) \geqslant \mu_{n-1} - \mu_{n-2}$. From equation (5.96), $\mu_{n-1} - \mu_{n-2} = p^{-1} \int (g_{n-1}(y) - g_{n-2}(y)) dF(y)$. Hence if $g_{n-1}(y) \geqslant g_{n-2}(y)$, for all y, so is $g_n(y) \geqslant g_{n-1}(y)$ for all y. Therefore $\{g_n(y)\}$ is monotonic increasing in n. Hence so is $\{\mu_n\}$ monotonic increasing in n. However, from equation (5.100) $\mu_n \leqslant p^{-1}\{\mu_{n-1} + M\}$ if $G(0) \leqslant M < \infty$. Hence, since $p > 1$, $\{\mu_n\}$ is monotonic increasing and bounded and therefore converges to a limit μ.

Since $\mu F(\mu) + G(\mu)$ is monotonic increasing in μ (established by differentiating, since F has a density function) we now have

$$\mu \geqslant \mu_n = p^{-1}(\mu_{n-1}F(\mu_{n-1}) + G(\mu_{n-1})) \text{ for all } n$$
$$\geqslant p^{-1}(\mu F(\mu) + G(\mu))$$

and

$$\mu_n = p^{-1}(\mu_{n-1}F(\mu_{n-1}) + G(\mu_{n-1}))$$
$$\leqslant p^{-1}(\mu F(\mu) + G(\mu)) \text{ for all } n.$$

Hence $\mu \leqslant p^{-1}(\mu F(\mu) + G(\mu)) \leqslant \mu$ and the required result follows.

Appendix to Chapter 6

A6.1. Sufficient Statistics

It will be proved here that, if sufficient statistics exist in the classical sense, then they are also sufficient state variables for the D.P. model in the case where successive observations are independently distributed.

To do this we have to show two things, viz.

(*i*) that all probabilities can be expressed in terms of the sufficient statistic, and

(*ii*) that the sufficient statistic at the $(n+1)$th stage depends only on the sufficient statistic at the nth stage plus the intervening observations.

Using the definitions as given in Chapter 6, we first of all note that, if z_n is the (vector) sufficient statistic at the nth stage, then:

$$dF_n(x_1, x_2, \ldots x_n/\alpha) = d\Phi_n(z_n, \alpha) dX_n(x_1, x_2, \ldots x_n).$$

We then see that

$$dG_n(\alpha/x_1, x_2, \ldots x_n) = \frac{d\Phi_n(z_n, \alpha) dX_n(x_1, x_2, \ldots x_n) dG_0(\alpha)}{\displaystyle\int_\alpha d\Phi_n(z_n, \alpha) dX_n(x_1, x_2, x_3, \ldots x_n) dG_0(\alpha)}$$

$$= \frac{dG_0(\alpha) d\Phi_n(z_n, \alpha)}{\displaystyle\int_\alpha d\Phi_n(z_n, \alpha) dG_0(\alpha)}$$

$$dF_n(x_{n+1}/x_1, x_2, \ldots x_n) = \int_\alpha dF_{n+1}(x_{n+1}/\alpha) dG_n(\alpha/x_1, x_2, \ldots x_n)$$

$$= \frac{\displaystyle\int_\alpha d\Phi_n(z_n, \alpha) dF_{n+1}(x_{n+1}/\alpha) dG_0(\alpha)}{\displaystyle\int_\alpha d\Phi_n(z_n, \alpha) dG_0(\alpha)}$$

Thus, providing the observations are independently distributed, the *a posteriori* distributions of α and x_{n+1}, given $x_1, x_2, \ldots x_n$, depend only on z_n. A further discussion of the equivalence of the Baysian and classical definitions of sufficiency, again under the independence assumption, is given in Raiffa and Schlaiffer.[39]

For the second point, we note that

$$dF_{n+1}(x_1,x_2,\ldots x_{n+1}/\alpha) = d\Phi_{n+1}(z_{n+1},\alpha)dX_{n+1}(x_1,x_2,\ldots x_{n+1})$$
$$= dF_{n+1}(x_{n+1}/\alpha)dF_n(x_1,x_2,\ldots x_n/\alpha)$$
$$= dF_{n+1}(x_{n+1}/\alpha)d\Phi_n(z_n,\alpha)dX_n(x_1,x_2,\ldots x_n).$$

Therefore

$$d\Phi_{n+1}(z_{n+1},\alpha)/d\Phi_n(z_n,\alpha)dF_{n+1}(x_{n+1},\alpha) =$$
$$dX_n(x_1,x_2,\ldots x_n)/dX_{n+1}(x_1,x_2,\ldots x_{n+1}).$$

Thus we see that the first expression is independent of α. Taking two such values of α, such that $d\Phi_n(z_n,\alpha_1)/d\Phi_n(z_n,\alpha_2)$ is not constant for all values of z_n (and this, we assume, is possible), and equating these expressions, we see that z_{n+1} is some function of z_n and x_{n+1}, as required.

The outcome of these analyses is that, if $x_1,x_2,\ldots x_n$, are the variables subject to observation, which are described probabilistically as above, and s is any other state vector needed for completeness of description, then if $v_n(x_1,x_2,\ldots x_n,s)$ is the optimal value from the nth stage on, we can adequately represent this by $v_n(z_n,s)$, thus simplifying the computations.

A6.2. The Form of Policy in Section (6.4.1)

Let us assume that, for some n, an optimal action is S, i.e. take a further sample.

Then since $f(n) = \min \begin{bmatrix} k/(n+1) \\ c+f(n+1) \end{bmatrix}$

we must have $f(n) = c+f(n+1) \leqslant k/(n+1)$.

Now $\quad f(n-1) = \min \begin{bmatrix} k/n \\ c+f(n) \end{bmatrix}$.

Also

$$|f(n)-f(n+1)| \leqslant \max [k/(n+1)-k/(n+2); \ |f(n+1)-f(n+2)|\ ]$$
$$\leqslant \max_{t \geqslant 1} [k/(n+t)-k/(n+t+1)]$$
$$\leqslant k/(n+1)(n+2),$$

whence $\quad f(n) \leqslant k/(n+1)(n+2)+f(n+1).$

Thus $\quad c+f(n) \leqslant k/(n+1)(n+2)+c+f(n+1)$
$$\leqslant k/(n+1)(n+2)+k/(n+1)$$
$$= (n+3)k/(n+1)(n+2).$$

Thus $c+f(n) \leqslant k/n$ if

$$n(n+3) \leqslant (n+1)(n+2),$$

i.e. $0 \leqslant 2$.

Hence $c+f(n) < k/n$.

Therefore if an optimal action is S for n, then S for $(n-1)$ is also an optimal action. Hence the optimal policy is a predetermined sample size followed by choosing $\hat{\beta} = ms/(m+1)$.

A6.3. The Computational Algorithms of Section 6.4.2

(i) Bellman's Method of Successive Approximations

We see easily that, if $k \geqslant 2$

$$v_k(m,n) - v_{k-1}(m,n) \leqslant \max[0; p(m,n)(v_{k-1}(m+1,n) - v_{k-2}(m+1,n)) +$$

$$(1 - p(m,n))(v_{k-1}(m,n+1) - v_{k-2}(m,n+1))].$$

Hence if $v_{k-1}(m,n) \leqslant v_{k-2}(m,n)$ for all arguments m,n then $v_k(m,n) \leqslant v_{k-1}(m,n)$ for all arguments. However, $v_2(m,n) - v_1(m,n) \leqslant 0$ since $v_1(m,n) = u(m,n)$.

Therefore, the sequence $\{v_k(m,n)\}$ is monotonic decreasing in k and uniformly bounded below by zero for all m,n, and is therefore convergent to some function $v(m,n)$.

Since $\{v_k(m,n)\}$ is convergent, it is uniformly convergent over the finite set of three states, (m,n), $(m+1,n)$, $(m,n+1)$, generated by a fixed (m,n). The fact that $v(m,n)$ satisfies the original equation now follows, as with the proof of the convergence in the 'Optimal Path' problem, since, for a given (m,n), only the above three states are involved, and we can make $v_k(m,n)$, $v_{k-1}(m+1,n)$, $v_{k-1}(m,n+1)$ as arbitrarily close to $v(m,n)$, $v(m+1,n)$, $v(m,n+1)$ respectively, as we wish.

We need to show uniqueness, for otherwise we would not know if the sequence converged to the correct result. Let $v(m,n)$, $v^*(m,n)$ be two solutions, both satisfying the conditions specified in Section 6.4.2.

We have, if

$$\Delta(m,n) = \max_{m' \geqslant m, n' \geqslant n} [\,|\,v(m',n') - v^*(m',n')\,|\,],$$

$$\Delta(m,n) \leqslant \max[\Delta(m+1,n), \Delta(m,n+1)].$$

Now let $u(m,n) \leqslant \varepsilon(T) \leqslant c$ if $m+n \geqslant T$.
Then, for sufficiently large T,

$$v(m',n') = u(m',n') \text{ for } m'+n' \geqslant T$$

$$v^*(m',n') = u(m',n') \text{ for } m'+n' \geqslant T.$$

Repeating the above inequality a sufficient number of times, we get $\Delta(m',n') = 0$ for $(m'+n')$ sufficiently large. Hence $\Delta(m,n) = 0$ for all m,n, and, therefore, $v(m,n)$ is a unique solution to the problem.

A6.4. The Computational Algorithms for Section 6.4.3

i) Bellman's Method of Successive Approximations

We see that, for $k \geqslant 2$,

$$f_{k+1}(N,m,n) - f_k(N,m,n) \geqslant \sum_{0 < l \leqslant N} q(M^*, N-l, m, n)\{f_k(l, m+M^* - N+l,$$

$$n+N-l) - f_{k-1}(l, m+M^* - N+l, n+N-l)\},$$

where M^* is the optimal solution to the $(k+1)$ stage problem.

Therefore, if $f_k(N,m,n) \geqslant f_{k-1}(N,m,n)$ for all arguments, N,m,n, we see that $f_{k+1}(N,m,n) \geqslant f_k(N,m,n)$ for all arguments, N,m,n.

Now

$$f_2(N,m,n) - f_1(N,m,n) \geqslant$$

$$\sum_{0 < l \leqslant N} q(M, N-l, m, n) f_1(l, m+M-N+l, n+N-l)$$

for all $M \geqslant 0$, and, since $f_1(N,m,n) \geqslant 0$, we see that $f_2(N,m,n) \geqslant f_1(N,m,n)$ for all arguments, N,m,n.

Therefore, we see that $\{f_k(N,m,n)\}$ forms a monotonic increasing sequence in k. To show convergence, all we need to do now is to show that the sequence $\{f_k(N,m,n)\}$ is bounded for fixed N.

We see that $f_k(N,m,n)$ is actually equal to the expected cost over k stages, using an optimal policy, terminating the process when N items have been provided at least, and, should there be a final stage, ending up with $f_1(N,m,n)$ as defined. This expectation is conditional on m,n being given.

If we select a policy in which we always put into production a quantity equal to the outstanding deficit at any stage, and if $F_k(N,m,n)$ is the k stage expected cost of such a policy, we see that

$$f_k(N,m,n) \leqslant F_k(N,m,n)$$

and, if $n > 0$

$$F_k(N,m,n) = s + Nc + \sum_{0 < l \leqslant N} q(N, N-l, m, n) F_{k-1}(l, m+l, n+N-l).$$

Now suppose p were fixed, and we adopted the same policy. Then, if we define $F_k(N,p)$ as the expected cost using this policy, conditional on p, we easily see, either by expanding the equation for $F_k(N,m,n)$, or from *a priori* reasoning, that

$$F_k(N,m,n) = \int_p F_k(N,p) dG_{m,n}(p),$$

where, as in Section 6.4.2, $G_{m,n}(p)$ is the conditional distribution of p, given m,n.

Now let $E_k(N,p)$ be the expected number of stages required, either to complete the order, or exhaust the k stages, whichever is the first. Then

$$F_k(N,p) \leqslant (s+Nc)E_k(N,p).$$

If $N>0$

$$E_k(N,p) = 1 + \sum_{l=1}^{N} \binom{N}{l} p^l (1-p)^{N-l} E_{k-1}(l,p).$$

Obviously $E_{k-1}(l,p) \leqslant E_{k-1}(N,p)$. Hence:

$$E_k(N,p) \leqslant 1 + (1-(1-p)^N)E_{k-1}(N,p).$$

Repeating this argument, if $p \neq 1$,

$$E_k(N,p) \leqslant 1 + (1-(1-p)^N) + (1-(1-p)^N)^2 + \ldots +$$
$$(1-(1-p)^N)^{k-1}E_1(N,p)$$
$$= (1-(1-(1-p)^N)^k)/(1-p)^N$$
$$\leqslant (1-p)^{-N}.$$

Therefore we see that $f_k(N,m,n)$ will be uniformly bounded over m,n, for fixed N and all k if

$$\int_p p^m(1-p)^{n-N}dG_0(p) \bigg/ \int_p p^m(1-p)^n dG_0(p)$$

is uniformly bounded over m,n for all N.

A less restrictive condition requires only that the above quantity be uniformly bounded for all m above some finite m^*, since

$$F_k(N,m,n) \leqslant \alpha(s+Nc) + F_k(N,m^*,n)$$

where $\alpha = 1 + \text{integral part of } (m^*/N)$.

Therefore, under these conditions, the sequence $\{f_k(N,m,n)\}$ is monotone increasing and uniformly bounded for all m,n,k, and hence converges to some function $f(N,m,n)$. The convergence need not be uniform over N,m,n, but, since N never increases, and, for a given N, the sequence $\{f_k(N,m,n)\}$ is uniformly convergent on the set of points $(N-z,m,n)$, $(N-z,m+1,n)$, $(N-z,m,n+1)$, $0 \leqslant z \leqslant N$, the proof used in Section 6.4.2 can be modified to prove that the limiting function, $f(N,m,n)$, does, indeed, satisfy the basic functional equation.

It is fairly obvious, from the form of the sequence, that this solution is a solution to our problem. However, for rigour, it is useful to establish that the functional equation has only one solution for $f(N,m,n)$.

Let $f(N,m,n)$, $f^*(N,m,n)$ be two such solutions with $f(0,m,n) \equiv f^*(0,m,n) \equiv 0$.

Define $\Delta(N) = \max_{u \leqslant N} \max_{m,n} [\,|f(u,m,n)-f^*(u,m,n)|\,]$.

Then we derive:

$$\Delta(N) \leqslant \max_{\substack{M \geqslant N \\ m,n \geqslant 0}} \left[\left(\sum_{0 < l \leqslant N} q(M,N-l,m,n) \right) \Delta(N) \right].$$

We have assumed $M \geqslant N$, but there is, in this problem, no advantage in putting into production less then we need, since we are not learning how to produce items, but are only learning about the actual production quality.

The summed expression is the probability that less than N acceptable items will be produced and, hence, is a maximum when $M = N$ and is equal to $1 - q(N,N,m,n)$, where

$$q(N,N,m,n) = \int_0^1 p^m(1-p)^{N+n}dG_0(p)\Big/\int_0^1 p^m(1-p)^n dG_0(p).$$

$q(N,N,m,n)$ takes its minimum value over m, n when $n = 0$ and $m = \infty$ and hence if

$$Lt_{m\to\infty}\left\{\int_0^1 p^m(1-p)^N dG_0(p)\Big/\int_0^1 p^m dG_0(p)\right\} \geqslant \delta > 0$$

we see that $\Delta(N) \leqslant (1-\delta)\Delta(N)$, and since $\Delta(N) \geqslant 0$ we must have $\Delta(N) = 0$.

Therefore, under the condition on $Lt_{m\to\infty}\{q(N,N,m,0)\}$, $f(N,m,n)$ is a unique solution of the functional equation.

Referring to the condition required to establish the boundedness of $f(N,m,n)$, for a specific N, putting $n = N$, this expression reduces to

$$\int_0^1 p^m dG_0(p)\Big/\int_0^1 p^m(1-p)^n dG_0(p) < \infty$$

and this reduces to precisely what we require above, if we add 'uniformly bounded for all m' instead of simply 'finite'.

(ii) The Directed Method of Computation

We see easily that

$$|\, f(N,m',n) - f(N,m,n)\,|$$

$$\leqslant \max_M\left[\sum_{l=1}^{N} q(M,N-l,m'n)\{f(l,m'+M-N+l,n+N-i) -\right.$$

$$f(l,m+M-N+l,n+N-l)\} + \sum_{l=1}^{N}\{q(M,N-l,m',n) -$$

$$\left. q(M,N-l,m,n)\} f(l,m+M-N+l,n+N-l)\right].$$

Define

$$\Delta(N,m,n) = \max_{\substack{m' \geqslant m \\ n' \geqslant n \\ u \leqslant N}}\left[\,|\, f(u,m'n') - f(u,m,n')\,|\,\right]$$

$$z(N,m,n) = \max_{\substack{m' \geqslant m \\ M \geqslant N}} \left[\sum_{l \leqslant 1}^{N} q(M,N-l,m',n) \right] =$$

$$\max_{m' \geqslant m} \left[\sum_{l=1}^{N} q(N,N-l,m',n) \right]$$

$$= \max_{m' \geqslant m} [1 - q(N,N,m',n)]$$

$$h(N,m,n) = \max_{\substack{m' \geqslant m \\ M \geqslant N \\ 1 \leqslant l \leqslant N}} \left[\, |\, q(M,N-l,m',n) - q(M,N-l,m,n)\, |\, \right].$$

Then we see that: for some $M = \hat{M}$,

$$\Delta(M,m,n) \leqslant z(N,m,n)\Delta(N,m,n) + h(N,m,n)f(N,m+\hat{M},n).$$

This follows, since if $m' \geqslant m$, $l \leqslant N \leqslant M$, we have on the right hand side of the original inequality, $m' + M - N + l \geqslant m$, $n + N - l \geqslant n$ and hence,

$$|\, f(l,m'+M-N+l,n+N-l) - f(l,m+M-N+l,n+N-l)\, |\ \leqslant \Delta(N,m,n).$$

Also

$$f(l,m+M-N+l,n+N-l) \leqslant f(N,m+M,n).$$

Therefore, if $z(N,m,n) \neq 1$, for all $M \geqslant N$, we have

$$\Delta(N,m,n) \leqslant h(N,m,n)f(N,m+\hat{M},n)/\min_{m' \geqslant m} [q(N,N,m',n)].$$

Now, under the conditions assumed in the proof of Bellman's method of successive approximations, we have, for all M,

$$f(N,m+M,n) \leqslant (s+Nc) \left\{ \frac{\displaystyle\int_0^1 p^{m*}(1-p)^{n-N}dG_0(p)}{\displaystyle\int_0^1 p^{m*}(1-p)^n dG_0(p)} + \alpha \right\} \leqslant (s+Nc)\lambda(N,n),$$

say,

using the results obtained in the analysis of Bellman's method of successive approximations.

Now

$$\min_{m' \geqslant m} [q(N,N,m',n)] = Lt_{m' \to \infty} \{q(N,N,m',n)\}$$

$$= Lt_{m' \to \infty} \left\{ \int_0^1 p^{m'}(1-p)^{n+N}dG_0(p) \Big/ \int_0^1 p^{m'}(1-p)^n dG_0(p) \right\}$$

$$\geqslant \mu(N,n) > 0$$

as a consequence of the uniform boundedness assumption.

We therefore have:

$$\Delta(N,m,n) \leqslant h(N,m,n)\lambda(N,n)/\mu(N,n).$$

We now make a further assumption, viz. given $\varepsilon > 0$, $\exists m = m(\varepsilon,N,n)$ such that '$m \geqslant m(\varepsilon,N,n)$' implies '$h(N,m,n) \leqslant \varepsilon$'. A rigorous proof that this is true generally appears to be very difficult. An heuristic proof might follow from noting that for each p, such that $G_0(p) < 1$ there is an

$m(N,n,p)$ such that $q(M,N-l,m,n) \geqslant p^{M-N+l}(1-p)^{N-l}$ for $m \geqslant m(N,n,p)$, and hence $q(M,N-l,m,n)$ has, as a limit, as $m \to \infty$ the limit of the sequence of all p such that $G_0(p) < 1$.

Under these conditions, for $m > m(\varepsilon,N,n)$

$$\Delta(N,m,n) \leqslant \varepsilon \lambda(N,n)/\mu(N,n).$$

Returning to the functional equation we now have:

$$f(N,m,n) = \min_{M \geqslant N} [s + Mc + q(M,0,m,n)f(N,m+M,n) + \sum_{0 < l < N} q(M,N-l,m,n)f(l,m+M+l-N,n+N-l)].$$

Therefore, for all $M \geqslant N$,

$$f(N,m,n) \leqslant s + Mc + q(M,0,m,n)(f(N,m+M,n) - f(N,m,n))$$
$$+ q(M,0,m,n)f(N,m,n)$$
$$+ \sum_{0 < l < N} q(M,N-l,m,n)f(l,m+M+l-N,n+N-l).$$

As in Chapter 5, we therefore derive

$$f(N,m,n) =$$

$$\min_{M \geqslant N} \left[\frac{\{s + Mc + q(M,0,m,n)(f(N,m+M,n) - f(N,m,n)) + \sum_{0 < l < N} q(M,N-l,m,n)f(l,m+M+l-N,n+N-l)\}}{(1 - q(M,0,m,n))} \right].$$

The solution procedure is now straight forward.

(i) Choose m^* large enough to make $|f(N,m^*+M,n) - f(N,m^*,n)|$ as small as possible, (as a consequence of the convergence of $\Delta(N,m,n)$ to zero as m becomes large). We might guess at m^* and check the smallness of this difference later on, or use the expression for $\Delta(N,m,n)$.

(ii) Assuming $f(l,m',n')$ is known for all $0 \leqslant l < N$, and all $m' > m$, $n' > n$ we can then compute $f(N,m,n)$ as accurately as we want to (depending on the choice of m^*).

(iii) We can then compute $f(N,m,n)$ directly for all $m < m^*$.

To complete the proposed algorithm we need to be able to compute $f_1(N,m,n)$ for all m, n, and this can be computed as in (i) for sufficiently large m, in accordance with the convergence of $\Delta(1,m,n)$. More specifically,

$$f(1,m,n) \sim \min_{M \geqslant N} [(s + Mc)/(1 - q(M,0,m,n))].$$

It is worth noting that these results reduce to those in Chapter 5 for the non-adaptive case.

REFERENCES

1. M. AOKI. On optimal and sub-optimal policies in the choice of control forces for final value systems. *I.R.E. natn Conr. Rev.*, pt. 4, 1960, pp. 15–21.
2. —— On the minimum of maximum expected deviation from an unstable equilibrium position of a randomly perturbed control system. *I.R.E. Trans. autom. Control*, 7, no. 2, 1962, pp. 1–12.
3. —— Dynamic programming approach to a final value control system with a random variable having an unknown distribution function. *I.R.E. Trans. autom. Control*, 5, no. 4, 1960, pp. 270–83.
4. —— *Dynamic programming and numerical experimentation as applied to adaptive control systems.* Ph.D. Thesis, University of California, 1960.
5. R. ARIS. *The optimal design of chemical reactors.* Academic Press, 1961.
6. S. AZEN. *Some applications of polynomial approximation to dynamic programming.* Rand Corporation, RM–3728–PR, August, 1963.
7. M. BARTLETT. *Stochastic processes.* Cambridge University Press, 1956.
8. R. BECKWITH. *Analytical and computational aspects of dynamic programming processes of high dimension.* Ph.D. Thesis, Purdue University, 1959.
9. R. BELLMAN. *Dynamic programming.* Princeton University Press, 1957.
10. —— On a routing problem. *Q. appl. Math.*, 16, 1959, pp. 87–90.
11. —— Dynamic programming and adaptive processes—mathematical foundations. *I.R.E. Trans. autom. Control*, 5, no. 1, 1960, pp. 5–10.
12. —— *Adaptive processes—a guided tour.* Princeton University Press, 1961.
13. —— & R. KALABA. On communication processes involving learning and random duration. *I.R.E. natn Conv. Rec.*, pt. 4, 1958, pp. 16–20.
14. —— —— Dynamic programming and statistical communication theory. *Proc. natn Acad. Sci. U.S.A.*, 43, no. 8, 1957, pp. 930–933.
15. —— *A problem in the sequential design of experiments.* Rand Corporation, p. 586, 1954.
16. —— *Applied dynamic programming.* Princeton University Press, 1962.
17. —— Equipment replacement policy. *J. Soc. ind. appl. Maths.* 3, 1955, pp. 133–6.
18. —— *Dynamic programming of continuous processes.* Rand Corporation R–27, 1954.
19. —— Functional approximations and dynamic programming. *Mathl Tabl natn Res. Coun., Wash.*, 13, 1959, pp. 247–51.
20. —— —— & J. LOCKETT. *Dynamic programming and ill-conditioned linear systems.* Rand Corporation RM–3815–PR, December 1963.
21. H. DODGE. Sampling inspection plans. *An. Math. Statist.*, 14, 1943, pp. 264–79.
22. J. S. DRANOFF. Application of dynamic programming to counter-current flow processes. *Opns. Research*, 9, no. 3, 1961, pp. 388–401.
23. —— *et al.* Letter to the Editor. *Opns. Research*, 10, no. 3, 1962, pp. 410–11.
24. D. ELLIS. *An abstract setting for the notion of dynamic programming.* Rand Corporation, 1955, P. 783.
25. J. FISHER. A class of stochastic investment problems. *Opns. Research*, 9, no. 1, 1961, pp. 53–65.
26. C. HOLT, J. MUTH, F. MODIGLIANI & H. SIMON. *Planning production, inventories and work force.* Prentice-Hall, 1960.
27. R. HOWARD. *Dynamic programming and Markov processes.* Technology Press, 1960.
28. G. KIMBALL. *Notes on dynamic programming.*
29. B. O. KOOPMANS. The theory of search, III. The optimum distribution of searching effort. *Opns. Research*, 5, 1957, pp. 613–26.

30. A. LOWAN. Tables of functions and zeros of functions. *Appl. Math. Ser.* **37**, November 1954, pp. 185–91.
31. I. McDOWELL. The economic planning periods for engineering works. *Opns. Research*, **8**, no. 4, 1960, pp. 533–42.
32. A. MANNE. Linear programming and sequential decisions. *Mgmt Sci.*, **6**, no. 3, 1960, pp. 259–67.
33. J. M. NORMAN. *Heuristic methods in dynamic programming*. Ph.D. Thesis, Centre for Business Research, Manchester University, 1966.
34. —— *Use of expectations in dynamic programming*. Working Paper No. 35, Centre for Business Research, Manchester University, 1964.
35. S. N. NORAHARI PANDIT. Addendum on a routing problem. *Opns. Research*, **9**, no. 1, 1961, pp. 129–32.
36. A. PARIKH. *Some theorems and algorithms for finding optimal paths over graphs with engineering applications*. Ph.D. Thesis, Purdue University, 1960.
37. M. POLLOCK & W. WIEBERSON. Solutions of the shortest route problem—a review. *Opns. Research*, **8**, no. 2, 1960, pp. 224–30.
38. L. PONTRYAGIN. *The mathematical theory of optimal processes.* Interscience, 1962.
39. H. RAIFFA & R. SCHLAIFER. *Applied statistical decision theory*. Harvard Business School, 1961.
40. W. SADOWSKI. A few remarks on the assortment problem. *Mgmt Sci.*, **6**, no. 1, 1959, pp. 13–24.
41. W. STARBUCK. *A generalisation of Terborgh's approach to equipment replacement*. Institute Paper No. 20, Institute for Quantitative Research in Economics and Management, School of Industrial Management, Purdue University, 1962.
42. G. TERBORGH. *Dynamic equipment policy*. McGraw-Hill, 1949.
43. J. VON NEUMANN. *Theory of games and economic behaviour*. Princeton University Press, 1953.
44. A. WALD. *Statistical decision functions*. John Wiley, 1950.
45. D. J. WHITE. *Studies in dynamic programming*. Ph.D. Thesis, Birmingham University, 1962.
46. —— Dynamic programming, Markov chains and the method of successive approximations. *J. math. Analysis Applic.*, **6**, no. 3, 1963, pp. 373–6.
47. —— Optimal revision periods. *J. math. Analysis Applic.*, **4**, 1962, pp. 353–65.
48. —— *Dynamic programming and the value of an investment opportunity*. Working Paper No. 14, Centre for Business Research, Manchester University, 1963.
49. —— & J. M. NORMAN. *Interim report on portfolio investigation*. Working Paper No. 4, Centre for Business Research, Manchester University, 1963.
50. —— Comments on a paper by McDowell. *Opns. Research*, **9**, no. 4, 1961, pp. 580–4.
51. —— *Sub-optimality of linear decision rules*. Working Paper No. 17, Centre for Business Research, Manchester University, 1963.
52. —— Dynamic programming systems of uncertain duration. *Mgmt Sci.*, **12**, no. 1, 1965, pp. 37–67.
53. —— —— Control of cash reserves. *Opl. Res. Q.*, **16**, no. 3, 1965, pp. 309–28.
54. —— The allocation of stocks to warehouses. *Opns. Research*, **10**, no. 4, 1962, pp. 724–6.

INDEX